the

PORTRAIT

of the

PREACHING

PASTOR

who

PLEASES

the

LORD

CURTIS BRAUN

LUCIDBOOKS

Dedicated to Laura, Pax, and Keryx. Trust and follow the Lord Jesus Christ no matter the cost. The fear of man brings a snare, but the one who trusts in the Lord will be protected. *"Do not fear those who kill the body but cannot kill the soul. Rather fear Him who can destroy both soul and body in hell"* (Matthew 10:28).

Father, in your mercy, raise up faithful men to be pastors. Do this for your glory. I pray this in Jesus's name. Amen.

Turn your eyes upon Jesus
Look full in His wonderful face
And the things of earth will grow strangely dim
In the light of His glory and grace.

Contents

Chapter 3: A Man Who Has the Grace of God Poured Out on His Life to Have a Burden for the Proclamation of the Gospel

Preface

A growing burden and zeal led me to write this book explaining what a biblical God-made, God-commissioned pastor looks like. Many misconceptions and much misinformation exist when it comes to understanding what a biblical pastor is and what he is commissioned to do. Many people think that attending seminary makes a man a pastor, rather than God.

But that is simply not true; too many pastors are rich in followers and money but poor in character. Some pastors claim to know the gospel, yet they refuse to preach on the attributes of God, repentance, hell, and true saving faith. Some claim to be evangelists but are sacramentalists and teach salvation by water baptism or the Lord's Supper. Others claim to be representatives of Christ, yet they do not know and cannot explain Christ's work of propitiation on the cross. Some pastors are charismatic and have winsome personalities but are unskilled in teaching and sloppy in handling God's Word. Although some pastors are knowledgeable about church growth strategies, they are ignorant about Scripture. There are men who give lectures from the pulpit but never preach from the pulpit.

Some love and desire to be liked and honored by men but run from confrontation and refuse to address false teachers who teach false gospels. Others seek to be known by men but don't seek to know God or walk before Him. Many pastors think that persecution only occurs in Third World nations but don't realize that preaching the truth may cause their own congregation to hate and revile them.

Man lowers the bar for the office of pastor, waters down the qualifications, strips the pastorate of biblical duties, and makes the office to fit their own passions and desires. Therefore, I believe that it is critical for us to recover a biblical portrait and understanding of the position and duties of the preaching pastor.

God has gifted skilled men to the church to feed, guide, and guard the church, to equip the saints, build up the body, and bring her to maturity so that she is not deceived by false doctrine, but rather, grows through the truth into Christ-likeness. *The Portrait of the Preaching Pastor* is organized to take a broad and thoroughly biblical look at the scope of the preaching pastor's role. I want to avoid the common practice of looking primarily at 1 Timothy 3:1–7 and Titus 1:5–9 and focusing solely on the character of the pastor rather than understanding that God pours out His grace on a man and makes him approved, commissioned, sufficient, and enabled to fulfill the work of a pastor, evangelist, and teacher while that man, though still a sinner, maintains and advances in Christlikeness. It is God who gets the glory for making, equipping, and giving the church gifted men to do His will. This book seeks to honor

God by drawing a faithful portrait of the biblical pastor whom God gives to His church.

Finally, I heartily acknowledge that the Lord Jesus Christ saved me from a life of adultery, pornography, lying, and manipulation. Though I was in the church, I was not a part of Christ's kingdom. Though I attended church on Sunday, I was a hypocrite of the worst kind. Though I knew the Lord's prayer, the Apostle's Creed, the Ten Commandments, and more, I did not know the Lord. The Lord is willing and able to save the most perverted, hypocritical, corrupt, vile, wretched, polluted, and idolatrous sinners of whom I could be considered foremost. The Lord was gracious to cause me to be born again, grant me repentance, and grant me saving faith. Along with the apostle Paul, this is my testimony:

> *I have been crucified with Christ. It is no longer I who live, but Christ who lives in me. And the life I now live in the flesh I live by faith in the Son of God, who loved me and gave himself for me.*
>
> —Galatians 2:20

Acknowledgments

To Laura, Pax Emmanuel, and Keryx Kyrie: I love you all very much. Remember, all who desire to live a godly life in Christ Jesus will be persecuted. Do not be ashamed of the Lord and His gospel. Rather, let us go to Him outside the camp and bear the reproach He endured. Stand firm in the faith and let nothing move you. Be strong in the Lord and His Word. Love the Lord your God with all your heart, and with all your soul, and with all your mind, and with all your strength. Seek the Lord with all your heart and serve Him only. Be steadfast, immovable, always abounding in the work of the Lord. Always give yourself fully to the work of the Lord because you know that your labor in the Lord is not in vain. Whatever you do, whether you eat or drink, do it all for the glory of the Lord. Lastly, repent and put your faith in the Lord Jesus Christ. Deny yourself, take up your cross, and follow Him.

To Keryx and Pax: The man who is described in this book is the man I pray that you will become. I'm not praying that you enter pastoral work, but rather that God would pour out His grace on your lives and make you into men that love the Lord, love the Word, serve the Lord, live in all godliness, and glorify Him. Desire to be this man with all your heart. He is a man who is blessed by the Lord.

To I'll Be Honest, Grace to You, and Ligonier Ministries: Thank you for your faithful ministries, which have helped build up our family in the faith.

Introduction

The portrait of the preaching pastor who pleases the Lord reveals a man who has these marks:

- **He is a man commissioned, made, and equipped by God.** He is a man that the Lord has regenerated, converted, and saved (Ephesians 4:4–8). The Lord has given and gifted this man to the church for equipping the saints, building up the church, and uniting her in the unity of the faith and knowledge of the Son of God so that the church is not carried about by every wind of doctrine, trickery of men, demonic lies, and deceitful schemes (Ephesians 4:11–14). He is not above or below fellow elders, overseers, and shepherds, but is a co-laborer (1 Peter 5:1, 1 Corinthians 3:9). He is a man who has been made and given to the church by the Lord and has been gifted and enabled by the Holy Spirit (Ephesians 3:7, 4:11; Acts 20:28) to preach the Word (2 Timothy 4:2) and shepherd the flock of God

(1 Peter 5:2) as one who must watch over the souls of the sheep (Hebrews 13:17) and who will give a final account of his ministry to the Lord who is the Good Shepherd, the Chief Shepherd (2 Timothy 4:2, John 10:11, 1 Peter 5:4).

- **He is a man who has the grace of God poured out on his character.** His preaching and teaching ministry must be fulfilled with a good conscience, a pure heart, and untainted motives (1 Timothy 1:5); sincere faith (1 Timothy 1:5, 4:12); godliness (1 Timothy 3:1–11, 6:11); steadfastness (1 Timothy 6:11); courageousness and boldness (2 Timothy 1:7); love for that which is good (Titus 1:8); uprightness, holy, and disciplined (Titus 1:8); godly in speech and conduct and demonstrating a life of purity (1 Timothy 4:12); gentleness and a lack of violence (1 Timothy 3:2, 6:11); faithful to his wife (1 Timothy 3:1); above reproach, sober-minded, self-controlled, respectable, and hospitable (1 Timothy 3:2); having a good reputation with those outside the church (1 Timothy 3:7); not being a recent convert (1 Timothy 3:6); able to manage his own household well (1 Timothy 3:4–5); not a drunkard or quarrelsome or loving money and dishonest gain (1 Timothy 3:3); shepherding the flock of God willingly and eagerly and not out of compulsion or shameful gain (1 Peter 5:2); not lording over and domineering the flock (1 Peter 5:8); fleeing the love of money, worldliness, and youthful lusts (1 Timothy 6:11, 2 Timothy 2:22); and demonstrating a progression in Christlikeness (1 Timothy 4:16).

- **He is a man who has the grace of God poured out on his life to have a burden for the proclamation of the gospel and the Lord.** He maintains godliness and Christlikeness all while preaching the gospel with all boldness and no hindrance (Acts 28:31), having a burden to proclaim the gospel (1 Corinthians 9:16), guarding the gospel (1 Timothy 6:20, 1 Timothy 1:14), defending the gospel (Philippians 1:7), confirming the gospel (Philippians 1:7), and doing the work as a herald and proclaimer of the gospel (2 Timothy 4:5).

- **He is a man who has the grace of God poured out on him to teach, preach, and love God's Word.** He maintains godliness and Christlikeness all while teaching and handling the Word with precision and care (2 Timothy 2:15) and being skilled in teaching the Word (1 Timothy 3:2). He must use the gifts that God has given him (2 Timothy 1:6) being obedient to God as a soldier is obedient to a commanding officer (2 Timothy 2:3–4), disciplining himself and following God's commandments as an athlete would be disciplined and compete according to the rules (2 Timothy 2:5), working tirelessly for the Lord as a patient farmer who works the land in hope for a crop (2 Timothy 2:6). He must preach the Word, reprove with the Word, rebuke with the Word, exhort with the Word (2 Timothy 4:2); and be devoted to the public reading, teaching, and exhortation of the Word (1 Timothy 4:13). He must preach and teach while fighting the good fight of faith (1 Timothy 1:18, 6:12; 2 Timothy 4:7) and trusting in the inspired, authoritative, infallible, inerrant Word of God to be all-sufficient for teaching, reproof, correction, and training in righteousness for the salvation of those who are lost as well as those who are saved (2 Timothy 3:16–17, 1 Corinthians 1:18).

- **He is a man who has the grace of God poured out on him to stand firm in the faith and oppose false teachers.** He must also be able to discern false teaching and identify those who are false teachers (1 Timothy 4:1–5, 6:3–10; Ephesians 4:14; Jude 22–23), command them to stop their false teaching (1 Timothy 1:3–4), rebuke false teachers (Titus 1:13), silence false teachers (Titus 1:11), teach opponents and false teachers in the hopes that God grants repentance (2 Timothy 2:24–26), face the apostasy of unbelievers and the deceitfulness of false teaching and false teachers with godliness (2 Timothy 3:1–13), and shun false teachers who are unrepentant (Titus 3:10–11; 2 Timothy 3:5; Romans 16:17; 2 John 9–11).

- **He is a man who has the grace of God poured out on him to suffer persecution.** He must maintain godliness while suffering persecution for the gospel (2 Timothy 1:8) and suffer persecution for Christ's Bride (2 Timothy 2:8–10) while understanding that he will be both betrayed and supported by people in the church (2 Timothy 1:15–18, 2:17–18, 4:9–14). He must suffer persecution knowing that he may be put to death for the cause of the gospel while gladly accepting this fate with the hope of pleasing the Lord, the Righteous Judge (2 Timothy 4:6–8). Though the task of carrying out this ministry is weighty and overwhelming, it is God who commissions the faithful pastor, leads him in triumph, and makes him sufficient for the task (2 Corinthians 2:14–17).

- **He is a man who has the grace of God poured out on him to face sin in the church.** He must also deal with sin in the church (Matthew 18:15–20), instruct the church on how to deal with sin (Matthew 18:15–20), confront sinning elders in the church and identify those who are not qualified to be elders (1 Timothy 5:17–25), call women to be submissive in the church so that they do not to fight for authority over men (1 Timothy 2:9–12), not be drawn into public debates and quarreling over words that destroy the listeners (2 Timothy 2:14), and bring about orderly worship in the church (1 Corinthians 14:37–38). He is to identify and discern men who meet the qualifications of a faithful pastor and deacon and not hastily put them into ministry (1 Timothy 3:1–13, 5:22; 2 Timothy 2:2).

- **He is a man who should be blessed by the sheep he shepherds.** Such a faithful pastor is worthy of double honor from the sheep he shepherds (1 Timothy 5:17). The sheep under his care should joyfully and lovingly honor him, respect him, greatly esteem him, and submit to him (Hebrews 13:17, 1 Thessalonians 5:12–13). The sheep must also mimic the elder so far as the elder mimics Christ (1 Corinthians 11:1). It is also the responsibility of the sheep to test what the elder says (1 John 4:1–6) and ensure that he does not go beyond what Scripture says (1 Corinthians 4:6).

Chapter 1

A Man Commissioned, Made, and Equipped by God

And he gave the apostles, the prophets, the evangelists, the shepherds and teachers, to equip the saints for the work of ministry, for building up the body of Christ.

—Ephesians 4:11–12

In this chapter, we will seek to understand who makes the true pastor, how he is made, and what Christ's purpose is for him in the church. One of the clearest portions of Scripture explaining how a pastor is made and Christ's purpose for the pastor is found in Ephesians 4:11–16. We will exposit this portion of Scripture to understand how Christ gifts His church with competent and skilled men whose duty it is to build up the body of believers, the church. However, before we jump into Ephesians 4:11–16, we will briefly exposit Ephesians

4:1–10. Here are some of the main points that we'll cover in this chapter:

- A man is saved by grace before God makes him a pastor (Ephesians 4:4–6).

- Christ gives the gift of pastors to His church (Ephesians 4:11).

- *Pastor, elder, shepherd,* and *overseer* are different terms for the office of pastor (1 Timothy 3:1–7, Titus 1:5, Ephesians 4:11).

- Christ appoints, equips, and makes pastors sufficient and qualified to be ministers (1 Corinthians 3:5–6).

- All pastors are co-laborers; no pastor is above or below fellow pastors (1 Peter 5:1).

- Pastors feed, guide, and guard the church (4:12–13).

- Pastors equip the church for ministry, to unite the saints in truth and the knowledge of Christ (Ephesians 4:12–13).

- Pastors are to guard the church against false teachers (Ephesians 4:14).

- Pastors are to do the work of teaching and evangelism (Ephesians 4:11).

- Pastors are to be imitators of Christ and are to walk, speak, and conduct their lives in truth and godliness (1 Corinthians 11:1, Ephesians 4:15).

I therefore, a prisoner for the Lord, urge you to walk in a manner worthy of the calling to which you have been called, with all humility and gentleness, with patience, bearing with one another in love, eager to maintain the unity of the Spirit in the bond of peace.

—Ephesians 4:1–3

As we begin this chapter, let's look back at how Paul explained God's purpose for the church in the first three chapters of Ephesians:

- In Ephesians 1:3–6, Paul explains how believers were predestined for salvation in Christ by God the Father in love.

- In Ephesians 1:6–10, Paul explains that redemption and the forgiveness of sins were accomplished in Christ.

- In Ephesians 1:11–14, Paul explains that in Christ, all believers have an eternal redemption and inheritance.

- In Ephesians 1:15–23, Paul explains that believers have all the resources, power, and wisdom in Christ who is the Head of the church and sovereign over all things.

- In Ephesians 2:1–10, Paul explains the believer's previous fallen condition, being made new with

Christ, being raised with Christ in the heavenlies, being saved through Christ, and being created in Christ for good works.

- In Ephesians 2:11–3:13, Paul explains how Christ brought peace for both Jew and Gentile and reconciled both groups to God, brought unity to the church, and made the Gentiles fellow heirs with Jews through the gospel of Christ Jesus.

- In Ephesians 3:14–21, Paul prays for believers to have the fullness, strength, and knowledge to comprehend the breadth, length, height, and depth of Christ and for this knowledge to lead to maturity and the fullness of God.

Having explained the bountiful riches of believers who are in Christ, Paul begins to exhort the Ephesians to strive to maintain unity of the Spirit in the church (Ephesians 4:1–3). It is important to note that, in Paul's day, there was much controversy about whether Gentiles should be included in the church, which is why Paul is exhorting the church to strive for unity. The Jerusalem Council had to address the issue and affirm that Gentiles were included into the church by faith in Christ and not through circumcision or keeping the law of Moses (Acts 15:1–10). Peter had to be shown a vision three times that dietary laws had been abolished, and Gentiles were not to be seen as unclean (Acts 10:9–16). Peter explained to the apostles and brothers in Judea that Gentiles had received the Word of God and that they were included in the church because they believed in the Lord Jesus Christ (Acts 11:1–18). These are just a few examples of the hurdles that Jews and Gentiles had to overcome to understand that they were brothers and sisters and coheirs of salvation in Christ. Therefore, we see that the inclusion of Gentiles into the church was significant as the Jews previously saw Gentiles as unclean pagans.

Paul explained in Ephesians 2:11–3:13 that it was always God's plan for the Gentiles to be included in the church and members of the household of God. In Ephesians 4, Paul is calling for the Ephesians to walk worthy of this salvific call, which brought the Gentiles into the church of God and to strive for unity among all believers in love and with all humility, gentleness, and patience.

A Pastor Is Born from Above, Converted, and Saved by the Lord

There is one body and one Spirit—just as you were called to the one hope that belongs to your call—one Lord, one faith, one baptism, one God and Father of all, who is over all through all and in all. But grace was given to each one of us according to the measure of Christ's gift. Therefore it says, "When he ascended on high he led a host of captives, and he gave gifts to men."

—Ephesians 4:4–8

Paul makes an appeal to keep the unity of the Spirit. He makes this appeal in Ephesians 4:4–10 by describing how God brought true unity in the church through the salvific work of God, how Christ's victory purchased the redemption of men, and how Christ's victory secured His authority to distribute the spoils of His victory as gifts to men. In Ephesians 4:4–6 Paul reminds the Ephesians of the salvific work of the Triune God that brought them into unity with one another.

One may ask, "How does explaining Ephesians 4:4–10 help with answering the question of how God makes a pastor?" The answer lies in understanding that before the Lord ever makes a man a pastor, He first saves the man. Before God ever gifts and equips a man for the office and responsibility of a pastor, He saves the man. This is where our brief exposition of Ephesians 4:4–10 will pay dividends in helping us understand this principle.

In Ephesians 4:4–6 Paul states that there is one body (the church or all true believers), one Spirit (the Holy Spirit), one hope (the hope of inheritance and eternal redemption in Christ), the call (the effectual call of salvation), one Lord (the Lord Jesus Christ), one faith (the justifying faith in the revealed truth of Scripture about the person and work of Christ), one baptism (the baptism of the Holy Spirit), one God (the Triune God), and one Father (God the Father). In these short but powerful and descriptive verses, Paul is doing something that I believe many theologians miss. Paul mentions all three persons of the Godhead, and he uses salvation language to demonstrate and highlight the salvific work of the Triune God in the baptism of the Holy Spirit, which saves and brings sinners into the body of Christ and equips them for work. When we understand the baptism of the Holy Spirit, we see how the one Father, one God, one Lord, one Holy Spirit, one faith, one baptism, and the effectual call are all elements of the baptism of the Holy Spirit in Ephesians 4:4–6. We also see how unity is achieved in the body of believers through this salvific work of the Triune God. Below is a definition and diagram of the baptism of the Holy Spirit:

The baptism of the Holy Spirit is the sovereign monergistic work of salvation performed by God the Father, God the Son, and God the Holy Spirit. The Son asks the Father to send the Holy Spirit (John 14:16) [**Diagram Step 1**]. The Holy Spirit is given from the Father to the Son (John 14:16, 15:26; Luke 11:13) [**Diagram Steps 2 and 3**]. The Son pours out or gives the Holy Spirit in the Father's name (Matthew 3:11–12; Mark 1:8; Luke 3:16, 24:49; John 1:31–33, 14:16, 26; 15:26; 16:7; Acts 1:4–5, 2:17–18, 10:44–48, 11:16; Titus 3:6) [**Diagram Step 4**] through hearing the Word of God, the Gospel (James 1:18; Ephesians 1:13; Romans 1:15–17, 10:17; 1 Corinthians 1:21) [**Diagram Step 5**]. The Holy Spirit then regenerates or causes man to be born again (John 3:3–10, Titus 3:5, Ezekiel 36:25–27) which gives spiritual life to the previously spiritually dead man (Ephesians 2:1–3, Colossians 2:13) [**Diagram Step 6**]. Man, then repents, which is a gift granted by God (Acts 11:18, 2 Timothy 2:25), and man puts saving faith in Jesus Christ, which is also gifted and granted by God (Ephesians 2:8–9, Philippians 1:29, John 7:38–39) [**Diagram Step 7**]. Man is then justified by grace through faith in Christ (Titus 3:7), receives and is indwelt by the Holy Spirit (Galatians 3:2, 3:14; Ephesians 1:13; 1 Corinthians 6:19), and the Holy Spirit spiritually unites or immerses man with Jesus Christ and puts the man into the body of Christ and gives gifts to the man for the benefit of the church (1 Corinthians 12:7, 12:13; Romans 6:3–4) [**Diagram Step 7**].

The baptism with the Holy Spirit is not water baptism, and water baptism is not the baptism with the Holy Spirit, for only Christ can baptize with the Holy Spirit, and man can only baptize with water (Matthew 3:11–12; Mark 1:8; Luke 3:16; John 1:31–33, 3:8, 7:38–39, 14:15–17, 26; 15:26, 16:7; Acts 1:4–5, 2:17–18, 10:44–48, 11:16; 1 Corinthians 1:17). The baptism of the Holy Spirit is a one-time, instantaneous, and salvific work of God (1 Corinthians 12:13).

Diagram of Baptism of the Holy Spirit

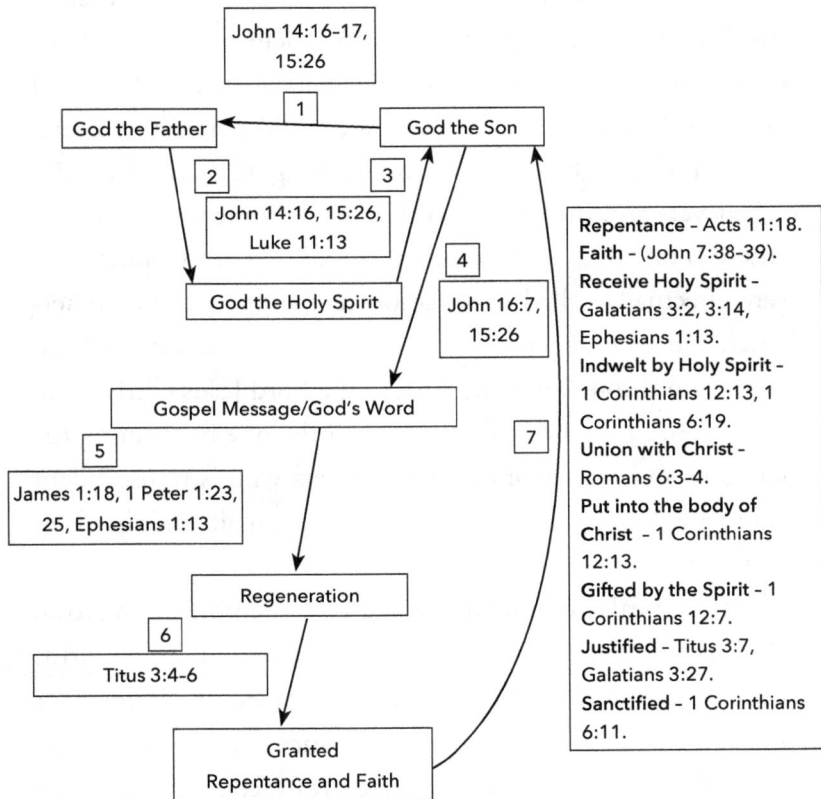

John 14:16-17, 15:26

1

God the Father ← God the Son

2   3

John 14:16, 15:26, Luke 11:13

4

God the Holy Spirit

John 16:7, 15:26

Gospel Message/God's Word

5

James 1:18, 1 Peter 1:23, 25, Ephesians 1:13

7

Regeneration

6

Titus 3:4-6

Granted Repentance and Faith

Repentance - Acts 11:18.
Faith - (John 7:38-39).
Receive Holy Spirit - Galatians 3:2, 3:14, Ephesians 1:13.
Indwelt by Holy Spirit - 1 Corinthians 12:13, 1 Corinthians 6:19.
Union with Christ - Romans 6:3-4.
Put into the body of Christ - 1 Corinthians 12:13.
Gifted by the Spirit - 1 Corinthians 12:7.
Justified - Titus 3:7, Galatians 3:27.
Sanctified - 1 Corinthians 6:11.

The salvific work of the baptism of the Holy Spirit is not something that happens only to pastors. All true believers in the Lord Jesus Christ have been baptized by the Holy Spirit. It is the work of God in salvation to bring sinful man into a right standing and reconciliation with God through the gospel message. When Paul commands the believers in Ephesus to strive for unity of the Spirit in the bond of peace with all humility, gentleness, patience, and love among believers in Ephesians 4:1–3, he makes his appeal by having them recall the salvific work of the Triune God, which reconciled them to God and put them in the body of Christ. We could paraphrase Ephesians 4:4–6 to highlight what Paul is saying regarding the unity of believers and the salvific work of the Triune God this way: "There is one body of true believers and one Holy Spirit. You were effectually called to salvation to the one hope of inheritance and eternal redemption in the one Lord who is Jesus Christ and through the one faith in the Lord Jesus Christ. You were baptized by the Holy Spirit with the one baptism by the one God and Father of all true believers who is transcendent and reigns over all, is imminent and through all, and dwells in all true believers."

Paul appeals for unity in the church by demonstrating to all believers that their common salvation and identity is in Christ. It's as if he's saying, "Remember your salvation. Remember who saved you. Remember the inheritance you have in Christ. Remember that Christ died and saved your fellow brothers and sisters. Remember that Christ died and saved both Jews and Gentiles." Paul sought unity for the Ephesians by reminding them of their identity and salvation in Christ.

Paul goes on to explain how grace and gifts were given to the body of believers in Ephesians 4:7–8: "*But grace was given to each one of us according to the measure of Christ's gift. Therefore it says, 'When he ascended on high he led a host of captives, and he gave gifts to men.'*"

So, the question that we should ask is this: How was Christ able to give grace and gifts to the body of believers? Paul answers this question when he cites Psalm 68:18 in verse 8. Psalm 68, written by David, pictures Yahweh as the Divine Warrior. This psalm, which is sometimes called a "triumphal hymn," pictures God as a warrior who delivers His people from their enemies and provides for and protects His people. When Psalm 68 was written, it would be common for the conquering king to take the spoils of war after his conquest. In this psalm, the Lord is pictured as the conquering king who returns to heaven after successfully subjugating His enemies as He also brings home the spoils and prisoners. In quoting Psalm 68:18, Paul is purposeful in speaking of Christ's victory on the cross and ascension into heaven; this conquering victory of Christ is described in Colossians 2:13–15 where it says:

And you, who were dead in your trespasses and the uncircumcision of your flesh, God made alive together with him, having forgiven us all our trespasses, by canceling the record of debt that stood against us with its legal demands. This he set aside, nailing it to the cross. He disarmed the rulers and authorities and put them to open shame, by triumphing over them in him.

At the cross, Christ triumphed over sin, death, and the devil. The penalty and power of sin was defeated, and the devil and all the demons were put to open shame by Christ's victory.

At the cross, it was demonstrated that Christ is the power and wisdom of God (1 Corinthians 1:24).

Not only did Christ triumph over sin, death, and hell at the cross, but with His victory came glory and spoils. Isaiah 53:12 prophesies about Christ's victory and about God dividing the spoils of Christ's victory to those for whom Christ died where it says:

> *Therefore I will divide him a portion with the many, and he shall divide the spoil with the strong, because he poured out his soul to death, and was numbered with the transgressors; yet he bore the sin of many and makes intercession for the transgressors.*

This is exactly what Paul is referring to in Ephesians 4:7–8. Christ's victory ransomed many for whom He died and gave Him the spoils and rewards, which He distributes to His church.

In Ephesians 4:9–10, Paul further explains Psalm 68:18 by stating that Christ's ascension also meant that He descended, which speaks of the Divine Warrior's humiliation prior to His exaltation:

> *(In saying, "He ascended," what does it mean but that he had also descended into the lower regions, the earth? He who descended is the one who also ascended far above all the heavens, that he might fill all things.)*

In these verses, Paul interprets and provides an explanation of Psalm 68:18 by stating that Christ's ascension also meant that He descended which speaks of the Divine Warrior's humiliation prior to His exaltation. When Paul says that the one who descended is the one who ascended; He makes the argument that Christ, the Divine Warrior, was victorious in His mission on earth and ascended back to heaven as the conquering champion. Paul captures this in Philippians 2:5–11, which describes Christ's humiliation in verses 6–8 and Christ's exaltation in verses 9–11. After Christ's ascension back to heaven, He was given authority to baptize with the Holy Spirit and distribute spiritual gifts (Acts 1:4–5). Although Ephesians 4:9–10 can be difficult to interpret, they become much easier to understand when seen as an interpretation to Psalm 68:18.

As we close this brief exposition of Ephesians 4:4–10, it should be manifestly clear that before God ever makes a man a qualified and competent pastor, He regenerates, converts, and saves the man. Therefore, we can know that a true pastor is one who has come to true repentance and saving faith in the Lord Jesus Christ; he has heard and believed the gospel of his salvation. A true pastor been born from above and baptized by the Holy Spirit. A true pastor is indwelt by the Holy Spirit and uniquely gifted by the Holy Spirit to do the work of a pastor. If a man is unconverted and unregenerate, he does not even meet the criteria of being a convert (1 Timothy 3:6) and, therefore, he does not have the basis for becoming a true pastor. Let's transition into an exposition of

Ephesians 4:11–16 to understand Christ's purpose for the true pastor.

A Pastor Is Given by Christ to the Church

And he gave the apostles, the prophets, the evangelists, the shepherds, and teachers.

—Ephesians 4:11

There are many misconceptions regarding who takes and makes a man a God-pleasing pastor. One misconception is that going to seminary is what makes a man a pastor and equipped for ministry. While seminary can provide training, education, and discipline, attending a seminary is not what makes a man a pastor. Furthermore, it is not the vote, consensus, or a council of religious seminary or church men who make a man a pastor; nor is it religious accomplishment, years of service, childhood rearing, or any of the like that make a man a pastor. These are all a pernicious misunderstanding that a man can be made a pastor by any other means then by God himself. It is God who takes a man and makes a man a pastor and gifts His church with skilled and competent pastors for the building up and edification of His church. As we saw previously in Ephesians 4:4–8, God will always save, regenerate, and convert a man before He makes the man a God-commissioned true pastor.

Therefore, the first point we see is that Christ is the one who gave apostles, prophets, evangelists, shepherds, and teachers to the church. Christ is the initiator in making a man a pastor, not man deciding to become a pastor. When Jesus is instructing His disciples on the night of His betrayal, He makes this statement in John 15:16: "*You did not choose me, but I chose you and appointed you that you should go and bear fruit and that your fruit should abide, so that whatever you ask the Father in my name, he may give it to you.*" Notice what Jesus says. He is stating that the divine prerogative for salvation, discipleship, and even building His church starts with Him. The disciples didn't choose Jesus; Jesus chose them first.

Likewise, Jesus tells Peter and the disciples that He will build His church (Matthew 16:18–20). It's not man that chooses Christ first. Rather, it is God who chooses the man first. It is God who appoints him and commissions him. Man can scheme, plan, and devise ways to put other men in the position of elder, overseer, or pastor in a church, but it is God and God alone who makes a man qualified to be a pastor. Man does not choose Christ first. Rather, Christ chooses man and appoints him to bear fruit that will last.

Paul makes similar statements in several of his epistles on this God-commissioned calling. In 2 Corinthians 3:5–6, Paul makes this statement about how he and his co-laborers are enabled to carry out the duties and responsibilities of a pastor: "*Not that we are sufficient in ourselves to claim anything as coming from us, but our sufficiency is from God, who has made us sufficient to be ministers of a new covenant.*" Paul is describing how he became a minister of the new covenant. It was through Christ that Paul or any minister becomes sufficient to be a new covenant pastor. In fact, the word for "made us sufficient" is *hikanos,* which can also mean adequate or competent. In this context, this word is used to describe the minister meeting a certain standard and being fit to teach and carry out this God-ordained office. Paul and any God-ordained and God-gifted man is made sufficient by God and God alone.

In Paul's second letter to Timothy, he describes how God saved him and appointed him as a preacher, an apostle, and a teacher of the gospel: "*For which I was appointed a preacher and apostle and teacher*" (2 Timothy 1:11). When Paul says that he was appointed as a preacher, apostle, and teacher, it is important to note that he writes this word in the passive voice rather than the active voice. In other words, God was the acting agent, and Paul was the passive agent who was acted upon by God. Paul is stating that this commission and appointment was the work of God and not the work of man, not any self-willed or self-determined effort that was of his own accord; nor was it by any work or council of man. In fact, when Paul went up to Jerusalem to see Peter and James to confirm that the gospel he was preaching was correct, Peter and James both confirmed that God alone had entrusted Paul with the ministry to preach the gospel to the Gentiles, and they gave him the right hand of fellowship (Galatians 2:1–9).

In Paul's first letter to Timothy, he describes who appointed him for ministry when he makes this statement in 1 Timothy 2:7, "*For this I was appointed a preacher and an apostle (I am telling the truth, I am not lying), a teacher of the Gentiles in faith and truth.*" Once again, when Paul says that he was appointed as a preacher, apostle, and teacher, he writes this word in the passive voice rather than the active voice. It was not Paul's decision to make himself a preacher, teacher, and apostle of the gospel. No! It was God who was the acting agent who made, commissioned, and equipped Paul for this work.

In Paul's letter to the Ephesians, he is crystal clear on how he became a minister of Christ and the gospel and who made him a minister: "*Of this gospel I was made a minister according to the gift of God's grace, which was given me by the working of his power*" (Ephesians 3:7). We see here that Paul was made or became a minister of the gospel according to the gift of God's grace. Notice that Paul became a minister according to God's power. In fact, the word *made* comes from the original word *ginomai*, which means "to come into being" or "become." The word *ginomai* is also written in the passive voice, which simply means that Paul was not the acting agent who made himself a minister. Once again, the passive voice shows us that God was the acting agent who made Paul a minister. We should also see that Paul was made a minister according to the gift of God's grace. It is always God who is the acting agent who gifts, makes, graces, and equips a pastor to carry out the pastoral duty according to His mighty power and grace. In his letter to the Corinthians, Paul states that not all are apostles, not all are prophets, not all are teachers (1 Corinthians 12:29). It is the divine and sovereign prerogative of God who determines who will be a God-commissioned pastor. Seminaries can provide useful training, but they do not make a man a qualified and competent pastor. Church councils that vote men into positions of leadership or pastoral roles may be able to discern whether a man has been gifted to be a God-qualified pastor, but their vote does not make the man a qualified and competent pastor. Childhood rearing, teaching, and bringing up a child in the fear and admonition of the Lord is of great value and benefit. However, this does not make a man a God-commissioned pastor. It is God and God alone who gifts His church with qualified and competent pastors.

The second point we should see is that God has given His church apostles, prophets, evangelists, shepherds or pastors, and teachers. To give the text adequate attention, we will seek to understand what it means to be an apostle, prophet, evangelist, shepherd, or teacher.

The apostles in this context would be the twelve apostles. We can know that Paul is referring to the twelve apostles because there are a couple texts that state how Christ built the church. In Ephesians 2:19–20 it says this regarding the establishment of the church: "*So then you are no longer strangers and aliens, but you are fellow citizens with the saints and members of the household of God, built on the foundation of the apostles and prophets, Christ Jesus himself being the cornerstone.*" We see here that Christ is the cornerstone of the church, and from other texts, we also see that He is the builder, owner, and Head of the church (Matthew 16:18–20, Colossians 1:18). What we also see is that Christ gave the apostles as a foundation. And in 1 Corinthians 12:28, Paul states that Christ first appointed the apostles, second prophets, and third teachers.

Therefore, we can know that the twelve apostles are who Paul has in mind.

The apostles that Paul would have in mind would include Peter, Andrew, James, and John (the sons of Zebedee), Philip, Bartholomew, Thomas, Matthew, James the son of Alphaeus, Thaddaeus, Simon the Zealot, and either himself or Matthias. Judas, the betrayer, would not be included as an apostle and it would be a fair guess to say that Paul would have been the twelfth apostle rather than Matthias (1 Corinthians 15:9). There are impostors who appoint themselves as apostles in Christendom today. However, a theological definition of an apostle clarifies why the title of "apostle" is given only to these twelve men. The following attributes help us understand the qualifications which made an apostle:

- Considered someone who had seen the Lord and was able to testify of Him and His resurrection from personal knowledge (John 15:27; 1 Corinthians 9:1; Acts 1:21, 22:14– 15).

- One who had been called to this office by Christ (Luke 6:13, Galatians 1:1).

- One who was infallibly inspired and, thus, secured against all error and mistake in their public teaching, whether by word or by writing (John 14:26, 16:13).

- One who had the power of working miracles (Acts 2:43).

Thus, we see that the twelve apostles would fit these qualifications. They were the foundation of the church that Paul speaks of (Ephesians 2:19–20). They were eyewitnesses of Christ's ministry, were called by Him, were entrusted with preaching and teaching, or writing the Word, and they were given the power of working miracles to authenticate their teaching. The early church was devoted to the teaching of the apostles (Acts 2:42). We also see the apostles understood that the priority of their apostolic commission was to devote themselves to preaching the Word of God: "*And the twelve summoned the full number of the disciples and said, 'It is not right that we should give up preaching the word of God to serve tables'*" (Acts 2:42). When it came to choosing between a noble task of caring for neglected widows and preaching the Word of God, the apostles saw that preaching the body and doctrine of truth was their priority. They were devoted to the gospel and God's Word, which included the person and work of Christ, the response to Christ, sin, death, hell, salvation, and Christian living. Thus, we see that Christ is the Head and Cornerstone of the church, and Christ gave the apostles as the foundation to build up the church through their teaching, preaching, and working of miracles, which authenticated their message (Hebrews 2:3–4).

It's also important to note that just as Christ gave His church true apostles, the devil has false apostles who pretend to be true apostles. Paul speaks of this in 2 Corinthians 11:12–15 where he warns of false apostles and deceitful workmen who disguise themselves as apostles of Christ and servants of righteousness just as Satan disguises himself as an angel of light. Just as Christ had His true apostles, so the devil has false apostles who teach another Christ, another gospel, and have another spirit (2 Corinthians 11:4, 1 John 4:6).

Next, we see that Christ gave prophets. As we saw in 1 Corinthians 12:28, the apostles were given first, and the prophets were given second. The word *prophet* is derived from *prophétés* with *pro* meaning "before" and *phēmi* meaning "to speak" or "one who speaks forth." A prophet is one who speaks forth God's message. The function of a prophet varies throughout the Bible. There were prophets such as Nathan who spoke forth the Word of God but did not perform miracles. The prophets Elijah and Elisha both spoke forth the Word of God and performed miracles. The prophet Isaiah performed a miracle (2 Kings 20:11), spoke forth the Word of God, and spoke of prophetic events that would occur in the future (Isaiah 53). Therefore, we see that the function of the prophet was to always speak forth the Word of God and at times, they performed miracles or predicted future events.

In the New Testament, we see that there were prophets in the early church. This includes prophets who were in Jerusalem and went to Antioch; one prophet named Agabus foretold of a great famine (Acts 11:27–28). Prophets in the church at Antioch received revelation from the Holy Spirit on setting apart Barnabas and Saul for missionary work (Acts 13:1–13), and we also learn that Judas and Silas were prophets, sent from the Jerusalem Council who encouraged and strengthened brothers in Christ at Antioch through their words (Acts 15:32). Lastly, we see that a prophet named Agabus from Judea spoke by the Holy Spirit and predicted that Paul would be bound by the Jews in Jerusalem and given to the Gentiles (Acts 21:7–14). Therefore, we see that the early church prophets prophesied events that were to come, received revelation from the Holy Spirit, and spoke forth the Word of God.

John MacArthur makes a strong point that both the office of the apostles and prophets have ceased and are replaced by the office of pastors and evangelists.[1] The case he makes for this is incredibly strong especially when we consider Ephesians 2:20 where Paul declares that Christ is the cornerstone, and the apostles and prophets are the foundation. There is no other cornerstone nor is there any other foundation than the apostles and prophets. The church is being built up as a holy temple off Christ as the cornerstone and the apostles and prophets as the foundation (Ephesians 2:2–22). Therefore, it is a strong, logical, and biblical understanding that the office of apostles and prophets have ceased and have been replaced with the office of pastors, evangelists, and teachers.

Note that just as Christ gave His church true prophets, Satan also has false prophets. John warns of this in 1 John 4:1 where he says, "*Beloved, do not believe every spirit, but test the spirits to see whether they are from God, for many false prophets have gone out in the world.*" Therefore, we can know that there will always be many of Satan's false prophets who claim allegiance to Christ and pretend to speak on behalf of Christ but who are actually false prophets that carry a false and damning gospel.

Next, we see that Christ gave the church evangelists. The word *evangelist* comes from *euaggelistés*, which is a messenger who proclaims the good news of Jesus Christ. The office of the evangelist is still present in today's church. These men are gifted to proclaim the gospel message with clarity and conviction. They proclaim the gospel message with warning and exhortation. One may ask, "What is the specific gospel message they proclaim?" The next two sections present an abbreviated version of the good news and the bad news that the evangelist proclaims.

The Pastor's Message of the Bad News of Sin and Hell

Man has sinned by breaking God's law by either not doing what God's law demands (James 4:17) or doing what God's law prohibits (James 2:10) by any thought (Matthew 5:28), word (Matthew 5:22), deed (Matthew 5:39), or intent (Matthew 6:1). God hates (Psalm 5:5, 11:5), abhors (Psalm 5:6), is angered with (Psalm 7:11), and is ready to destroy and punish those who sin (Psalm 7:12–13) because sin is warfare against Him (James 4:4), and God considers sin an abomination (Proverbs 22:12) and evil (Psalm 7:9). Because God hates sin, He must deal with sin according to who He is. Because God is infinite (1 Timothy 1:17), loving (Psalm 136, 1 John 4:17), just (Genesis 18:25, Deuteronomy 32:4, Job 34:10, Jeremiah 17:10, Ezekiel 18:1–32), good (Psalm 25:8, Mark 10:18), faithful (Lamentations 3:22–23), omniscient (Psalm 147:5, Hebrews 4:13), immutable (James 1:17, Numbers 23:19), omnipresent (Jeremiah 23:23–24), and holy (Isaiah 44:6, 45:5), He must punish sin. For God to leave sin unpunished would violate and act in opposition to His character. Therefore, God must punish sin. The punishment for sin is hell, which is a place of God's full wrath; it is a place of blackest darkness (Jude 13, Matthew 22:13), filled with the furious, all-powerful, concentrated, raging, and vengeful fire of God that devours and consumes His enemies (Matthew 5:22, 5:29, 13:42, 13:50, Hebrews 10:26–31). Hell is filled with the lost who are weeping and angry against God; they are unrepentant, Christ-rejecting (Matthew 11:20–24), and Christ-neglecting sinners (Hebrews 2:1–3). The lost will spend all eternity being punished for every sin they ever committed (Revelation 20:12) with no hope of escape (Luke 16:26) and with only the expectation of excruciating torments to their body, soul, and spirit (Matthew 10:28) and an undying conscience that will haunt them day and night, forever and ever, with no reprieve (Luke 16:25).

The Pastor's Gospel Message

The gospel is the good news of salvation that God has authored and owns (Romans 1:1). God had promised His plan of salvation through His prophets and Holy Scripture and has fully revealed the good news of salvation through Scripture (Romans 1:2), which is the authoritative, inspired, inerrant, infallible, and all-sufficient Word of God (2 Peter 1:20–21, 2 Timothy 3:16-17). The good news concerns the person and work of the Lord Jesus Christ. Jesus is the Jewish Messiah and Son of the Living God (Matthew 16:16, Romans 1:1–4). Jesus is God, and He is coequal and coeternal with God the Father and God the Holy Spirit (John 5:17–18, 10:30, 10:38, 14:10). Jesus is the eternal, only begotten, one-of-a-kind, Son of God (John 3:16). Jesus is the Anointed One of God (Luke 4:18–19). Jesus is the Savior of the world (Luke 2:11). Jesus is the Creator and Sustainer of the Universe (John 1:1–14). Jesus is the King of Israel (John 1:49). Jesus is the Son of David (Matthew 1:1–16, Luke 3:23-38). Jesus was born of a virgin (Matthew 1:23, Galatians 4:4). Jesus was the Word made flesh (John 1:14). Jesus was physically born into this world as a man (Matthew 1:25). Jesus is thus truly God and truly man (Philippians 2:5–11).

The work of Jesus is that He lived a sinless life (Matthew 26:59–60, 1 Corinthians 5:21) and fulfilled all righteousness found in the law and the prophets (Matthew 5:17–20, Luke 24:44–46). He declared Himself to be the Christ (Matthew 16:16), the only begotten Son of the living God through His teaching (John 3:16, Matthew 22:41–46), which was attested to by His miracles and display of divine power (John 10:37–38). Jesus offered himself as a spotless and blameless sacrifice for sin (John 1:29, 1 Peter 1:19) to propitiate the righteous anger of God the Father for all the sins of God's people (John 10:11, Romans 3:25, Isaiah 53, 1 Peter 2:24). Christ bore the full and omnipotent wrath of God the Father on the cross, which was due to man (Matthew 26:39, 27:45–46; Luke 22:44). His sacrifice propitiated the righteous anger of God and reconciled (Romans 5:10–11) and brought peace from man to God and God to man (Matthew 27:51–53; John 19:30; Romans 5:1; 1 Peter 2:25). His substitutionary sacrifice and death also redeemed sinful man to Holy God by forgiving man's sin (Hebrews 8:12, Ephesians 1:7) and imputing Christ's righteousness to man (1 Corinthians 5:21, Isaiah 53:1–12, Romans 4:3–5). Jesus was resurrected from the dead on the third day by His own power (John 10:18), by God the Father (Galatians 1:1) and God the Holy Spirit (Romans 8:11), which affirmed His person, His teachings, and salvific work for sinners (Romans 4:25). He ascended to the right hand of the Father (Luke 24:51) and is empowered with all authority to bring about the plan of salvation for all His people (Matthew 28:18) by causing them to be born again (John 3:1–10) and justified by His grace (John 3:16, 3:18, 3:36). He will also return to bring all His own to heaven with Him (John 6:37–40, 14:1–3) to be glorified (John 17:24) while also judging and condemning Satan, demons, and sinful man to hell (Matthew 25:31–46, Revelation 20:7–15). The benefits of the person and work of Christ are available to those who respond to the gospel call of repentance toward God and faith in the Lord Jesus Christ (Mark 1:15, Acts 20:21).

Repentance is a gift from God and radical change in mind (Acts 5:31, 11:18, 2 Timothy 2:25) in which the sinner understands his sin against God and is thus, poor in spirit (Matthew 5:3, Luke 18:9–14), has godly sorrow and mourns over his sin against God (Matthew 5:4, 2 Corinthians 7:10), and turns away from his sin and sinful former way of life (Ephesians 4:22) and turns toward God for righteousness and salvation (Matthew 5:5–6; Luke 3:3–17; Acts 17:30, 20:21; 1 Thessalonians 1:9). Saving faith is a gift from God (Ephesians 2:8–9) whereby a sinner has knowledge of Jesus's person and work such that a sinner will respond to Christ's person and work by denying themselves (Matthew 16:24, Mark 8:34, Luke 9:23), picking up their cross (Matthew 10:38, 16:24; Mark 8:34; Luke 9:23), and lovingly (Luke 14:26–27, James 4:7) and obediently (2 Thessalonians 1:8, Romans 1:5) submitting (James 4:6, Matthew 11:28), and committing their life to Jesus (Matthew 10:37–39, 16:24–26; Mark 8:34–37; Luke 9:23–26, 14:25–33) and trusting in Him only for salvation (Romans 10:13, John 3:16, John 3:36, Acts 4:12). Thus, conversion is the turning away from sin in repentance and to the Lord Jesus Christ in faith for salvation (Acts 20:21, 1 Thessalonians 1:9, Ephesians 4:22–24, Colossians 3:9–10, Mark 1:15).

This is the message that evangelists and pastors proclaim. They proclaim the fallen condition of man and the eternal torments and punishment of hell that man justly earns. They also pronounce the good news of Jesus Christ as found in Scripture. They pronounce who Jesus is and what He did. They explain the propitiating, reconciling, expiating, redeeming, justifying, regenerating, sanctifying, and glorifying work of Christ. They also exhort and call men to Christ by commanding that all men repent and come to Christ in saving faith. God gives such men to the church to proclaim this gospel message in the church as well as to the lost. Evangelists are bold proclaimers of Christ; they have an unusual love for the lost and preach the gospel with conviction and urgency. They seek to reach the lost in the world as well as the lost in the church. They are unwavering in the gospel message; they dare not pervert, twist, alter, or modify the gospel message. They are Christ's precious gift to His church. Paul gave this very command to Timothy to carry out the work of an evangelist in 2 Timothy 4:5 where he says this, "*As for you, always be sober-minded, endure suffering, do the work of an evangelist, fulfill your ministry.*"

It's important that we reflect on the importance of the evangelist. They carry in their message the difference between eternal life and eternal death. The gospel message accepted is salvation, but the gospel message rejected or neglected is condemnation. Without the gospel, there is no hope and no salvation. The gospel is the power of God for salvation, and the kingdom of God and the church grow with every soul that is saved through this gospel.

Next, we see that Christ gave the church shepherds or pastors. In the original language this comes to us as *poimén*, which is a shepherd. The first point we should make is that shepherds and pastors (*poimén*), elders (*presbuteros*), and overseers or bishops (*episkopos*) are the same office and position. For the purposes of this book, I'll continue to use the terms *pastor* and *elder* interchangeably since those are the terms most frequently used today. Although these terms all refer to the same position, the different titles detail the multifaceted aspects of the office.

The Pastor Feeds, Guides, and Guards the Flock

The term *poimén* or shepherd is used to describe the office of the pastor or shepherd. In John 21:15–19 when Jesus is recommissioning Peter, He gives Peter two commands to feed the sheep and one command to shepherd the sheep. In Acts 20:28–29 when Paul is speaking to the Ephesian elders and is preparing to leave to go to Jerusalem, he commands the elders to:

> *Pay careful attention to yourselves and to all the flock, in which the Holy Spirit has made you overseers, to care for the church of God, which he obtained with his own blood. I know that after my departure fierce wolves will come in among you, not sparing the flock.*

In just these few verses we see that the office of the pastor is responsible for the following:

- Feeding the sheep with the Word of God (John 21:15–19).

- Guiding the sheep with the Word of God (John 21:15–19).

- Guarding the sheep from false teachers with the Word of God (Acts 20:28–29).

The term *overseer* comes from *episkopos*. It is a compound word derived from *epi*, which means "over" and *skopos* which means "watcher" or "guardian." The term conveys the idea of a man who literally "keeps an eye on the flock." This term denotes a person who oversees the spiritual well-being of the souls of his congregation and the functions of the church. He watches over the sound doctrine and moral conduct of his own life as well as those in the church. The term *presbuteros* emphasizes the age and maturity of the pastor. It's not that the pastor is old, but rather, he is someone who is respected because of wisdom, spiritual maturity, and strong faith.

The second point we should understand about the pastor is that all pastors are coequal and co-laborers. We learn this in 1 Peter 5:1–2 where Peter says this to the fellow elders: "*So I exhort the elders among you, as a fellow elder and a witness of the sufferings of Christ, as well as a partaker in the glory that is going to be revealed: shepherd the flock of God that is among you.*" When Peter says that he is a fellow elder, he is stating his equality with fellow elders. In fact, the word for "fellow elder" is *sumpresbuteros*, which means "co-presbyter" or "co-elder." Likewise, Paul says this regarding himself and Apollos being coequal pastors in 1 Corinthians 3:9, "*For we are God's fellow workers. You are God's field, God's building.*" When Paul says that he and Apollos are fellow workers, he uses the word *sunergos*, which means "fellow worker" or "co-worker." This word emphasizes collaboration and partnership rather than elevated status and purpose. It's important to notice that although Paul and Peter both had apostolic authority, when it came to the title and office of a pastor, they considered themselves coequal with fellow elders.

In the modern church landscape, we use titles such as lead pastor, senior pastor, associate pastor, and so on. From a biblical perspective, there is no associate pastor, lead pastor, or senior pastor. There are simply coequal pastors who are commissioned by God to carry out the duties of the office of the pastor. Of course, pastors within a local church may have different areas of focus. For example, one pastor may focus on preaching and teaching new members; another pastor may focus on preaching and teaching to the youth; another pastor may focus on preaching and teaching to shut-ins; and another pastor may focus on preaching and teaching for missions. One pastor may perform more preaching and teaching on Sundays and perhaps be more of a spokesman such as Peter was. However, the point that should be emphasized is that pastors are coequal. God-commissioned pastors or elders are all equally commissioned and are uniquely gifted and capable of fulfilling the God-ordained call and office of the pastor. It is important to emphasize this point because there is a misunderstanding that associate pastors or youth pastors aren't responsible for oversight, correcting error in the church, confronting sin among pastors, and more. Such an understanding is alien to Scripture and unbiblical. All pastors are coequal and responsible for teaching, preaching, shepherding, and fulfilling the office and duties of the pastor.

The third point we should understand about the pastor's role is his immense accountability to the Lord for the sheep that he's been entrusted with. Hebrews 13:17 charges the pastor with this immense responsibility:

> *Obey your leaders and submit to them, for they are keeping watch over your souls, as those who will have to give an account. Let them do this with joy and not with groaning, for that would be of no advantage to you.*

Here we see the immense accountability of this office. Pastors are responsible for shepherding the souls of the sheep; therefore, it matters to God how they carry out their ministry. It matters to God how they deliver sermons, how they teach, and how they preach. It matters to God whether the pastor is sloppy or careful with His word. It matters to God how the man conducts his life in the public eye. It matters to God how the man conducts his life in private when no one is looking. It matters to God how the man mimics Christ. It matters to God when the pastor is wrong or errant in his teaching. This job of shepherding souls is serious. The seriousness of this responsibility is illustrated in Ezekiel 3:16–21. The Lord makes Ezekiel a watchman for the house of Israel and warns Ezekiel that he will be held accountable if he does not warn the wicked to turn from their wicked says. We see this in Ezekiel 3:17–19:

> *"Son of man, I have made you a watchman for the house of Israel. Whenever you hear a word from my mouth, you shall give them warning from me. If I say to the wicked, 'You shall surely die,' and you give him no warning, nor*

speak to warn the wicked from his wicked way, in order to save his life, that wicked person shall die for his iniquity, **but his blood I will require at your hand.** *But if you warn the wicked, and he does not turn from his wickedness, or from his wicked way, he shall die for his iniquity,* **but you will have delivered your soul.**" (emphasis added)

Thus, we see the seriousness and heavy responsibility of being a pastor. Ezekiel was charged with being a watchman, and he would be held accountable for the blood of the wicked whom he refused to warn. He did not have the option not to warn the wicked. It was not a recommendation to withhold warning the wicked. As a faithful watchman, Ezekiel was responsible for warning the wicked and exhorting them to repent. Likewise, the pastor is responsible for overseeing the souls of those whom the Lord has entrusted to him. Pastors are to guard the flock, guide the flock, and feed the flock. They will give an account to the Lord for the souls they shepherded and the faithful service they rendered.

Finally, we see that Christ gave the church teachers. The word *teacher* comes to us from *didaskalos*. This word carries with it an image of a man who is acknowledged as a skilled and competent teacher—a man who communicates and instructs from the Word of God. Without exception, all pastors must be skilled and gifted teachers. All pastors must be skilled in teaching God's Word and dedicated to understanding it and teaching it. The pastor is to know the Word, so he is able to live the Word, so he is able to teach the Word. Without sound teachers, there will be no sound doctrine and that will lead to an unsound and "undoctrinal" church.

Thus, we see that when God gifts a pastor to the church, the man is a born again, converted, and saved. The man is equipped by the Lord to feed, guide, and protect the sheep and will be accountable for his faithfulness in shepherding of the sheep. The man is also skilled to teach the Word of God and is also an evangelist.

> *To equip the saints for the work of ministry, for building up the body of Christ, until we all attain to the unity of the faith and of the knowledge of the Son of God, to mature manhood, to the measure of the stature of the fullness of Christ.*
>
> —Ephesians 4:12–13

As we transition to Ephesians 4:12–13, we will begin to see why the apostles, prophets, evangelists, pastors, and teachers have been given to the church. These are the current offices held in today's church since the offices of apostles and prophets have gone away. This book is primarily concerned with the office of pastor, which includes the functions of evangelism and teaching; therefore, we will focus on understanding what Ephesians 4:12–13 says about the purpose for which the pastor was given to the church by Christ.

First, we see that pastors are a gift to the church for the purpose of equipping or perfecting the saints for the purpose of unifying the church in the faith and knowledge of Christ, so the church becomes mature and Christlike. We could even say that this describes the "feeding" and "guiding" purpose of the pastor. We also see that the pastor equips the church for the work of ministry. The word for equip comes from *katartizó* which means to "equip," "perfect," or "prepare." This word carries with it the idea of equipping something for a task or perfecting a person or thing so that it is in good working order and fully functional. It conveys the idea of making something whole by fitting it together and arranging it properly. So how does the pastor equip, feed, and guide the church? The pastor equips the sheep by feeding the sheep the Word of God so that they may grow in maturity. Peter exhorts his listeners in his first epistle that they are to grow by consuming Scripture: *"Like newborn infants, long for the pure spiritual milk, that by it you may grow up into salvation"* (1 Peter 2:2). Just as an infant is dependent on milk from their mother for life and growth, so the new Christian is dependent on Scripture for growth and maturity. In fact, in the NIV Bible, 1 Peter 2:2 says that believers are to *"crave"* the milk of Scripture. The word *crave* comes from *epipotheó*, which means "to strain after," "desire greatly," or "have affection for." The undiluted and unadulterated Word of God is what the pastor is to give the church for growth and preparation of ministry. Not only does the Word provide growth, but it also guides. It becomes a lamp to one's feet and a light to one's path (Psalm 119:105). The Word acts as a guide, so we may not sin against God (Psalm 119:11). The Word is a guide and puts false ways far from the believer

(Psalm 119:29). We could even paraphrase Ephesians 4:12–13 this way: "Christ gave pastors to His church to equip His saints for work so that His church may be built up in the unity of the Christian faith and the knowledge of Christ so that His church may become mature and Christlike."

Note that Christ did not give pastors to the church so membership would increase or to make a building look attractive. Christ did not give pastors to the church to entertain man or to increase activities in the church. No, Christ gave pastors to the church to equip it for ministry work, bring it to unity in the Christian faith, and become mature.

We should also note that without the truth of God's Word, there is no true unity. Truth and error are not tolerant of one another. Light and darkness do not fellowship with one another. Righteousness and unrighteousness share no commonality. Just as truth brings unity, falsehood brings division to the unity. Adrian Rogers captures the very essence of why the pastor must unite the church in truth:

It is better to be divided by truth than to be united by error. It is better to speak the truth that hurts and then heals, than to speak falsehood that comforts but then kills. It is not love and it is not friendship if we fail to declare the whole counsel of God. It is better to be hated for telling the truth than to be loved for telling a lie. It is better to stand alone with the truth than to be wrong with the multitude.[2]

Therefore, we see the absolute necessity for the pastor to feed the sheep the true Word of God to equip the church for works of ministry and guide the church.

Next, we should ask ourselves, "How is the church built up?" We can understand this in two ways. The church is built up when sinners hear the gospel of their salvation, believe in Christ, receive the Holy Spirit, and are put into the body of Christ (Ephesians 1:13). John MacArthur has rightly said that the church advances one soul at a time. We see Luke explain this very truth in the book of Acts where three thousand souls were added to the church after Peter's sermon at Pentecost (Acts 2:47). We also see this truth when Peter spoke before the Sanhedrin, and five thousand men were added to the church (Acts 4:4). Therefore, we can be sure that the church is built up as the gospel is proclaimed, and sinners are saved. We also see that the church is built up when it becomes mature and Christlike. Thus, we see that the church is built up when souls are being saved and when the church is growing in Christlikeness and becoming mature.

But how do pastors lead the church to attain the knowledge of the Son of God and mature into Christlikeness? The answer is quite simple. In Hebrews 12:1–2, the author tells us how this can be done:

> *Therefore, since we are surrounded by so great a cloud of witnesses, let us also lay aside every weight, and sin which clings so closely, and let us run with endurance the race that is set before us, looking to Jesus, the founder and perfecter of our faith, who for the joy that was set before him endured the cross, despising the shame, and is seated at the right hand of the throne of God.*

The author of Hebrews tells us how to attain this knowledge: We must have a ministry that is focused on Jesus. Notice here that the author is specifically pointing to Christ enduring the cross and scorning its shame. Why would the author do this? It is because the author and perfector of our faith is the very one who was completely submitted to the will of His Father. As Christ looked ahead to the wrath of God He was going to suffer, His soul was grieved even unto death, and yet He submitted to His Father's will (Matthew 26:38–39). Christ knew there would be suffering before celebration. In this very same way, the pastor must equip His people to follow Christ's example of submitting to the Father. The pastor must show his flock that the path to Christlikeness is by wholehearted loving submission and trust in Christ and following His example. When Christ is the object of one's wholehearted affection, love, and trust, he will be submitted to Christ, he will follow Christ, he will do Christ's will, and he will become more Christlike. This is how the pastor leads the church to attain the knowledge of the Son of God and bring her to maturity.

Paul also gives us another picture of how the pastor brings about the knowledge of the Son of God that brings maturity. In 2 Corinthians 3:18, Paul says this about those with unveiled faces, or rather, those who have believed the gospel and are transformed into Christ's image: *"And we all, who with unveiled faces contemplate the Lord's glory, are being transformed into his image with ever-increasing glory, which comes from the Lord, who is the Spirit"* (NIV). The word for "contemplate" comes from *katoptrizó*, which means "to look as in a mirror" or "contemplate." John MacArthur rightly said that looking to and contemplating Christ is essential for all three aspects of salvation: justification, sanctification, and glorification.[3]

We look to Christ for our justification and right standing with God (Romans 3:24). We look to Christ for our sanctification and being conformed to the image of Christ (Romans 8:29). We look to Christ until we're brought to glory (2 Timothy 4:8). Looking, gazing, and contemplating Christ is essential for bringing about unity of faith in the church, growing in the knowledge of Christ, and being conformed to His image. We must learn to think of sin as Christ thinks of sin. We must learn to think of hell as Christ thinks of hell. We must warn of hell as Christ warns of hell. We must think of repentance as Christ thinks of repentance. We must think of saving faith as Christ thinks of saving faith. We must have a true understanding of who Christ is and what He accomplished, not a false understanding of Christ's person, work, and teachings. We must think of sanctification as Christ teaches us to think about being conformed to His image. We must think about persecution for the sake of Christ's name with joy rather than disdain. We must think of false teachers and falsehood the way Christ teaches us to think about false teachers and error. We must be thinking, praying, giving, forgiving, living, eating, sleeping, drinking, working, parenting, worshipping, and doing everything else according to what Christ teaches and commands. Jesus prayed for this very reality in His High Priestly prayer in John

17:17: "*Sanctify them in the truth; your word is truth.*" The pastor has no better means to bring about the knowledge of the Son of God then by feeding the church the truth of Christ in Scripture.

So how else does a pastor equip the saints, bring unity, and the knowledge of the Son of God? Paul says it simply in Ephesians 5:1–2: "*Therefore be imitators of God, as beloved children. And walk in love, as Christ loved us and gave himself up for us, a fragrant offering and sacrifice to God.*" Paul would argue that the answer is to be imitators of Christ. The pastor who feeds and guides the church will explain who Christ is, what Christ accomplished, and what Christ commands of us. The pastor himself is to be a living, talking, and walking representation and devoted follower of Christ. Paul exhorts and gives this very command to be Christlike to the Corinthians: "*Be imitators of me, as I am of Christ*" (1 Corinthians 11:1). Therefore, we see that Christ gives the church pastors who are skilled in teaching, skilled in preaching, and sound in doctrine—pastors who proclaim Christ and His gospel and who are living, talking, and walking examples of Christ. When the saints and the pastor walk in Christlikeness, this equips the church, brings unity, and leads the church into a greater knowledge of Christ, "*so that we may no longer be children, tossed to and fro by the waves and carried about by every wind of doctrine, by human cunning, by craftiness in deceitful schemes*" (Ephesians 4:14).

The second point we'll see as we transition into Ephesians 4:14, is the growing and guiding office of the pastor to bring about maturity in the church, goes hand in hand with guarding the church. As we learned from the apostle John, many false prophets have gone out into the world (1 John 4:1). We learn from Peter that false teachers secretly bring in destructive heresies that damn the listeners (2 Peter 2:1–3). We learn from Paul that false teachers will come from outside the church and inside the church and damn men's souls through their words (Acts 20:26–32). We learn from Jesus that false prophets and false teachers will come to believers (Matthew 7:15–20). Therefore, we see that the God-commissioned pastor equips the church in the truth and in the knowledge of Christ to guard against false teachers and false doctrine.

In Ephesians 4:14, Paul uses two analogies. The first analogy pictures a small infant or child in a boat in the midst of dangerous conditions; the infant or child would not have the strength or stability to avoid being thrown around in the boat by waves and could potentially even be thrown out of the boat. Therefore, this is a vivid picture of the vulnerability of a young Christian, showing how false teachers and worldly doctrine endanger the believer. In fact, the phrase *"tossed to and fro by the waves"* comes from *kludónizomai*, which means "tossed by waves," "unsettled," or "to be agitated." It conveys a sense of instability, lack of direction, and vulnerability to external forces. The damning false doctrine that false teachers propagate, which is hidden by a layer of truth, is serious and deadly. The pastor is to guard the flock from such heretics and wolves.

The second analogy is that of young children being carried about by every wind of doctrine or false teaching. The word for *"carried about"* comes from *peripheró*, which means to "carry around" or "pass around." This is a picture of one who is whirled around by violent swinging that would make a person dizzy. Just like swirling winds, which change direction quickly, exposure to different false doctrines can be a danger for the young Christian. God does not want this for His children; rather, He wants His children to mature and stand firm in the faith instead of being thrown around and carried about by false doctrines (1 Corinthians 16:13). The pastor is to guard the church against men who teach false doctrine. The pastor is to have the church keep a firm grip on the truth, so it avoids being pulled, driven, tossed about, and led into error.

Paul also describes the character of these false teachers; he calls them cunning. This word comes from *kubeia*, which means "trickery," "deceit," or "craftiness," which conveys the idea of cunning manipulation. Charles Spurgeon warned of the trickery of falsehood: "Beware! Error often rides to its deadly work on the back of truth!"[4] The deadliness of false teachers is that they have doctrines that mix truth and error, making it difficult to detect which part is untrue. Not only are false teachers cunning and deceitful, but they are also "crafty." This word comes from *panourgia*, which can also mean "cunning." This word implies a shrewdness that is not necessarily positive since the shrewdness involves manipulation or deceitful practices. Rather than godly integrity and speaking and walking with truth in love, false teachers are marked by worldly or satanic deceit. They are crafty and cunning, practicing clever manipulation, which makes error look like the truth.

Paul also describes these false teachers as scheming, a word that comes from *methodeia*, which means "wiles" or "craftiness." This term is used to describe the deceptive strategies and tactics used by the devil to lead believers astray; it implies a deliberate and systematic approach to deception. When used in a negative sense, "scheming" implies strategies that often have logic and design; these are devilish and demonic designs and systems that are propagated using men (1 Timothy 4:1). The designs of the devil are often attractive, always deceptive, and often ensnaring. Charles Spurgeon said this about the devil's schemes:

> He will attack you sometimes by force and sometimes by fraud. By might or by sleight he will seek to overcome you, and no unarmed man can stand against him. Never go out without all your armor on, for you can never tell where you may meet the devil. He is not omnipresent, but nobody can tell where he is not, for he and his troops of devils appear to be found everywhere on this earth.[5]

Finally, we see that these schemes are deceitful and false. In fact, the word for deceit comes from *plane*, which means "error," "delusion," or "wandering." This word is used to convey the idea of leading someone away from the truth by using error. The pastor is to protect the sheep against such false teachers that come to the church as pastors (Matthew 7:15) and servants of righteousness (2 Corinthians 11:14–15), but who are truly perverse and self-condemned heretics (Titus 3:11).

The world is full of false Christianity, and the pastor is to be saturated with scriptural truth so that he is a living lie detector. Below are examples of churches and denominations in false Christianity that allow and propagate both damning false gospels and falsehood:

- Roman Catholic church – Mary as co-mediatrix; purgatory; baptismal regeneration; works-based salvation.

- Lutheran church – baptismal regeneration.

- Episcopal church – baptismal regeneration; LGBTQ advocacy; permitting women pastors, teachers, and elders.

- United Church of Christ – baptismal regeneration; LGBTQ advocacy; permitting women pastors, teachers, and elders.

- United Methodist church – baptismal regeneration; permitting women pastors, teachers, and elders.

- Liberal Reformed churches (Alliance of Reformed Churches, Reformed Church in America, and many other denominations) – permitting women pastors, teachers, and elders.

- Presbyterian Church USA (PCUSA) – LGBTQ advocacy; permitting women pastors, teachers, and elders.

- Various Churches – Health, wealth, and prosperity gospel.

Christian, beware! False Christianity is prevalent throughout the world.

Rather, speaking the truth in love, we are to grow up in every way into him who is the head, into Christ, from whom the whole body, joined and held together by every joint with which it is equipped, when each part is working properly, makes the body grow so that it builds itself up in love.

—Ephesians 4:15–16

Paul gives the practical means by which the church is to become Christlike; in fact, Paul makes a comparison between truth and falsehood. Rather than being cunning, crafty, deceitful, and false, the church will grow into Christlikeness by *"speaking the truth in love."*

The first point we should see in Ephesians 4:15–16 is that the church will grow into maturity by "truthing." The phrase *"speaking the truth in love"* comes from the original word *alétheuó*, which means "to speak truth," "do truth," or "maintain truth." In its participle mood, this word means more than simply speaking truth; it means living the truth in both speech and conduct, which reflect a transformed and regenerated life through the gospel of Jesus Christ. Peter speaks of this godly example when he describes elders as, *"not domineering over those in your charge, but being examples to the flock"* (1 Peter 5:3). The true pastor is to be a walking, talking, yet imperfect example of Christ to the flock. He is to not only speak the truth in love, but he is also to walk the truth in love. He is not to be cunning, crafty, deceitful, fleshly, or self-willed. Rather, he is to be one who is submitted to the truth of the Word—one who teaches the truth of the Word and lives the truth of the Word.

The second point we should note is that truth is rigid and absolute. The truth contains hard sayings and easy sayings. Jesus's radical call to saving faith in Luke 14:26–27, 33 would be considered a hard saying:

> *If anyone comes to me and does not hate his own father and mother and wife and children and brothers and sisters, yes, and even his own life, he cannot be my disciple. Whoever does not bear his own cross and come after me cannot be my disciple. . . . So therefore, any one of you who does not renounce all that he has cannot be my disciple.*

Paul spoke harshly at times when he called the Galatians foolish or morons for giving heed to a different gospel (Galatians 3:1). Paul spoke harshly about false teachers stating that he wished the Judaizers would castrate themselves for teaching salvation by circumcision, ritualism, and the law (Galatians 5:12). The Bible says that there is no other way to the Father except through Christ, which makes all other religions false (John 14:6). The Bible says that men who permit women to be pastors are to not be recognized as spiritual or as prophets and spokesmen for God (1 Corinthians 14:37–38). The Bible has very defined and absolute truths. The pastor who equips and unites the church to bring about maturity is the pastor who gives the whole counsel of God which includes the easy and hard truths of Scripture. There is no verse or doctrine that the pastor seeks to leave out or avoid.

The third point we see is that "truthing" is always done in love—a love for Christ, love for believers, and love for the lost. In Paul's second letter to Timothy, he testified that he suffered all things for the sake of the elect that they may obtain the salvation, which is in Christ Jesus (2 Timothy 2:10). Paul said that he would become all things to all people for the sake of the gospel that the lost may be saved and that he may share with them in its blessings (1 Corinthians 9:22–23). Paul was both a staunch warrior for the truth and a compassionate lover of the lost. Paul loved the brethren, and he loved the lost. He taught the truth and lived the truth for the sake of Christ and lost souls. The pastor is to be a walking example of the truth in love, speech, and conduct.

The fourth point we see is that Christ is the head of the church, and the church is held together and sustained by Christ. It is not the role of the pastor to be the head of the church or to hold the church together. Rather, the pastor's role is to fulfill the duties and obligations of this office, which are set forth in Scripture. It is the duty of the pastor to explain Scripture, exhort with Scripture, pray for the church, proclaim the gospel, feed the flock, guide the flock, protect the flock, and live the truth lovingly. It is God who will work through the Word and give growth to the church (1 Corinthians 3:6–7). Christ gifts the church with pastors to do the work of a pastor, but it is Christ who is the Head of the church, the Sustainer of the church, and the one who gives growth to the church. Another way to state this reality of Christ being the Head and sustainer of the church is that Christ takes a condemned man, saves the condemned man by grace, gifts, and enables the man to be a God-commissioned and sufficient pastor, gives the pastor instructions for caring for His church, and builds up His church through the ministry of the God-commissioned pastor. As we can see, it is not the pastor who is the hero of the church; it is solely Christ who is the hero and captain of the church.

As we close this chapter, we have learned much about the pastor:

- Before a man is ever a pastor, he is saved by grace (Ephesians 4:4–10).

- It is God who makes, equips, and gifts a pastor to His church (Ephesians 4:11).

- *Pastor, elder, shepherd,* and *overseer* are simply different terms for the office of pastor.

- Christ makes pastors sufficient and qualified to be ministers (1 Corinthians 3:5–6).

- All pastors are co-laborers, and no pastor is above or below fellow pastors (1 Peter 5:1).

- Pastors do the work of teaching and evangelism (Ephesians 4:11).

- Pastors feed, guide, and guard the church (4:12–13).

- Pastors equip the church for ministry, to unite the saints in truth and knowledge of Christ (Ephesians 4:12–13).

- Pastors are to guard the church against false teachers or false pastors (Ephesians 4:14).

- Pastors are to be imitators of Christ and are to walk, speak, and conduct their lives in truth and godliness (1 Corinthians 11:1, Ephesians 4:15).

- God receives all glory for the church as He is the Head, Sustainer, and grower of His church (Ephesians 4:16).

As we end this chapter, consider this excerpt from a sermon by Tim Conway, a pastor at Grace Community Church in San Antonio, who had this to say about the man whom God makes a pastor:

Some people have this idea that you go to Bible college, or you go to seminary, and you become [a pastor]. Let me ask you this, has God come to you and given you something that you did not have before? Has God entrusted you with a stewardship? Has God given you a ministry? Has God revealed something to you? Has God given you gift? Has God given you power to be able to carry this out? . . .

Men, if you do not have something that is by the will of God, how do you know that it's by the will of God? Because God came from outside you and gave you something that you didn't have before that. Too many men want to pronounce themselves as pastors. They want to pronounce themselves as teachers but let me tell you something. It's a stewardship of God's grace that's given to men for the sake of others and if you've been given such a stewardship, others will recognize that you have such a stewardship of God's grace given to you. Why? Because it's for them. It's for their advantage. It's for their upbuilding. If nobody's built up. If nobody's advantaged. If nobody's helped. If nobody gleans grace from what you're doing . . . brethren, the last thing the church needs is self-pronounced anything . . . .

Brethren, God is still the God who is sovereign in the church. It's by the will of God that there is an apostle, and it is by the will of God that there is any kind of teacher, or preacher, or anybody gifted for any ministry. This comes from God. He is sovereign in the church. We need to grasp this. Men, you need to grasp it. Don't enter any ministry if you just have some inclination, some self-serving desire to do so if God has not broken into your life from the outside, come to you and made you what you weren't before, gifted you in a way you were not gifted before, given you a ministry, the grace of God being given to you, poured out onto your life, poured out on your gift, poured out on your character, where you know God has come. This is real Christianity. This is the Christianity of Scripture. It is God coming in, it is God stepping in, it is God doing something. That's what we need to recognize.[6]

Chapter 2

A Man Who Has the Grace of God Poured Out on His Character

Keep a close watch on yourself and on the teaching. Persist in this, for by so doing you will save yourself and your hearers.

–1 Timothy 4:16

In this chapter, we will examine how God pours out His grace on a man's character. Not only will we examine the character of the man God has commissioned to fulfill the office of pastor, but we will also examine the very opposite characteristics of the false teacher or false pastor. In doing so, we will be able to hold the diamond against the black velvet backdrop. We will be able to see strong contrasts between the true pastor and the false teacher. The purpose for writing this chapter in this manner is to draw out the contrasts between a true pastor and a false teacher. Not only do we want to recognize a true pastor, but we also want to be able to identify false teachers, for Christ has promised that we will recognize false teachers by their fruit (Matthew 7:16, 20). Likewise, we will also be able to discern the man who may be a true Christian but does not meet the qualifications to become a pastor. Drawing the portrait and character of the true pastor and false teacher, will help us discern and ensure that we don't put a true Christian into the office of pastor hastily if the church discerns that God has not gifted the man for that office. To understand how God pours out His grace onto the true pastor's character, we will review passages in 1 Timothy, 2 Timothy, Titus, and other portions of Scripture. We will also review passages in Matthew, 1 Timothy, 2 Timothy, Titus, 2 Peter, Jude, and other portions of Scripture to see the character of the false teacher. Let's get started by examining the key character traits of the true pastor.

A Man of Good Conscience

From Scripture we see that the true pastor must be a man with a good conscience (1 Timothy 1:5, 1 Corinthians 4:4). First Corinthians 4:4 tells us that Paul conducted his ministry as a servant of Christ and faithful steward: *"For I am conscious of nothing against myself, yet I am not by this acquitted; but the one who examines me is the Lord"* (NASB1995). When Paul is saying that he is not conscious of anything against himself, he is stating that according to his conscience, he has carried out his ministry faithfully. This word for conscience comes from the original word *suneidon* with *syn* meaning "with" and *eidon* meaning "to see" or "to know." It means to be aware of or conscious of something; it is used to describe an awareness of seeing and understanding, often in a moral or spiritual context. The conscience is the faculty by which individuals discern ethical and moral choices, which reflect what is in the heart. The conscience also discerns what is morally good and bad; the conscience either accuses or excuses one's actions. The conscience can either be made sensitive or dulled by the morality or ethical standard around it.

For example, if someone is told that committing adultery is only the physical act of adultery between a married spouse and someone the individual is not married to, then the conscience is informed that adultery is merely physical. However, pornography, fornication, lustful thoughts, and visiting houses of ill-repute may be acceptable because the conscience hasn't been informed that these other acts are sinful acts of sexual immorality as well. However, if the conscience is informed that adultery is looking at a woman with lustful intent, then the conscience has been informed and made more sensitive to a higher level of godly morality (Matthew 5:28).

Similarly, if someone is told that it is wrong to steal someone else's possessions, then the conscience has been informed that stealing is unacceptable. However, they may not know that when someone does not perform their duties at work, this is also a form of stealing. Likewise, an employer who underpays employees is also committing a form of stealing.

When Paul tells Timothy to stay in Ephesus to charge certain persons not to teach a different doctrine, he tells Timothy that this must be done with a good conscience (1 Timothy 1:5). Paul says the conscience must be a "good" or *agathos* conscience. *Agathos* refers to that which is intrinsically good, and which aligns with God's nature and will. The pastor's words, actions, and conduct must be conducted with a conscience that has been informed by the Word of God to discern what is good and pleasing to the Lord. Paul had even testified before the council in Jerusalem that he had lived before God with a good conscience (Acts 23:1). Having a conscience that absorbs, is informed, and becomes sensitive by the Word of God does not mean that the pastor is sinless. Rather, it means that the pastor who has an informed conscience made sensitive by the Word of God becomes aware of more sin in his life, and he is enabled and illuminated to see himself as the chief of sinners (1 Timothy 1:16). Therefore, we see that a God-commissioned pastor is one whose conscience is made sensitive by the Word of God and who understands that his conduct and secret motives are seen by God, and he carries out his ministry with a good and godly conscience (Romans 2:16).

Contrary to the true pastor who has a good conscience, the false teacher does not possess a sensitive conscience, but has a seared conscience. First Timothy 4:1–2 says this regarding false teachers: "*Now the Spirit expressly says that in later times some will depart from the faith by devoting themselves to deceitful spirits and teachings of demons, through the insincerity of liars whose consciences are seared.*" Here, we understand that not only is the false teacher a hypocrite, meaning that they say one thing and do the opposite or stand in the place of a spokesman for God but are not His spokesman, but we also see that they are liars who have a seared conscience. The word for seared comes from *kautériazó*, which means "burned with a hot iron" or "cauterized." It implies a process by which the conscience is rendered insensitive or unresponsive; this is the conscience of the false teacher. It is not sensitive to sin, error, or God's truth. The conscience has been made dull and unresponsive by running the red light too many times and not heeding God's warnings. False teachers are able to speak lies with little trouble; they can teach falsehood and error with no sensitivity that their mishandling and perversion of God's Word will one day be judged. They can find ways to justify their sin before men and ignore that God sees the heart (Luke 16:15). Thus, we see the false teacher has a seared conscience as opposed to a good conscience.

A Man with a Pure Heart and Sincere Faith

The true pastor is a man with a pure heart and sincere faith (1 Timothy 1:5). As mentioned, earlier, when Paul commanded Timothy to stay in Ephesus to charge certain people not to teach a different doctrine, he charged Timothy to do this with a pure heart and sincere faith. Paul is not charging Timothy to do this with a sinless heart. Rather, he wants Timothy to do so with a pure heart, totally devoted, dedicated, and undivided toward the Lord. A pure heart is a heart that seeks to do the will of God with no corrupt or selfish desires. A pure heart isn't concerned with receiving applause from men, receiving a comfortable life and salary, being liked by men, or receiving any sort of earthly kickbacks. No, this is a heart that seeks the approval of God by being devoted to the will of God, which is found in the Word of God (Galatians 1:10). In the Sermon on the Mount, the Lord pronounced blessing on those with a pure heart and promised they would see God, which means they would know God, enter God's kingdom, and inherit eternal life (Matthew 5:8).

We also see that Paul commanded that Timothy carry this out with sincere faith. The word for sincere comes from *anupokritos*, which means "unfeigned," "without hypocrisy," or "genuine." Essentially, Timothy is to have an authentic faith meaning that his behavior and conduct are free from hidden agendas and hypocrisy. The true pastor is not out for more followers, bigger church membership, a bigger building, a bigger salary, elevated status, elevated titles, honor of men, or any of the like. No, the work and ministry he performs is done with sincere faith and no hypocrisy. The true pastor carries out his ministry willingly and not under compulsion, but as God desires (1 Peter 5:2). Thus, we see that the true pastor has a devoted heart for the Lord, which is sincere and free from hidden agendas.

Contrary to the true pastor who has a pure heart and sincere faith, the false teacher serves their own evil desires. In

Romans 16:17–18, Paul warns about the selfish motives of false teachers:

> *I appeal to you, brothers, to watch out for those who cause divisions and create obstacles contrary to the doctrine that you have been taught; avoid them. For such persons do not serve our Lord Christ, but their own appetites, and by smooth talk and flattery they deceive the hearts of the naive.*

Here, we see that false teachers do not serve Christ with a pure heart or sincere faith. Rather, they serve their own selfish desires. They may feign service to Christ, but by their contrary doctrine and deceitful ways, they only serve their own selfish desires. Paul says of these false teachers that they serve their "*own appetites.*" The word *appetite* comes from *koilia*, which means "belly" or "abdomen" but is a general term covering any organ in the abdomen. Metaphorically, *koilia* can also mean "the inner man" and is used this way in John 7:38. Perhaps the false teachers can earn a living wage, perhaps they love the honor, perhaps they love the title, or perhaps they love the ease of the job. Regardless of their true motives, they have their own selfish reasons, and they don't have a pure heart and sincere faith.

We also see what makes them so dangerous is that they use smooth talk or *chréstologia*, which means "a kind address," "gentle word," or "useful word," and flattery or *eulogia*, which means "praise," "blessing," or "a good word." Thus, the reason they are so deceptive is because they speak kindly and with much flattery, and they do so while introducing false doctrine that opposes the gospel and God's Word. Therefore, we see that they are not pure in heart or sincere in faith. Rather, they selfishly serve themselves, deceive others with flattering speech and smooth talk, and create divisions and obstacles through teaching false doctrine.

A Man Who Conducts His Life in Godliness

Scripture states that the true pastor is a man who conducts his life in godliness (1 Timothy 6:11). Toward the end of Paul's first letter to Timothy, he gives Timothy the following command in 1 Timothy 6:11: *"But as for you, O man of God, flee these things. Pursue righteousness, godliness, faith, love, steadfastness, gentleness."* Godliness comes from the original word *eusebeia*, which means "piety toward God" or "devotion." This word refers to a reverent and devout attitude toward God, which is characterized by a life that reflects God's holiness and commands. It includes inner piety as well as an outward life that reflects the inner piety and God's will. The true pastor shows godliness in his marriage, the raising of his children, the way he conducts worship, the Bible studies he leads, the care he provides to the church, the way he addresses opponents, the way he handles persecution, the way he handles slander, the way he handles money, the way he handles relationships, and more. The true pastor conducts both his teaching and walk of life in godliness, for he knows that by doing so, he saves himself and others (1 Timothy 4:16). He is a man who conducts his speech in godliness as well (1 Timothy 4:12). Therefore, we see that the true pastor will manifest godliness in his life.

Contrary to the true pastor who is godly, the false teacher is licentious and blasphemes the way of truth. Peter describes this ungodly behavior in 2 Peter 2:2 where he says, *"And many will follow their sensuality, and because of them the way of truth will be blasphemed."* Sensuality has been translated from *aselgeia*, which means "licentiousness," "wantonness," "outrageous conduct," or "conduct shocking to public decency." *Aselgeia* implies violent spite, which rejects restraint and indulges in lawless insolence or wanton caprice. The Greeks described this as a disposition of soul that resents all discipline. William Barclay adds a helpful comment on this:

> It is that attitude of the soul which has never borne and never will bear the pain of discipline . . . it is not that he arrogantly and proudly flaunts it; it is simply that he can publicly do the most shameless things, because he has ceased to care for decency at all.[7]

There is a lack of restraint with the false teacher; they can propagate error and false doctrine without shame or concern. They can conduct certain areas of their lives with no moral restraint. This lack of restraint in either their teaching or their conduct blasphemes the way of truth. The word *blaspheme* comes from *blasphémeó*, which refers to speaking evil against or refusing to acknowledge good, and it reverses that which is good. Blaspheming the way of the truth can be correctly understood from two different perspectives. The first way a false teacher could blaspheme the way of truth by their sensuality is by giving correct doctrine, but having their life disagree with the correct doctrine. For example, a pastor who said that one must repent and put their faith in Jesus but was actively committing adultery with another woman would certainly be blaspheming the way of truth because, by his words, he is claiming he belongs to God, but his life vehemently opposes the truth. This could cause his listeners to dismiss the true doctrine because of the hypocrisy of his life. Another way a false teacher could blaspheme the way of the truth is by teaching a false doctrine that accepts a sensuous lifestyle and, thus, blasphemes the gospel call to saving faith or blasphemes the believer's sanctified walk of life. Thus, we see that the false teacher can be licentious in his doctrine and walk of life contrary to the true pastor who is godly in both his doctrine and walk of life.

A Man Who Is Steadfast in the Lord

Steadfastness is a core character trait of the true pastor. He is to remain steadfast in the Lord, obeying the command that Paul gives to Timothy in 1 Timothy 6:11: *"But as for you, O man of God, flee these things. Pursue righteousness, godliness, faith, love, steadfastness, gentleness."* This word *steadfastness* comes from *hupomoné*, which means "endurance" or "remaining under." This word conveys the idea of remaining faithful and patient under pressure and maintaining one's faith and hope despite challenges. This characteristic reflects a trust in God's character and promise. It is a picture of one bearing up under a heavy load and describes the quality of character, which does not allow one to surrender to circumstances or succumb under trial. Rather than compromising with the world, false religion, false Christianity, and walking in worldliness rather than holiness, the true pastor endures hardship while trusting in the Lord and walking in holiness. Though much of false Christianity will accept women as pastors, the true pastor stands his ground and opposes this even if he is called a chauvinist. Though widespread use of sacramentalism or salvation by sacraments is accepted as true Christianity, the true pastor stands his ground and opposes these false systems even though he may be called unloving and slandered. The true pastor is a broad-shouldered, resilient, uncompromising, persevering, and steadfast servant of God.

Contrary to the true pastor who is steadfast in the Lord, false teachers profess to know God, but they deny Him by their works, and they despise authority (Titus 1:16, 2 Peter 2:10). In 2 Peter 2:10, we get another characteristic of the false teacher where Peter says they *"despise authority."* The word *despise* comes from *kataphroneó* meaning to "scorn," "disregard," "esteem lightly," "hold in contempt," or "disdain." The word *authority* comes from *kuriotés* and means "lordship." False teachers do not persevere and remain steadfast in the Lord. No, they despise Christ's lordship. They despise when their systematic theology disagrees with the Lord's teaching. They despise having to obey difficult or certain commands of the Lord. They lightly esteem the Lord's commands. They create their own self-willed interpretations of Scripture that contradict God's Word. Ultimately, they reject the authority of God's Word. When they encounter a verse, they don't understand, they twist it. When they're shown their sin, they justify it. They are skilled at rejecting God's authority in various ways. Rather than remaining steadfast in the Lord like the true pastor, they despise the lordship of Christ and desire to do ministry their own way and thus deny Christ by their works.

A Man Who Draws His Power from God to Be Lovingly Courageous and Self-Disciplined

The true pastor is a man who has power from God and is lovingly courageous and self-disciplined (2 Timothy 1:7, 1 Timothy 3:2). In Paul's second letter to Timothy, he sought to encourage Timothy who may have been becoming reserved, timid, or even cowardly by saying, *"for God gave us a spirit not of fear but of power and love and self-control"* (2 Timothy 1:7). We can know that Timothy was becoming timid and cowardly because Paul says that God does not give us a spirit "fear." The word for fear comes from *deilia*, which means "cowardice" or "timidity." In this context, *deilia* refers to a shameful state of fear because of a lack of courage, moral strength, or mental resolve. It is natural for the natural man to be timid and cowardly in the face of persecution and hostility. This was true especially during Timothy's time when death and martyrdom were prevalent in the early church. However, Paul tells us that

God does not give a pastor such a cowardly demeanor. Rather, God makes the man powerful to speak the Word of God with all boldness and without hindrance (Acts 28:31). God makes the true pastor a powerful man of strong resolve. God did this very thing for Ezekiel as it says in Ezekiel 3:7–9:

> But the house of Israel will not be willing to listen to you, for they are not willing to listen to me: because all the house of Israel have a hard forehead and a stubborn heart. Behold, **I have made your face as hard as their faces, and your forehead as hard as their foreheads. Like emery harder than flint have I made your forehead. Fear them not, nor be dismayed at their looks,** for they are a rebellious house. (emphasis added)

So, just as Ezekiel was given power, courage, and resolve to prophesy against stubborn Israel, so God makes His true pastor stand with steely resolve against the world, against opposition, and the man's own natural fears. The man can stand with a face and forehead as hard as flint because God has done this work in the man's life, and the man stands strong out of love for God and love for people. This is a supernatural enabling that comes only from the Holy Spirit.

We also see that the true pastor is self-disciplined. This word comes from *sóphronismos*, meaning "self-control," "self-discipline," or "prudence." This word implies a state of self-control and moderation where one's thoughts and actions are governed by the wisdom and prudence of God. Though the man may suffer terribly, become greatly discouraged, face hardships in his ministry, and face betrayals, the man remains controlled and disciplined because he has immersed himself in prayer and the Word of God (1 Timothy 4:15).

Contrary to the true pastor who is courageous and self-disciplined, we see that the false teacher has a form of godliness, but not the true transformative and regenerative power of the Holy Spirit (2 Timothy 3:5). In Paul's second letter to Timothy, he warns of the outward religious appearance of apostates and false teachers who lack the transforming power of the Holy Spirit in 2 Timothy 3:5 where he describes them as "*having an appearance of godliness, but denying its power. Avoid such people.*" Here we see that there are false teachers who appear godly. In fact, the word for "*form*" comes from *morphosis*, which means "form," "outline," or "semblance." This word refers to the outward form or appearance, which does not necessarily represent inner transformation. It is true that false teachers and false Christianity have a form of godliness. The Roman Catholic Church has hymns, catechisms, crosses, robes, gowns, liturgy, and prayers, but it lacks the true gospel. So, just as the Roman Catholic Church has a form of godliness and Christianity, so too false teachers have an outward semblance of godliness but lack the transformation and regenerating work of the Holy Spirit, which changes the affections and will of an individual to love and be devoted to Christ. Jesus described the Pharisees this same way when He says this in Matthew 23:28: "*So you also outwardly appear righteous to others, but within you are full of hypocrisy and lawlessness."* It is true that false teachers have an outward appearance of righteousness, but on the inside, there is simply hypocrisy and lawlessness. Spend enough time with a false teacher and you will find that they don't take God's commands seriously.

Spend enough time with a false teacher and you will find that they are really hypocrites that do not do the work they're called to do. Spend enough time with a false teacher and you will find that they would rather talk about other things rather than God and Christ because they are hypocrites. Spend enough time with a false teacher, and you will find that they do not handle the Word of God with care and precision, but with sloppiness and error. The false teacher does not exhibit holy boldness, courageousness, and self-discipline. Rather, they simply have an outward semblance of godliness without power as opposed to the true teacher who has been regenerated and given a spirit of power, love, and control.

A Man Who Loves What Is Good

The true pastor is a man who loves that which is good and meets the qualifications that Paul gave Titus where he described a true pastor as a man who is *"hospitable, a lover of good, self-controlled, upright, holy, and disciplined"* (Titus 1:8). The phrase *"lover of good"* comes from *philagathos*, which means "loving what is good." This word is used to describe that which is inherently virtuous and beneficial. To be a lover of what is good is to be a lover of what God loves. To put this characteristic negatively is to say that the man is a hater of what God hates. Because God loves marriage, the true pastor is to hate divorce and adultery. Because God loves truth, the pastor is to hate slanderous, coarse, and filthy language. Because God's gospel is the truth and message of salvation, the true pastor hates false gospels. The true pastor is a man of God who seeks to love what God loves and hate what God hates. To be a lover of good is to be a hater of what is evil and perverse.

Contrary to the true pastor who loves good, the false teacher loves what is evil and filthy and is described like a dog returning to its own vomit and a sow that, after washing herself, returns to wallow in the mire. In 2 Peter 2:22, Peter describes false teachers who have learned the truth but return to their licentious doctrine and life where he says this: "*What the true proverb says has happened to them: 'The dog returns to its own vomit, and the sow, after washing herself, returns to wallow in the mire.'*" Peter pictures false teachers who know the truth of the gospel but decide to return to a false gospel as a graphic and ugly picture of a dog eating its own vomit. It would not be uncommon in the ancient world to see a dog vomit and eat its own vomit. The vomit would be foul, potentially carry disease, and would stink. Just as a dog who returns and smells, licks, chews, and swallows vomit, so Peter pictures false teachers as a dirty animal who licks, smells, chews, and swallows up a putrid gospel and abhorrent life. Likewise, pigs returning to the mire pictures the same grotesque nature of false teachers. It is one of pigs returning to a pile of mud, manure, and urine and rolling around in a vile sludge of filth. In the very same way, false teachers are pictured as those wallowing in a vile sludge of abhorrent doctrine that damn their souls and damn the souls of their listeners. Paul says that these false teachers are those who speak perverse, corrupt, and distorted things (Acts 20:30). Thus, we see that false teachers are not lovers of good. No! They are lovers of what is foul, evil, putrid, corrupt, perverse, and wicked.

A Man Who Is Holy

The true pastor must live a life marked by holiness. Among the qualifications Paul outlined for being a true pastor (Titus 1:8), it is a clear call that the man is to be holy: "*But hospitable, a lover of good, self-controlled, upright, **holy**, and disciplined*" (emphasis added). The word *holy* comes from *hosios*, which means "holy," "pious," or "devout." This word is used to describe that which is set apart. In this context, this would be used to describe a life that is set apart or consecrated to God as opposed to a life that is secular or profane. Being holy does not mean that a man is sinless. A helpful understanding of this comes from Steven Cole who says:

> This refers to practical holiness, being separate from sin and evil behavior. It does not mean being separate from sinners, because the Lord Jesus was the friend of sinners. But the devout man does not carouse with sinners in their sin. Rather, he seeks to lead them to repentance. The devout man takes God and the Word

of God seriously. He doesn't take the things of God as a joke. He lives in obedience to God's Word.[8]

Thus, we see that the true pastor is a holy man who has reverence and fear toward God and who lives out this holiness.

Contrary to the true pastor who is holy, the false teacher is marked as one who is defiled (Matthew 23:24). Jesus condemns the Pharisees for neglecting the weightier matters of the law such as justice, mercy, and faith while focusing on the lighter matters of the ceremonial law in Matthew 23:24: "*You blind guides, straining out a gnat and swallowing a camel.*" The Pharisees would go to extreme lengths to keep from defiling themselves, by straining out a gnat, which was the smallest unclean animal (Leviticus 11:23). However, by rejecting the important matters of the law and rejecting Jesus, they were swallowing a camel or the largest unclean animal (Leviticus 11:4) and were defiling themselves to the largest extent possible by leading others away from Christ, which showed their utter blindness. In the same way, false teachers do not recognize that they are defiled and unholy and they make their followers defiled, unholy, and double sons of hell (Matthew 23:15). Yes, they appear religious, but they propagate false religion and false Christianity that is unholy, defiled, and worthy of being condemned.

A Man Who Is Self-Disciplined

Discipline is another essential characteristic of the true pastor that Paul included in Titus 1:8. The word *disciplined* comes from *egkratés*, which means "self-controlled" or "temperate." This word conveys the idea of having control over one's desires and impulses. This control does not come from a man's own effort; it comes when a man gives control to Christ and is thus, God-controlled. Barclay has a helpful comment about self-control or discipline; he says, "Self-control does not contemplate a situation in which a man is emasculated of all passion; it envisages a situation in which his passions remain, but are under perfect control and so become his servants, not his tyrants."[9] The true pastor is not one who is being tempted, loving the world, and being led astray by its passions (1 John 2:15–17). Demas was mentioned in Paul's second letter to Timothy as one who forsook Paul because he loved the present world (2 Timothy 4:10). In fact, Paul told Timothy to have godly contentment and flee youthful lusts (1 Timothy 6:6–8, 2 Timothy 2:22). Thus, the true pastor is not one who is stripped of his convictions, strength, or passions. Rather, he is one who submits himself to God and has these convictions, strengths, and passions under God's control. Thus, the true pastor is one who has been enabled to control his desires rather than have his desires controlling him.

Contrary to the true pastor who is disciplined, the false teacher is one whose heart is trained in greed and is ignorant and unstable. When Peter describes false teachers, he explains that they are those whose hearts have been trained or exercised in greed (2 Peter 2:14). The word for "*greed*" comes from *pleonexia*, which means "covetousness" or "the desire for more things" including lust for a greater number of temporal things that go beyond what God determines is eternally best. The word for exercised comes from *gumnazó*, which means "to exercise," "to train." False teachers are those who are exercised in covetousness. Their church is never big enough. Their salary is never compensating enough. They need more recognition, more praise, more followers, and more fame. They need their members to fill out pledge cards so they can see how much money the church will have. Their hearts will never be satiated or content. Rather than exercising self-control by giving God control and not being controlled by temporal things, the false teacher cannot help but crave and desire that which will not eternally last and scorn that which is in God's best eternal interest.

Additionally, we see that the false teacher is ignorant and unstable as Peter comments on how they sometimes misuse Paul's more difficult teachings: "*There are some things in them [Paul's writings] that are hard to understand, which the ignorant and unstable twist to their own destruction, as they do the other Scriptures*" (2 Peter 3:16). In this verse, Peter points out that ignorant and unstable false teachers twist Paul's letters to their own destruction. The word "*ignorant*" comes from the original word *amathés*, meaning "unlearned." The false teacher is ignorant because they refuse to learn from Christ. The word *unstable* comes from *astériktos*, meaning "one who was not established" and thus, they are unstable. It describes someone who literally does not have a staff to lean on—hence, a person who cannot be relied on because they are not steady. They are not disciplined and careful when it comes to Scripture. Rather, they are self-willed, stubborn, and careless when it comes to

God's Word. By being unlearned and ignorant, they create self-willed interpretations of Scripture that are destructive. They tear down rather than build up. They are blind guides who lead the blind into a pit (Matthew 15:14). They have errant doctrine, which leads them to errant conclusions about Scripture, which eventually leads to errant and unholy walks of life that are undisciplined. Thus, we learn that the false teacher is ignorant, unstable, and trained in greed whereas the true pastor is self-disciplined.

A Man Who Is Faithful to His Wife

The true pastor who is married is a man who is faithful to his wife (1 Timothy 3:2). The language here speaks of a pastor literally being a "one woman man." The true pastor who is married is to love his wife as Christ the loved church and gave Himself up for her (Ephesians 5:25). The man is to love his wife self-sacrificingly. He is to be purposeful and diligent to teach her Scripture and lead her in holiness (Ephesians 5:26, 1 Corinthians 14:34–35). He is to protect, guide, and guard his wife. The man is to care for and love their wife as he would care for his own body (Ephesians 5:28–29). The man is to recognize his wife as the weaker vessel and support her knowing that though the wife is a weaker vessel, he is a weak vessel as well and depends on the Lord for strength (1 Peter 3:7). This means that the true pastor is not to engage in pornography, in flirtatious talk with other women, in flirtatious and unprotected text messaging with other women, in sharing emotional connections with other women, in spending personal time with other women, in seeking out opportunities to work with women for un-Christlike intentions, or in watching sexually charged videos or images of other women. The true pastor is not to gain the approval of other women by exposing his body with un-Christlike intentions, by flaunting power and wealth, or by any fleshly means. He is dedicated to his wife for the purposes of caring for her soul by teaching her Scripture, caring for her body as he would care for his body, guarding and guiding her, and raising their children in godliness and the instruction of the Lord.

Contrary to the true pastor who is a one-woman man, the false teacher has eyes full of adultery (2 Peter 2:14). This means false teachers view women as potential adulterers or as sexual objects. They devise ways to seduce women, to prey on women to fulfill their sexual desires, to talk flirtatiously with women, and to manipulate women. They are masters of severing marriages. They are experts in finding vulnerable women. They are skilled in taking a conversation to debased and immoral levels. They specialize in meeting secretly with women under the guise of trying to help them. They look for vulnerable women (2 Timothy 3:5). They put women in positions of power so they can interact with them. They try to appeal by fleshly means to attract other women. They can use counseling sessions to appear genuine and comforting but have intentions of building emotional relationships. They love pornography. They cannot stop devising ways to feed their insatiable adulterous hearts. As opposed to the pastor who is a one-woman man, the false teacher has eyes full of adultery.

A Man Who Is Above Reproach

The true pastor is a man who is above reproach (1 Timothy 3:2). The word for "above reproach" comes from *anepilémptos*, which is derived from *a* meaning "not" and *epilambanō* meaning "to seize" or "to take hold of." This word also describes someone whose character and conduct are irreproachable; the individual has nothing in their life for which he could be accused, arraigned, or disqualified. It is not simply an acquittal. No, it is the absence of any valid accusation that could be lodged against this person. One's behavior is irreproachable because he is "never caught doing wrong." The pastor is not sinless, but his speech, teaching, and conduct of life is blameless. Examples of a man who is not above reproach could include a man who is continually stealing from the church offering, a man who has forsaken his wife to run off with another woman, a man who violently beats and abuses his children, a man who is involved in illegal activity, a man who is a slanderer or a malicious gossip, a man who openly advocates disobedience to God's Word. John MacArthur makes this comment about a pastor being irreproachable:

> Paul is not speaking of sinless perfection but is declaring that leaders of Christ's church must have no sinful defect in their lives that could justly call their virtue,

their righteousness, or their godliness into question and indict them. There must be nothing in their lives to disqualify them as models of moral and spiritual character for believers under their care to emulate.[10]

Contrary to the true pastor who is above reproach, the false teacher follows their sensuality and revels in their deceptions. In 2 Peter 2:13, Peter says this regarding the false teacher who does not hide their revelry or deception: "*They count it pleasure to revel in the daytime. They are blots and blemishes, reveling in their deceptions, while they feast with you.*" The word for "*revel*" comes from *truphé*, which means "indulgent living," "effeminate luxury," or "softness." It conveys the idea of a lifestyle characterized by self-indulgence and moral laxity rather than a life of humility, self-control, and spiritual discipline. This speaks of moral and spiritual breakdown from overindulgence that deteriorates the soul and body. Thus, we see that false teachers can live indulgently in the daylight as opposed to carrying this conduct out at nighttime, which shows they are unrepentant and show no shame. Not only do they revel audaciously by living immoral and indulgent lives, but they also revel in their deceptions. Rather than be concerned and repentant about living a life of self-indulgence while teaching damning doctrines, they live indulgently and boldly proclaim their damning false gospels. When it comes to spreading their damning doctrine and falsehood, they boldly proclaim these heresies by putting them in catechisms, creeds, confessions, online videos, online sermons, and books for everyone to see.

They are blots and blemishes. They are filth spots. They are dirty and diseased. Thus, we see that the false teachers can revel in overindulgence all while spreading deception rather than the true pastor who is above reproach.

A Man Who Is Gentle, Not Violent

The true pastor is a man who is gentle and not violent (1 Timothy 3:3, 6:11). The word for "gentle" comes from *epieikés*, which means "mild," "fair," "reasonable," or "moderate." This word implies a disposition that is not overly strict, harsh, or violent, but rather one that is patient and understanding. This word describes the Christian who does not insist on the letter of the law but is willing to compromise where no moral issue is at stake. It is the attitude of taking wrong rather than of avenging the injuries received. It is true that the Christian faith is full of dogmatic truths where there can be no compromise, yet Christ who was full of divine truth was also full of divine compassion and mercy. Christ did not break a bruised reed or quench a smoldering wick, meaning He dealt gently with sinners (Matthew 11:19–20). Though Christ would preach hell and judgment, He also declared that He came to call the sin-sick sinner to repentance (Luke 5:32). Though Christ denounced towns for refusing to repent (Matthew 11:20–24), He was merciful and saved a murderous, false teaching, heretic such as Paul (Acts 9). So, we see that the true pastor is gentle; he has uncompromising beliefs and is unwavering in the truth. Yet, the true pastor deals gently with sinners. He is not easily excited. He is not quick to take revenge. He is not one who practices the art of holding grudges. Rather, he is a model of Christ who proclaimed divine truth, stood firm, and condemned cities and false teachers for not repenting; yet, he was divinely gentle, forgiving, and compassionate toward lost sinners.

Contrary to the true pastor who is gentle, the false teacher abuses his power and lords his authority over those beneath him (1 Peter 5:3, Matthew 23:4). In 1 Peter 5:3, Peter gives a description of how the pastor is not supposed to shepherd his flock when he describes the shepherd as "*not domineering over those in your charge, but being examples to the flock.*" The word for "*domineering*" comes from *katakurieuo*, meaning "to subdue," "to exercise dominion over," or "lord over." This word describes the act of exercising dominion or authority over others with a connotation of oppressive or authoritarian control where one party exerts power in a domineering or controlling manner. The term depicts a heavy-handed use of authority and can even indicate the use of authority to one's own advantage by manipulation or intimidation. Jesus denounced the Pharisees for such behavior when He indicted them for tying up heavy burdens that were hard to bear, laying them on the people's shoulders, and not lifting a finger to help them, all while practicing self-righteous hypocritical false religious activities to be seen by others, greeted respectfully by others, and honored by others (Matthew 23:4–7). Jesus also indicted false teachers for exalting themselves rather than humbling themselves (Matthew 23:12). Here the false teachers used their elevated religious status to be honored rather than to serve; they desired to be honored rather than help. Likewise, when the Lord denounced the religious leaders in Luke 11, we see that the Pharisees had become oppressive: *"As he went away from there, the scribes and the Pharisees began to press him hard and to provoke him to speak about many things, lying in wait for him, to catch him in something he might say"* (Luke 11:53–54). When Christ denounced the Pharisees for their blind and damning religious leadership, the Pharisees began to be hostile and quarrel with Christ. In fact, verse 54 says they were looking to entrap Christ with their questions much like a hunter entraps the game he is hunting. These false teachers will not take correction and will not admit when they're wrong. In fact, when they're shown to be wrong, we see through Christ's example with the Pharisees that they become enraged and refuse to give up their power or humble themselves. Thus, we see that the false teacher is one who is not gentle, but one who abuses their power and can be oppressive and dominating all while gaining honor and retaining power for themselves.

A Man Who Is Respectable

The true pastor is a man who is respectable (1 Timothy 3:2). The word for respectable comes from *kosmios*, which means "orderly," "respectable," "virtuous," or "well-behaved." The term describes someone who conducts themselves in a manner that is fitting and appropriate, reflecting a sense of decorum and propriety. It conveys the idea of being attractive because one's life is well-arranged and orderly. The true pastor's life is not chaotic and unorganized like that of the secular world. This is not to say that the pastor runs his life like a military institution either. However, it is to say that the pastor has purpose, is organized, and is orderly in how he conducts his ministry and personal life. The true pastor is a man who has a well-ordered and respectful life that is in harmony with Christian values and teachings.

A Man Who Is Hospitable

The true pastor is a man who is hospitable (1 Timothy 3:2). The word for hospitable comes from *philoxenos*, which means "loving strangers." This word is derived from *philos* meaning "loving" or "friend" and *xenos*, meaning "stranger" or "foreigner." This pictures the virtue of showing love and care to strangers and guests. It implies a readiness to welcome and provide for those who are not part of one's immediate family or community. This word conveys the practical application of being generous, welcoming, and cordial of visitors, guests, and strangers. It also implies giving practical help to anyone in need, which may include time, resources, and encouragement. This is not the type of hospitality that looks for a return or kickback from the one who is being helped. This virtue of hospitality is also not for the advantage of gaining a good name or receiving praise from men; rather, it is a display of genuine love and concern for strangers to meet their need in earnestness, truth, and sincerity. This is a self-sacrificing love for strangers that mimics the Lord Jesus Christ who did not come to be served, but to serve (Matthew 20:28). This is not a man who sits around his own circle of friends and is closed off to others. Not at all. This is a man who seeks and searches out strangers to know them, to meet their needs, and to love them. Thus, we see the true pastor is a hospitable lover of strangers.

Contrary to the true pastor who is hospitable, false teachers treat others with contempt. Jesus had observed that there were some who trusted in themselves—their own form of righteousness—and treated others with contempt before he told the parable of the Pharisee and the tax collector (Luke 18:9). The false teaching Pharisees were self-righteous and treated others with contempt; that is, they despised others, ignored them, and regarded them as nothing. The self-righteousness of the Pharisees was a contributing factor to why they showed contempt for the very ones they were to be shepherding. In Matthew 9:36 we read how Jesus felt when He saw the helpless state of the people of Israel under the Jewish religious leadership: *"When he saw the crowds, he had compassion for them, because they were harassed and helpless, like sheep without a shepherd."* The word *"harassed"* comes from *skulló*, which means "flayed," "skinned alive," "mangled," or "harassed." *"Helpless"* comes from *rhiptó*, which means "thrown down" or "hurled." In effect, the religious leaders spiritually skinned, flayed, and cast away the people of Israel; the religious leaders did nothing to feed, guide, or guard the sheep. So too, false teachers despise and show contempt for the sheep and even strangers or nonmembers in the church by not feeding them, not guiding them, and not guarding them. In Ezekiel 34:1–10, the Lord promised that He would be against such shepherds who showed contempt for the flock by not feeding and healing the sheep, treating them harshly, and scattering them. Thus, we see the false teacher does not love strangers or show hospitality; rather, they show contempt for strangers and even the sheep of God.

A Man Who Is Sober-Minded

The true pastor is sober-minded (1 Timothy 3:2); the word *sober-minded* comes from *néphalios*, which means "sober," "temperate," or "self-controlled." It can be used to describe a state of sobriety or abstaining from excessive wine consumption, but it can also convey the idea of being clear-minded and vigilant and keeping one's life free from world-dominating influences or circumstances. The man who is sober-minded submits all things, including every thought, to Christ as it says in 2 Corinthians 10:5: "*We destroy arguments and every lofty opinion raised against the knowledge of God, and take every thought captive to obey Christ.*" The sober-minded man has learned to think and see things as Christ sees them. He takes arguments, philosophies, religious talk, and worldly wisdom and makes them captive to Christ. His measuring stick is the Word of God. He is sober minded because he has a biblical worldview. He does not get his wisdom or instruction from the world. Rather, he takes every thought captive to obey Christ. Thus, the true pastor is able to see the world through the mind of Christ and make spiritual evaluations; he is not dominated and mastered by the circumstances of life (1 Corinthians 2:14–16).

Contrary to the true pastor who is sober-minded, the false teacher is like an irrational animal, a creature of instinct, born to be caught and destroyed; he is always learning but never able to come to a knowledge of the truth (2 Peter 2:12, 2 Timothy 3:7). In 2 Peter 2:12, Peter describes false teachers as an irrational animal born to be captured and destroyed. These false teachers are not sober-minded individuals who can see spiritual realities. No, they are blind guides (Matthew 23:26). Yes, false teachers may have books and read their Bible, but as Paul says to Timothy in 2 Timothy 3:7, they are *always learning but never able to arrive at a knowledge of the truth.*" They're never able to come to a saving knowledge of the truth. Though they bear the title of a pastor, they give worldly advice. Though they have a Bible, they still counsel as the world counsels. John has this to say about the worldly counsel and wisdom these false teachers give: "*They are from the world; therefore they speak from the world, and the world listens to them*" (1 John 4:5). They are not profound because they are not submitted to God's Word. Peter compares these false teachers to animals who only act on instinct. However, unlike animals who serve a purpose when they're caught and killed for food or other useful purposes, these false teachers only serve a benefit when they die and are thrown into hell, putting an end to their false teaching. The greatest benefit these false teachers provide is when they die and stop propagating damning doctrine that damns other men's souls. The greatest benefit these false teachers provide is when they are eventually captured and sent to hell. Thus, false teachers are irrational creatures who are not sober-minded. The greatest benefit they provide the world is when God is glorified by throwing them into hell.

A Man Who Is Peaceable

The true pastor is not a drunkard or a violent man, but peaceable. In 1 Timothy 3:3, Paul says that the pastor "*is not being a drunkard.*" This word *drunkard* comes from *paroinos*, which is derived from *para* meaning "beside" or "near" and *oinos* meaning "wine." It describes one who is habitually overindulging in wine, which conveys both a lack of self-restraint and dependency or addiction to alcohol. Paul is not saying that the elder must never consume alcoholic beverages, but he is saying is that the pastor must not be given over to, overindulge, be controlled by, or dependent on alcohol. The Bible gives strong warnings of the devastation that comes from drinking and becoming intoxicated by alcoholic beverages (Proverbs 23:26–35). The true pastor is to heed these warnings. Some churches require that the pastors and elders completely abstain from alcohol. Though there is no biblical mandate that a pastor must completely abstain from alcohol, he must be aware of the dangers associated with drinking alcohol, and if he does consume alcohol, he must be discerning and not consume alcohol in such a way that leads the flock astray or brings reproach on himself and the church.

Paul also says that the true pastor must not be a violent

man. The phrase "*violent man*" comes from *pléktés*, which means a "striker," "contentious person," or a "brawler." This word is used to convey the idea that someone is violent or a bully either by physical, emotional, or spiritual means. This word describes someone who is prone to striking others either physically or metaphorically—one who has a proclivity for conflict. The pastor must not be someone who retaliates either verbally, physically, or spiritually. In 2 Timothy 4:17 Paul says that he was deserted by all his followers during his first defense; yet he hoped that this act of cowardice and betrayal would not be held against those who deserted him. He exemplified an attitude of forgiveness rather than retaliation. Though Paul was abandoned and deserted, he did not seek retaliation against those who abandoned him; instead, he forgave them. Likewise, Paul exhorted the Romans to never avenge themselves but to leave vengeance up to God and to repay evil with good, which exemplified the attitude of a child of God (Romans 12:19–21, Matthew 5:43–48). Just like Paul, the pastor is not to strike back and attack; he is not to be a malicious slanderer when wronged. He is not to be a man who seeks to get in the last word. He is not to be a man who seeks conflict. Meekness does not mean weakness, and kindness does not mean compromise. This does not mean that the pastor is to be a man with no backbone who never defends himself. Even Paul was forced to defend himself and his ministry when his character and ministry was under attack by false teachers in 2 Corinthians 3:1–6. However, we see that the true pastor is not a man given to physical, emotional, or spiritual abuse, or violence and conflict. Rather, the true pastor is to be gentle and self-controlled.

The true pastor is to be peaceable. The word "*peaceable*" comes from *amachos* with "*a*" meaning "not" and *machē* meaning "fight" or "battle." It can also mean "not contentious" or "abstaining from fighting." This word conveys the idea of someone who avoids disputes and conflicts and maintains harmony and unity in the Christian faith when possible. In fact, this word stresses not having an ill-natured readiness to fight without good cause. Being peaceable does not mean he compromises and tries to maintain harmony when error is propagated. We are called to contend for the faith (Jude 3) and fight the good fight of faith (1 Timothy 6:12), but we are not called to be contentious and obnoxious. In fact, Jesus pronounces blessing over this beatitude in Matthew 5:9 when He says, "*Blessed are the peacemakers, for they shall be called sons of God.*" The peacemakers are those who have made peace with God (Romans 5:10–11), carry the message of peace in the gospel (2 Corinthians 5:19), and strive for peace with all people (Romans 12:18). A peacemaker is a man who is not looking for a debate, not looking for quarrels, not looking for fights, not looking to break unity, and not looking to agitate while remaining firm and unwavering in the Christian faith. Paul gives this very instruction to Timothy in 2 Timothy 2:14, "*Remind them of these things, and charge them before God not to quarrel about words, which does no good, but only ruins the hearers.*" Engaging in debates, fights about words, and contentious arguments are not the way of the godly man and true pastor.

The true pastor knows that these things are not profitable and only do harm. The true pastor's knee-jerk reaction is reconciliation rather than retaliation.

Contrary to the true pastor who is peaceable, false teachers are given to controversy, quarreling over words, and debate (1 Timothy 6:3–5). As we learned earlier, false teachers live licentious lives and can live in revelry, which includes the overindulgence of wine so no further discussion is needed to understand how false teachers may abuse alcohol or other mind-altering pharmaceuticals (2 Peter 2:2, 13). In 1 Timothy 6:3–5, Paul says this regarding false teachers and their argumentative spirit:

> *If anyone teaches a different doctrine and does not agree with the sound words of our Lord Jesus Christ and the teaching that accords with godliness, he is puffed up with conceit and understands nothing. He has an unhealthy craving for controversy and for quarrels about words, which produce envy, dissension, slander, evil suspicions, and constant friction among people who are depraved in mind and deprived of the truth, imagining that godliness is a means of gain.*

False teachers not only propagate false doctrine that does not agree with the teachings of Christ, but we understand from this passage that they have an unhealthy, diseased, and sick craving for controversy. The word *controversy* comes from *zétésis*, which means "debate" "questioning," or "dispute." In this context, it describes discussions or arguments that would lead to division or confusion, disrupting unity and bringing about ungodliness. Additionally, we see that the false teachers quarreled over words. This phrase *"quarrel about words"* comes from *logomachia*, which is derived from *logos*, meaning "word" or "speech" and *machē* meaning "battle" or "fight." This word literally means a "word fight" or "word battle;" this word is often associated with arguments or semantics over trivial matters rather than substantive matters such as the gospel, salvation, the person and work of Christ, and the authority of Scripture. Such word fights come from pride and being puffed up; they do not come from love. They come from the pride of someone who has a depraved mind and is deprived of the truth. Rather than seeking peace over trivial matters, false teachers seek debates and word battles out of pride and a depraved mind because they are deprived of the truth and are unregenerate.

A Man Who Manages His Household Well

The true pastor manages his own household well, with children being in submission and doing so with full respect (1 Timothy 3:4–5). The true pastor must be able to guide, provide, and maintain leadership in his household. This reflects the quality of his ability to lead by positively setting an example through nurture and protection rather than domination. As we discussed earlier, the man is to lead, care, protect, and nurture his wife. He is to manage and guide his children; he is to rule over his children without embittering them or being domineering. He is to bring his children up in the discipline and instruction of the Lord (Ephesians 6:4). The father is to raise his children up in the wisdom, instruction, knowledge, and prudence of Scripture (Proverbs 4). He is to ensure that his children obey him out of love and not fear; children are to obey their father out of honor and not out of coercion. The man is to do this with all honor. The word *honor* comes from *semnotés*, which means "dignity," "reverence," or "seriousness." It describes a quality that is worthy of respect and honor that is befitting the title of a Christian. The pastor's management and leadership are to be worthy of honor and dignity that can be seen by both believers and unbelievers. The man's ability to lead his wife, children, and the affairs of his household are an indication of whether he can lead the church with all dignity and honor.

A Man Who Is Mature in the Faith

The true pastor is not to be recent convert, but rather, mature regarding the faith (1 Timothy 3:6). The phrase *recent convert* comes from *neophutos*, which is derived from *neos* meaning "new" and *phuo* meaning "to grow" or "to plant." It literally means "newly planted," which is where "recent convert" or the idea of a new convert to Christianity comes from. Paul explains that the pastor must not be a recent convert because of the risk of being puffed up with conceit and falling in the judgment of the devil. Paul is concerned with the pitfalls that might come with pride for the new convert to Christianity. We saw that the Lord dealt with pride and the desire for greatness among His disciples when they argued over who among them would be the greatest. Christ had to remind them that they were to serve rather than rule as the Gentiles did (Luke 22:24–26). Peter was confident he would never betray the Lord, but the very boast he made was shattered that very night when he denied the Lord three times and could not even remain vigilant to pray with Him. We can learn from the apostles that pride can accompany spiritual leadership. This pride is the desire for greatness and exaltation rather than to serve; such pride can lead to devastating consequences. Peter exhorts his fellow co-pastors on the importance of remaining humble when he says this in 1 Peter 5:6–8: "*Humble yourselves, therefore, under the mighty hand of God so that at the proper time he may exalt you . . . . Be sober-minded, be watchful. Your adversary the devil prowls around like a roaring lion, seeking someone to devour.*" Pride goes before destruction, and a haughty spirit before a fall (Proverbs 16:18). Therefore, God requires that the pastor not be a recent convert for the purposes of protecting against pride and the snares of the devil who is seeking to devour and destroy.

One thing that should be mentioned is that the pastors and elders who are going to discern the maturity of a potential elder or pastor must be discerning in the testimony and validity of the potential pastor. For example, there are many testimonies from men who desire to be an elder which include statements such as these: "I've always been a believer," "I've been a Christian my whole life," or "I grew up in the church and have followed the Lord my whole life." Such a testimony does not square with Scripture, which tells us that we were children of wrath prior to being made alive with Christ (Ephesians 2:1–5). In short, the testimony must align with what the Bible says about regeneration, conversion, repentance, faith, and sanctification. The pastor who puts men into the position of pastor or elder hastily also shares in the sins of the pastor he commissioned (1 Timothy 5:22). Therefore, the pastor must also be discerning of the testimony and conversion of the potential co-pastor as well as their spiritual maturity.

Contrary to the true pastor who is a true believer, the false teacher is not a true Christian at all. The false teacher is one who shuts up the kingdom of heaven and makes false converts who are double sons of hell just as much as he is (Matthew 23:13–15). False teachers are ones who bring destruction upon themselves (2 Peter 2:1–3). False teachers are ones who are perverted, sinful, and self-condemned (Titus 3:10–11); they are disqualified regarding the faith (2 Timothy 3:9). Therefore, we see that false teachers do not even meet the requirement of being a convert to Christianity; they are outside the kingdom of God and are unregenerate.

A Man Who Has a Good Reputation with Outsiders

The true pastor is a man who has a good reputation with those outside the church (1 Timothy 3:7). The true pastor is not only known inside the church as a godly man, but he also has a good reputation with those outside the church. The word *reputation* comes from the word *marturia*, which means "testimony," "witness," or "evidence." Of course, this all implies that the true pastor is sound in doctrine and sound in the Word. So just as those inside the church know him to be self-controlled, respectable, hospitable, not violent, gentle, steadfast, godly, pure in heart, and sincere in faith, outsiders must see this same conduct and give witness to the man's character. A man who has a good reputation inside the church but doesn't have a matching testimony with the outside world can fall into the snare of the devil.

How would such a testimony fall into the snare of the devil? A man who has a bad witness outside the church brings disgrace and contempt onto the church. Jesus says we are to be the salt of the earth, and the light of the world and the Christian's good works is to bring glory to the Father (Matthew 5:14–16). However, a pastor who lives a compromised life, which bears a bad witness, will bring reproach upon Christianity and the church. True Christians are those who have been transferred from the kingdom of darkness to the kingdom of God's beloved Son, and they reflect His character. Christians who have a bad reputation with the outside world cause the Gentiles to blaspheme God (Romans 2:24). Additionally, fellow pastors who are not able to properly identify that a man has a bad reputation outside the church will bring reproach upon church leadership because the church leadership could not discern this by simply asking neighbors, coworkers, and acquaintances about the pastor's reputation. As you can see, when a pastor has a bad reputation outside the church, it blasphemes God and brings reproach upon His character and church. For this reason, the true pastor must have a good reputation with outsiders.

Contrary to the true pastor who has a good reputation, the false teacher is one who is disqualified from the faith, and their folly will be plain for all to see. In 2 Timothy 3:9, Paul compares false teachers to Jannes and Jambres who opposed the truth, and he makes this statement about the obviousness of identifying false teachers who are corrupted in mind and disqualified from the faith: *"But they will not get very far, for their folly will be plain to all, as was that of those two men."* Paul is saying that it will eventually become clear who false teachers are by their folly. The word *folly* comes from *anoia*, which means "without understanding," "foolishness," or "madness." It refers to irrationality or madness with actions or thoughts that are devoid of wisdom or sound judgment. For example, this could be a pastor who preaches truthfully that one is justified by faith alone in Christ alone; yet he claims that his son received saving faith and was justified in water baptism even as his son is committing adultery and addicted to pornography. True Christians and even outsiders would recognize the pastor's theological stupidity, and it would become manifest that something is wrong with the pastor's wisdom, counsel, and biblical understanding. Even someone outside the church would recognize that the son's immorality lacks the moral integrity that is consistent with Christianity. Additionally, Jesus promised that true Christians would be able to recognize false teachers by their fruits (Matthew 7:16, 20). Paul is simply stating that the false teacher's foolishness and opposition to the truth will be made manifest whereas the true pastor will have a good reputation inside and outside the church.

A Man Who Is Content with God's Provisions

The true pastor is to be content with what the Lord has given him and not be greedy for gain (1 Timothy 6:6–9, Titus 1:7). In 1 Timothy 6:6–9, Paul tells Timothy:

> *But godliness with contentment is great gain, for we brought nothing into the world, and we cannot take anything out of the world. But if we have food and clothing, with these we will be content. But those who desire to be rich fall into temptation, into a snare, into many senseless and harmful desires that plunge people into ruin and destruction.*

In these verses, Paul is drawing a comparison between the true pastor and the false teacher. Paul wants Timothy to understand that having a godly character with contentment is of great worth and gain. For Paul, contentment refers to being satisfied with what one has without the need for excess or reliance on external circumstances. This contentment emphasizes the reliance on God's provision and sufficiency in Christ rather than material wealth or self-reliance. In fact, Paul speaks of having godly contentment in having nourishment and coverings in verse 8. Paul also spoke of having such contentment in Philippians 4:11–12:

> *I am not saying this because I am in need, for I have learned to be content whatever the circumstances. I know what it is to be in need, and I know what it is to have plenty. I have learned the secret of being content in any and every situation, whether well fed or hungry, whether living in plenty or in want.*

Paul wanted Timothy to have such godly contentment and not to long for the things that perish.

In fact, Paul warned Timothy that those who desire to be rich fall into temptation and a snare and bring harm to themselves and their listeners. The love of material wealth can have devastating consequences. The true pastor is never to make decisions based on whether he will receive a salary, whether his salary will increase, whether the church's financial position will improve, or whether he will get the salary he wants. Likewise, the pastor is never to alter, modify, or change the message or Word of God because he's afraid of the financial implications and costs. Money is not to be the driving factor for contentment. Rather, the driving factor for contentment is glorifying God and pleasing the Lord (Galatians 1:10). Decisions that are made based on gaining wealth will have devastating consequences. We read that people will literally accumulate for themselves teachers to suit their own passions and will turn away from listening to the truth (2 Timothy 4:3–4). These people will find pastors who alter the message and the gospel and water down the Word of God, and they will compensate pastors financially to do so. Pastors who compromise the truth for monetary gain rather than pleasing the Lord will plunge people into ruin and pierce themselves with many sorrows (1 Timothy 6:10). Therefore, the man of God is to learn to be content with what the Lord provides and not be greedy for money and wealth.

Contrary to the true pastor who is content, the false teacher has a love of money (1 Timothy 6:10, 2 Peter 2:3). Peter says this about false teachers who exploit their listeners with false words: *"And in their greed they will exploit you with false words. Their condemnation from long ago is not idle, and their destruction is not asleep"* (2 Peter 2:3). The word *exploit* comes from *emporeuomai*, which carries the idea of "a place for trading or doing business." Peter is saying here that false teachers take advantage of their listeners for money. The outrageous televangelists who have huge mansions and private jets would certainly fall in this category, but Peter would also have in mind those who make their living off false teaching. For example, even though false teachers may not be getting rich off their trade, they are able to get what they want through their profession. This certainly carries the heavy implication that false teachers do this for money. As we noted earlier, false teachers can certainly be covetous for money, but they can also be covetous for power, prestige, preeminence, comfort, friends, and more. In Luke 16:14, Jesus warned that one cannot serve both God and money, and then he denounced the Pharisees for their love of money in Luke 16:14–15:

The Pharisees, who were lovers of money, heard all these things, and they ridiculed him. And he said to them "You are those who justify yourselves before men, but God knows your hearts. For what is exalted among men is an abomination in the sight of God."

Loving money, being devoted to it, and making spiritual decisions based on money are abominations to God. Such behavior is offensive, and it is repulsive to God when we make spiritual decisions based on money rather than pleasing Him. Peter gives an example of the false teacher, Balaam son of Beor, who forsook the right way because he loved gain from wrongdoing (2 Peter 2:15). Rather than choosing obedience to God, the false teacher lusts for filthy lucre (Titus 1:11). What is so upside down is that the false teacher thinks that godliness is a means of gain (1 Timothy 6:5); they believe that acting and standing in the office of a pastor is an acceptable means to gain wealth. What foolishness! Thus, we see that false teachers have a love for money and make spiritual decisions based on money rather than obedience to God.

A Man Who Is Not Self-Willed

The true pastor is not to be self-willed. We see this requirement in Titus 1:7 where Paul tells Titus, *"For the overseer must be beyond reproach as God's steward, not self-willed, not quick-tem-pered, not overindulging in wine, not a bully, not greedy for money*" (NASB2020). The compound word *self-willed* comes from *authadés*, which means "self-satisfied," "arrogant," or "stubborn." This word conveys the idea of someone who is obstinate and demonstrates a life of self-interest or self-pleasure that disregards other people's opinions or authority. The opposite of being self-willed is to be humble, and Peter exhorts the co-elders to humble themselves under the mighty hand of God so that at the proper time, they may be exalted (1 Peter 5:5). The true pastor is not to be self-willed but is to humble himself under the authority of God. The pastor is not to carry out his ministry under his own authority. Rather, he is to carry out his ministry humbly and under the authority, rule, and instruction of the Lord. Just as Moses built the Tabernacle according to the pattern he was shown (Exodus 26:30), so too the pastor is to fulfill his ministry exactly according to Scripture. Jesus captures this humble mindset when He tells His disciples this regarding their duty, "*So you also, when you have done everything you were told to do, should say, 'We are unworthy servants; we have only done our duty'*" (Luke 17:10 NIV).

Contrary to the true pastor who is not to be self-willed, the false teacher is one who rejects authority (Jude 8). When Jude says that apostates and false teachers reject authority, he means that these false teachers consistently reject or nullify authority. This speaks of a sense of disregarding or setting aside established norms or commands. It is a behavior that involves a deliberate decision to invalidate something that is authoritative or binding. This can be true of the false teacher who wants to have authority over others in the church. Rather than being a co-pastor or co-elder, they reject co-eldership and seek total authority. This can also happen when a false teacher is obstinate or disregards civil or government laws, such as purposefully evading taxes, laundering money, or deliberately breaking the law. Ultimately, this means setting aside and disregarding God's will. The false teacher will find ways to disregard God's will in their ministry. This could mean self-willed interpretations of Scripture, self-willed plans for the church, self-willed and self-selected church discipline, and more. Thus, we see that the false teacher is self-willed and obstinate; this may be revealed in several different ways.

A Man Who Is Not Quick-Tempered

Next, we should see that the true pastor must not be quick-tempered (Titus 1:7). This word *quick-tempered* comes from *orgilos*, which means "prone to anger." This word is used to describe someone who has a propensity for wrathful or irritable behavior and is easily provoked and cannot control his anger. This word also carries with it the picture of someone who is prone to anger, harbors resentment, and nurtures long-standing anger. Barclay has said this about this kind of anger:

> There are two Greek words for anger. There is *thumos*, which is the anger that quickly blazes up and just as

quickly subsides, like a fire in straw. There is *orgē*, the noun connected with *orgilos*, and it means inveterate (firmly established by long persistence) anger. It is not the anger of the sudden blaze, but the wrath which a man nurses to keep it warm. A blaze of anger is an unhappy thing; but this long-lived, purposely maintained anger is still worse. The man who nourishes his anger against any man is not fit to be an office-bearer of the Church.[11]

There is a time for righteous anger, but even righteous anger is to be controlled and must not lead to sin or give the devil a foothold, and an opportunity to trap or ensnare the person in sin (Ephesians 4:26). Thus, the true pastor is one who is not easily angered.

On the contrary to the true pastor who is not to be quick-tempered, the false teacher is one who is savage or brutal (2 Timothy 3:3). In Paul's letter to Timothy, he describes apostates and false teachers and gives this description in 2 Timothy 3:3, saying that they will be, "*heartless, unappeasable, slanderous, without self-control, brutal, not loving good.*" The word *brutal* comes from *anémeros*, which means "not tame," "fierce," "or savage." This word is used to describe someone as lacking the gentleness and control associated with domestication. It is used to describe someone who is unruly or lacking in moral restraint. It describes someone who is unfeeling and ruthless and who will pounce and attack anyone who gets in their way. The false teacher is willing to slander anyone who opposes them. They are ready to assassinate someone's character and stab them in the back. They are crouched and ready to gossip and defame others. They will not listen to reason, and they are the very opposite of gentle. Thus, we see that the false teacher is one who can be brutal and quick-tempered.

A Man Who Is Humble

The true pastor is a man who is humble. In 1 Peter 5:5, Peter commands the elders and his listeners to be humble toward one another: "*Clothe yourselves, all of you, with humility toward one another, for "God opposes the proud but gives grace to the humble.*" Additionally, in 1 Peter 5:6 Peter commands the elders and his listeners to be humble under God where he says: "*Humble yourselves, therefore, under the mighty hand of God so that at the proper time he may exalt you.*" Therefore, we see that the true pastor is to be humble toward the congregation, humble toward co-pastors, and humbled before God.

The word for *humble* comes from *tapeinoó* which conveys the idea of someone who is fully dependent on the Lord and shuns self-reliance and ego. It is the virtue of recognizing one's dependence on God for absolutely everything. What brings about true humility in the pastor? It is the recognition of sin, self, the Savior, and salvation. The humbled pastor knows of his sin against the Lord and the punishment he deserves which is hell. The pastor also understands Christ's person and work. He understands that Christ lived a perfect life, suffered the unimaginable wrath of God on the cross for his sins, and died as a substitutionary propitiation for his sins. The pastor has also accepted Christ's terms of salvation which are repentance toward God and faith in the Lord Jesus Christ. The pastor has been brought low by his sin, been emptied of self-exalting righteousness, and denied himself, took up his cross, and lovingly submitted his life to Christ and trusted in Him alone for salvation. This is what brings true humility for the pastor. It is the highly exalted view of his sin and Christ's glory and a Biblical reality and thorough grasp of his unworthiness and the foolishness of self-righteousness and self-will.

In true humility there is simply the Biblical understanding of who one is and who Christ is. The true pastor can see himself as an unworthy slave (Luke 17:10). The true pastor realizes that the only thing that he contributed to his salvation was his sin. True humility is poverty of spirit and a broken and contrite heart before the Lord (Matthew 5:3, Psalm 51:17). All boasting of human effort, human will, and human accomplishment vanishes in exchange for boasting in the cross of Christ (Galatians 6:14). Christ is the true pastor's preeminent model of humility. The true pastor sees Christ who did not count equality with God a thing to be grasped but emptied himself by being born in the likeness of man, taking on the form of a servant, humbling Himself under the Father's will, and was obedient to the point of dying on the cross (Philippians 2:5-8).

On the contrary, the false teacher is marked by pride and self-exaltation. Jesus denounced this attitude prior to giving His seven woes to the Pharisees. Jesus said that the Pharisees were those who laid heavy burdens on people but would not move a finger to help them (Matthew 23:4). Jesus castigated the Pharisees for practicing their deeds in front of men and loving the honor of men (Matthew 23:5-7). Jesus confronted the false teachers because they justified themselves before men (Luke 16:15) and gloried in their religious activity and self-righteousness (Luke 18:9-13). The proud false teacher will boast about their years of service, giving to the poor, teaching a Sunday school class, serving as an elder, serving in a music ministry, teaching a Bible study, and more. They are those who celebrate their religious achievements but have no place in their heart for confessing their sin before the Lord and seeing their wretched condition. The false teacher is not willing to see their sin as it really is. The false teacher is not willing to have their sin exposed and be humbled. Rather, the false teacher continues to practice wicked doctrine, deceitful schemes, and evil works because they hate the light and will not come to the light so that their evil works are exposed (John 3:20).

Modern Christianity is filled with both true pastors who lack humility as well as false teachers who are marked by pride. Pride can show up in many ways. For example, this could be a man who arrogantly tells the congregation that his sermons will not be scrutinized or judged even when he is consistently sloppy and makes errant statements concerning God's Word. This could be a Lutheran pastor who is shown that baptismal regeneration is a false gospel, and he refuses to look to Scripture to understand why he's wrong and haughtily retaliates by saying, "Stop cramming Scripture down my throat." This could be a reformed pastor who knows the Biblical mandate to turn away and shun false teachers but says, "I would not do it" and proudly flaunts his flagrant disobedience, false humility, and self-will over God's authority and commands. This could be a group of elders who outright refuse to teach the congregation on the Biblical qualifications of a pastor. Pride is pernicious. Pride is wicked. Proverbs 16:5, says this regarding God's disposition toward the proud: "*Everyone who is arrogant in heart is an abomination to the LORD; be assured, he will not go unpunished.*" To be proud is for one to fight against the Lord; and the Lord will oppose and fight against the proud (James 4:6). The true pastor is commanded to humble himself before God and be humble toward the congregation. The true pastor's humility is to stand in stark contrast to the false teacher's pride.

A Man Who Is Growing in Christlikeness

The last point we should see is that the true pastor is a man who demonstrates a progression in Christlikeness (1 Timothy 4:15). The character and conduct of the true pastor mimics Christ. In 1 Timothy 4:12, Paul commands Timothy to be a pattern for believers in speech, conduct, love, faith, and purity. The pastor is to do the pastoral work laid forth in Scripture, and he is to do all this while being a Christlike example to the flock. In 1 Timothy 4:15, Paul gives this command to Timothy regarding conduct and carrying out ministry: "*Practice these things, immerse yourself in them, so that all may see your progress.*" Not only is Timothy to fulfill the ministry, but he is also to do so while showing progression in Christlikeness. In fact, the word *progress* comes from *prokopé*, which means advancement or furtherance. This is speaking of making spiritual progress or advancement. Paul pursued this very goal of becoming Christlike. Paul did not consider himself perfect, but one thing he did, he strained and pressed on toward this goal to lay hold of it (Philippians 3:12–16). So, we see that the true pastor is one who pursues Christlikeness.

Contrary to the true pastor, the false teacher will go from bad to worse, deceiving and being deceived. In 2 Timothy 3:13 Paul explains that unbelievers and false teachers will become worse where he says, "*while evil people and impostors will go on from bad to worse, deceiving and being deceived.*" The word *impostors* comes from *goes*, which can be a sorcerer, enchanter, deceiver, or imposter. It is used to describe individuals who lead others astray through false teachings or supernatural claims that oppose the truth of the gospel. In the context of 2 Timothy 3, Paul is most likely talking about apostates and false teachers. Therefore, we can understand that false teachers and apostates will not progress in Christlikeness, but will advance in evil, deceiving others, and being deceived themselves. They will only increase in unholiness, pride, love for self, slander, opposition to truth, love of money, lack of self-control, arrogance, and not loving good (2 Timothy 3:1–9). They will only increase in opposing the true gospel and giving a damnable false gospel (2 Timothy 3:8). In 2 Peter 2:14, Peter says that false teachers are those who are, "*insatiable for sin.*" The word *insatiable* comes from *akatapaustos*, which means "not ceasing from" or "not abandoning." There is nothing that stops these false teachers from their sins. This word *insatiable* gives the idea that they are relentless in their sin; they cannot be commanded, coerced, or convinced to stop their sin. If they are commanded to stop preaching a false gospel, they double down on their damning doctrine. If they are confronted and shown their error, they persist in their error. They cannot stop or cease from their sin because they are enslaved and in bondage to their sin (John 8:34). They are adept in justifying, downplaying, and ignoring their sin. These false teachers will talk about their self-righteous deeds but never their sinfulness. Thus, the picture of the false teacher is not one who progresses in Christlikeness, but one who progresses into deception, evil, sin, and self-deception.

As we close this chapter, we begin to see how the true pastor has had the grace of God poured out on his character in a supernatural way that stands in opposition to the world, false religions, and false Christianity. The true pastor is a man who has been regenerated, gifted by God, and has had the grace of God poured out on his character. However, the false teacher's character stands in stark contrast to that of the true teacher. Just as many godly characteristics and qualifications mark the true pastor, certain ungodly characteristics mark the false teacher.

Chapter 3

A Man Who Has the Grace of God Poured Out on His Life to Have a Burden for the Proclamation of the Gospel

For when I preach the gospel, I cannot boast, since I am compelled to preach. Woe to me if I do not preach the gospel!

—1 Corinthians 9:16 NIV

In this chapter, we will see how the grace of God is poured out on the true pastor to have a burden for preaching the gospel of the Lord Jesus Christ. Far too often, it is assumed that when a man stands in the pulpit and delivers a sermon, he is preaching when he may not be preaching at all. Some men stand in the pulpit and give lectures but do not preach. Some men stand in the pulpit and tell jokes, rather than preach with soberness and solemnness.

Therefore, we will seek to understand what we mean by the term *biblical preaching*. And after we understand biblical preaching, we will seek to understand the gospel that the pastor is to deliver. Sometimes, pastors give truths or components of the gospel but fail to present the whole gospel, and they exclude the essential elements of the gospel. Therefore, in this chapter we will address three major topics: preaching and the origin of the pastor's gospel, the bad news, and the true gospel. Let's also keep in mind that one of the ways the church is built is when unregenerated sinners are converted Christ. Therefore, God gives the church pastors and evangelists who preach the gospel, so it is built up when the lost are transferred from the domain of darkness into the kingdom of God's beloved Son (Ephesians 4:11–13, Colossians 1:13).

Preaching

In 1 Corinthians 9:16, Paul says that he is *"compelled to preach . . . the gospel"* (NIV). *Compelled* comes from *anagké*, which means compulsion or constraint. This word conveys the unavoidable obligation that compels a certain immediate action or response. It is the compulsion and necessity that occurs due to the pressure of circumstances and refers to the course of action, which is inevitable. Paul wasn't compelled to chat the gospel, debate the gospel, whisper the gospel, or suggest the gospel. No, Paul had the obligation to preach the gospel. There was an absolute, undeniable, and pressing necessity for Paul to preach the gospel of the Lord Jesus Christ.

The word *preaching* comes from the original word *kérussó*, which means to "proclaim" or "herald." In ancient times, a herald had authority to proclaim a message because he spoke for the king. The herald would go and announce the king's message. The herald was to have certain qualities and attributes to carry out this important role. For example, he had to have a voice of certainty. In fact, auditions were held to ensure that the herald had a powerful voice and had an honest disposition to protect against tampering or exaggerating the message. He was not to announce the king's message with words such as *perhaps, maybe,* or *probably*. His voice, posture, and delivery were to match the seriousness of the message he was delivering. The herald also needed to be accurate, precise, and faithful to the message he proclaimed. In fact, the herald was allowed to ask the king questions to ensure that he understood the message as well as the intention of the message so he could proclaim the message with the same spirit and attitude of the king.

Additionally, when delivering his message from the king, there were things that he was not allowed to do. He was not allowed to enter debates, discussions, or chats. The herald was not to enter negotiations. The herald would come with the king's message and whether it was an order for the nation's surrender or an edict from the king, the herald would go throughout the towns and villages and announce the king's message. The herald would not be quiet; he would bring forth the message with the full conviction and authority of the king. The herald would not dare to misrepresent the king's message, add to the king's message, leave anything out from the king's message, or announce the message quietly. In fact, in ancient times, the herald was to announce the message with a gravity and authority that required the listeners to obey. The herald would boldly, loudly, and clearly articulate the message of the king to all the people with conviction and authority. To tamper with the message was tantamount to being unfaithful to the king.

In this very same way, the pastor is to be a preacher of the gospel. He is not to enter debates or negotiations when preaching the gospel. He is to deliver the gospel with the full authority and conviction of Christ the King. He is not to change Christ's gospel message or water it down and soften it to suit the ears of carnal men. No! He is to proclaim and herald this message as if Christ Himself were delivering the gospel message. He is to announce that life and death, heaven and hell, and commendation or condemnation are at stake with accepting this gospel.

Richard Owen Roberts has an excellent description of the difference between preaching and teaching. He recounts a dialogue he had with a business acquaintance who had traveled to America to understand the preaching landscape and gives the following insights into the difference between preaching and teaching:

> When I was with him in his home and full of expectations I said, "Now tell me about your trip to the states and about the great preaching that you heard."

He balled up his fist which was very large. We were at the dinner table, and he gave it an incredible wallop and all of the dishes jumped, and he said to me, "I didn't hear a single sermon preached in America!"

"Well why? Were you taken ill? Was it impossible to complete your itinerary?"

"No!" he said to me. "It was because you don't have preachers in America. All you've got are teachers."

And naively I said to him, "In your mind, what is the difference between preaching and teaching?"

And once again, he balled up his fist and walloped the table so that I wondered why it didn't just simply collapse. And he said to me, "This is not a matter of my personal opinion! Here is a long-established fact! To teach is to inform, to preach is to move!" And he went on to explain that the teacher informs those who are listening to him of things they may not know, but the preacher, he finds the people *here* and he knows they belong *there*. And in preaching, he moves them from where they are to where they belong.[12]

Roberts then addressed the audience at the G3 Conference where he was speaking and added the following salient comments:

Now I know that's not what some of you think. We've heard it said this morning that teaching and preaching are the same. That the words are used interchangeably. Well, you may use them interchangeably and I'm not going to try and correct you. If you want to be dumb, that's your choice. But I know that all across America there are countless numbers of people going to church and coming away disappointed. In many cases, their heads were so packed full of information they never acted upon that they're at the point of over saturation. I find people are hungry to be moved by God's Word and by God's Spirit from where they are to where they belong."[13]

There have been many powerful descriptions which characterize the nature of preaching. It's helpful to see what other men have said regarding this topic of preaching:

- Vance Havner said, "It is not the business of the preacher to fill the house. It is his business to fill the pulpit."[14]

- Dwight L. Moody stated, "The best way to revive a church is to build a fire in the pulpit."[15]

- Jonathan Edwards has said this regarding preaching, "I should think myself in the way of my duty to raise the affections of my hearers as high as possibly I can, provided that they are affected with nothing but truth."[16]

From these statements we see that preaching must contain the content of the truth, but it also contains fervency, intensity, urgency, energy, authority, and sobriety. There is fervency for the glory of God and the gospel. There is intensity which is driven by conviction. There is urgency which presses upon the listener their duty to hear and obey God's Word immediately. There is energy because the man is preaching with excitement about the one and only God and His word. There is authority because God's Word is binding and absolute truth. There is sobriety because the subject matter is serious and solemn. Thus, the true pastor is one who is empowered not only to teach and inform, but to preach with conviction, boldness, and authority.

In the book of Acts, Luke describes how Paul preached, *"He lived there two whole years at his own expense, and welcomed all who came to him, proclaiming the kingdom of God and teaching about the Lord Jesus Christ with all boldness and without hindrance"* (Acts 28:30–31). Paul unashamedly was a preacher of the gospel and kingdom of God; in fact, Luke says that Paul preached with all boldness. The word *boldness* comes from *parrésia*, which means "confidence," "openness," or "all speech." This word refers to the quality of boldness and confidence in speech where one speaks with no fear. Wuest said of this word that it is, "freedom in speaking, unreservedness in speech, free and fearless confidence, cheerful courage, boldness, assurance . . . free and bold speaking, speaking out every word. Its dominant idea is boldness, confidence, as opposed to fear, ambiguity, or reserve."[17]

This is a God-enabled and gifted ability to proclaim God's Word and not water it down, tamper with it, twist it, pervert it, or corrupt it. And Luke adds that Paul proclaimed the gospel with no *"hindrance,"* which conveys the idea of being able to proceed without any barriers or restrictions. Every true pastor is not ashamed of the gospel (Romans 1:16). Every true pastor boasts in the cross of Christ (Galatians 6:14). Every true pastor feels the necessity to preach the gospel (1 Corinthians 9:16). Every true pastor is an "all speech," unhindered, proclaimer of the gospel. Just as the apostles prayed for boldness to preach the Word amid the threat of the Jewish leaders and Gentiles, so the true pastor is a man who is gifted and enabled and who prays for strength to speak the gospel with boldness, clarity, and no hindrance.

Not only is the true pastor a proclaimer of the gospel, but he also understands that the gospel never originated from him, was never authored by him, and doesn't belong to him. The gospel is the gospel of God. In Galatians 1:11–12, Paul offers this important clarification regarding the gospel he received:

For I would have you know, brothers and sisters, that the gospel which was preached by me is not of human invention. For I neither received it from man, nor was I taught it, but I received it through a revelation of Jesus Christ.

What a statement by Paul confirming the origin of the gospel! Notice that God is the owner and the author of the gospel. This gospel was planned, authored, fulfilled, and executed by

God. Man will get no credit for this gospel. Man will have no room for boasting with this gospel (Romans 3:27). The exclusive authorship and ownership of the gospel belongs to God. Therefore, any trifling with God's gospel is a serious matter. The true pastor dares not to change or alter the message because there is simply no other gospel (Galatians 1:6–7). The true pastor seeks to know the gospel and declare it with clarity (Colossians 4:3–4). The true pastor seeks to preach the gospel, not with eloquent words but with the power of the Holy Spirit and with conviction (1 Corinthians 1:17, 1 Thessalonians 1:5). The true pastor is simply to proclaim the gospel with full conviction, authority, fervency, boldness, urgency, energy, and sobriety.

So, what is the gospel? What is this gospel message that the pastor is to herald and proclaim? The word *gospel* is a compound word in the original language, which is *euaggelion*. The word *eú*, means "good, well" and *angellō* means to "announce" or "herald." This word comes to us as "good news" or "glad tidings" in English. Therefore, we should know that the gospel is a message of good news. However, if you were to ask many professing Christians what the gospel is, you would most likely get different answers from just about everyone you asked. For example, you may get a variety of answers such as this: The gospel will help you live a Christian life. The gospel is the Bible. The gospel is the first four books of the New Testament. The gospel is Jesus Christ. The gospel is all about the love of Jesus. The gospel is how to have your sins forgiven. The gospel is Christianity. The gospel is the good news. The gospel is how to go to heaven. In this chapter, we will seek to understand the gospel message that the true pastor is commanded to proclaim. However, before we go too far, it is essential that we know the bad news. The good news is not good news until we know the bad news. Just as we would put a diamond against a black backdrop to see the color, cut, clarity, and carat, we must compare the good news against the bad news. For when we thoroughly explore the bad news, the good news shines vibrantly in all its glory against the black backdrop of the bad news. There is no good news until the bad news is understood.

The Bad News - Sin

If we are to understand God's good news, then we must understand God's bad news. The bad news is not that we have credit card debt, a house payment, loss of a job, no food to eat, political issues, wars, a failing education system, illness, injury, bad in-laws, a car that won't run, low self-esteem, no friends, no spouse, no children, social inequality, income inequality, or any of the like. The bad news is that man has sinned against God, and God must deal with man's sin.

Therefore, we need to first define sin and understand it. *Hamartía*, from which we get the word *sin*, carries the meaning of "missing the mark" or "loss and forfeiture because of not hitting the target." First John 3:4 helps us begin to flesh out a definition of sin; "*Everyone who makes a practice of sinning also practices lawlessness; sin is lawlessness.*" John describes sin as lawlessness. The original word for *lawlessness* comes from *anomia*, which is translated as "lawlessness" or "anti-law." Thus, we can understand that sin is lawlessness or disobedience against God's law. John further defines sin in these words: "*All unrighteousness is sin*" (1 John 5:17 NASB2020). Unrighteousness comes to us from *adikia*, meaning "injustice" or "wrongdoing." Sin is injustice and wrongdoing against God because the sinner misses the mark of God's perfect law. Thus, we can understand that sin is anything that does not conform to God's standard of righteousness and justice. James gives us yet another definition of sin in James 4:17: "*So whoever knows the right thing to do and fails to do it, for him it is sin.*" Here we can see that sin is not only what we do to break God's law, but it also includes breaking God's law by failing to do what God's law requires. Thus, a good definition of sin would be as follows: Sin is breaking God's law by either not doing what God's law demands or doing what God's law prohibits by any thought (Matthew 5:28), word (Matthew 5:22), deed (Matthew 5:39), or intent (Matthew 6:1).

Next, we must understand how the God of the Bible deals with sinners who have broken His law and offended Him. Quite simply, we learn that the God of the Bible deals with sinners according to who He is. First, we would need to know something of the attributes of God—that He is eternal, loving, just, good, faithful, omniscient, immutable, omnipresent, holy, and more. The attributes of God dictate the necessity for God to punish sinners who violate and break His law.

Since God is eternal and man has offended the eternal God (1 Timothy 1:17), the question is, "What is a just punishment for a finite man who sins against an infinite God?" The obvious answer is that the punishment must be eternal because God, the offended party, is an eternal God. Therefore, the penalty for man sinning against God demands an eternal punishment because God is eternal.

Since God is a loving God (1 John 4:17), this means that there are things that God hates. For example, since God is the only true God, He must hate idolatry because it robs Him of His glory. Because God loves truth, He must hate falsehood and lies. Therefore, since God must hate evil because He is love, He must punish sinners who sin against Him and do the very things He hates because He is an eternal and loving God.

Since God is a just God and man has offended Him by sinning against Him, God must deal equitably and justly with those who have broken His law (Ezekiel 18:1–32). It is simply not in God's character to leave sin unpunished. God deals justly and equitably with sin. God is not a corrupt judge who will ignore sin; He is not a biased judge who will overlook sin. The God of the Bible is a God who deals justly with sinners who commit the very sins He hates. Even unholy man knows that it would be unjust to pardon a serial murderer with no punishment. Thus, God must deal justly with the sinner and see to it that every sin the sinner commits is eternally and justly punished because He is an eternal, loving, and just God.

Since God is good, He must punish sin (Psalm 25:8). To leave sin unpunished would not be good; it would be bad, evil, and wicked. Even the unregenerate man knows that a parent who throws a newborn baby in a dumpster commits a wicked and murderous act, which must be punished; it would be wicked for a judge to freely pardon a parent for such an atrocity. God cannot let sin go unpunished. In His goodness, God must punish sin because He is an eternal, loving, just, and good God.

God is holy, meaning that He is set apart, and there is nothing or no one like Him (Isaiah 44:6). He is totally separate in terms of all His attributes, which include His self-existence, sovereignty, immutability, self-sufficiency, omnipotence, omniscience, omnipresence, wisdom, faithfulness, goodness, justice, mercy, graciousness, love, and glory. It is quite clear, that all men are fallen and don't meet God's required level of holiness and perfection (Romans 3:23). Therefore, God must punish men according to their sin because He is an eternal, loving, just, good, and holy God.

It is also important to understand how the God of the Bible views sin and those who sin against Him. We see from the Bible that God hates sin (Psalm 5:5, 11:5), abhors sin (Psalm 5:6), is angered by sin (Psalm 7:11), and is ready to destroy and punish those who sin (Psalm 7:12–13) because sin is warfare against Him (James 4:4); God considers sin an abomination (Proverbs 22:12) and evil (Psalm 7:9). Because God hates sin, He must deal with sin according to who He is. For God to leave sin unpunished would violate and be in opposition to His character. Knowing that the God of the Bible must punish sin, we need to understand how God punishes sin. The God of the Bible does not change; He will always hate sin. The God who sent a flood to destroy humanity and left only eight survivors is the same God of the New Testament. The God who sent burning sulfur down on Sodom and Gomorrah and destroyed an entire city has not and never will change in His anger against sin.

The Bible teaches that God punishes sinners by sending them to hell. The doctrine of hell is quite possibly one of the least favorite and least taught doctrines in Scripture. However, it is a doctrine that must be covered. The doctrine of hell will make the glory of the gospel and Christ shine even brighter. The bad news of hell is more than bad news; it is terrifying. The bad news from God about hell is the worst news possible for man. The faithful and true pastor will preach on the punishment and horrors of hell and the necessity for God to send sinners to hell if they refuse to repent and put their faith in Christ. It is a necessity for the pastor to preach on hell.

The Bad News - Hell

Although this section cannot cover every aspect of the doctrine of hell, it will be thorough enough for the reader to understand the horrors of hell because the true pastor is commanded to preach the Word and whole counsel of God (2 Timothy 4:2). John the Baptist describes hell as a place of fire where every tree that does not bear fruit of repentance is cut down and thrown into the fire (Matthew 3:11). Jesus describes Hell as a furnace of fire; this pictures a concentrated fire (Matthew 13:42). The author of Hebrews describes Hell as a place that contains furious fire that consumes and devours the enemies of

God (Hebrews 10:27). Therefore, we know that hell is a place full of the omnipotent, wild, and zealous fire of God that consumes His enemies. The Bible does not give a picture of hell as a warm sauna or a nice warm campfire. The Bible describes hell as a place that burns with a wild and zealous fire that eternally and perpetually consumes and devours sinners with the omnipotent heat and righteous anger of God.

John the Baptist describes hell as eternal in that the fire never goes out but burns forever (Matthew 3:12). Jesus describes hell as being so horrible that it must be avoided at all costs when He says that it would be better to lose one of your members than to be thrown into hell (Matthew 5:29–30). Jesus said that just one sin is enough to merit someone being cast into hell (Matthew 5:28) because even one offense against God requires His punishment. Jesus describes Hell as a place of weeping and gnashing of teeth, which means it is a place where the sinner is in an eternal state of anger against God and unfathomable sadness and despair (Matthew 8:12). Jesus describes Hell as a place of destruction where one's whole body and soul are being eternally destroyed by the omnipotent and unrestrained wrath of God (Matthew 7:13, 10:28); it is a place where the whole of a man—body, soul, and spirit—is eternally being destroyed by the unmitigated wrath of God.

After death, unrepentant man does not go into a state of annihilation; nor does he go out of existence. He goes into an eternal state where his body, soul, and spirit are continually being destroyed; Jesus describes hell as inescapable (Luke 16:26).

In hell, the sinner will realize that the time to respond to the gospel has passed. In hell, a man will have full awareness that after one trillion years of torment, that one trillion years will be like a drop in the ocean compared to eternity. Jesus describes hell as being full of excruciating pain with no reprieve (Luke 16:24). Though man will desire the goodness that God gives in water, air, rest, and comfort, the man will find no such comfort for even a millisecond for all eternity. Hell is described by Jesus as a place that is full of mental anguish and torment—a place where there is only regret, sorrow, and haunting memories of rejecting Christ (Luke 16:25). All the debauched pleasures and self-deception that the man indulged in will give him no comfort. The lost opportunity and eternal regret of neglecting or rejecting Christ will be his haunting memory forever. Jude describes hell as the blackest darkness, which describes a place of such appalling gloom and a darkness that it can be felt (Jude 13). A hopeless and despairing darkness is what awaits man in hell. Hell is described as a place where man will have personal punishments and that every sin ever committed by the sinner will be paid back in full retribution by God (Romans 2:5). The idea of God delivering His full and all-powerful wrath back to the sinner for every sin they have ever committed is horrifying to consider.

Finally, hell is described as heavily populated (Matthew 7:13–14). Jesus said that many are on the broad road to destruction and that there are few who find eternal life. Therefore, we can know that there will be many in hell who rejected

Christ (Matthew 11:20–24), neglected Christ (Hebrews 2:1–4), and who were deceived into thinking they belonged to Christ but never came to a saving faith in Him (Matthew 7:21–23).

The soul-sobering reality of hell should cause anyone and everyone to test whether they are truly in the faith. When we contemplate the good news, let us always keep the bad news in mind. The bad news heightens the good news of Christ. The bad news should inextricably and unequivocally heighten our love for the Lord. The bad news will multiply a thousandfold the wonder of a verse such as Romans 5:8: *"But God demonstrates his own love toward us, in that while we were still sinners, Christ died for us"* (NKJV).

The Good News in Scripture

In Romans 1:1–3, Paul writes this regarding the importance of the Scripture and pointing to the person and work of Jesus Christ:

> *Paul, a servant of Christ Jesus, called to be an apostle, set apart for the gospel of God, **which he promised beforehand through his prophets in the holy Scriptures**, concerning his Son, who was descended from David according to the flesh and was declared to be the Son of God in power according to the Spirit of holiness by his resurrection from the dead, Jesus Christ our Lord.* (emphasis added)

Here, we see that good news was promised through the prophets in God's Word, and this good news concerned God's Son. In fact, Peter announced this very same truth when he preached at Solomon's Colonnade as recorded in Acts 3:18, *"But what God foretold by the mouth of all the prophets, that his Christ would suffer, he thus fulfilled."* So, we see that Christ is the fulfillment of what the prophets spoke of regarding the gospel; both Paul and Peter proclaim that Jesus is the fulfillment of what the prophets spoke of in the Old Testament. Though there are many prophecies about Christ in the Old Testament; below are just eight prophecies dealing with the suffering of Christ, which have been fulfilled:

- Moses wrote in Genesis 3:15 that the woman's promised Seed would bruise the head of the serpent, and that the serpent would bruise the heel of the Seed; fulfilled on Calvary (Mark 15:16–40, Matthew 26:57–27:50, Luke 22:47–23:49, John 18:1–19:30).

- The psalmist wrote that Christ would be betrayed by a friend in Psalm 41:9 and 55:12–14; fulfilled in John 13:18, 21.

- Zechariah wrote that Christ would be sold for thirty pieces of silver in Zechariah 11:12; fulfilled in Matthew 26:15.

- Zechariah wrote that Christ would be given for the price of a potter's field in Zechariah 11:13; fulfilled in Matthew 27:7.

- The psalmist, David, wrote that Christ would suffer intensely in Psalm 22:14–15; fulfilled in Luke 22:42, 44.

- Isaiah wrote that Christ would suffer for others (Isaiah 53:4–12); fulfilled in all the gospel accounts of Christ's betrayal, unjust trials, beatings, and crucifixion.

- Isaiah promised that Christ would be patient and silent under suffering in Isaiah 53:7; fulfilled in Matthew 26:63, 27:12–14.

- Micah wrote that Christ would be struck on the cheek in Micah 5:1; fulfilled in Matthew 27:30.

It is estimated that the likelihood or mere chance that eight prophecies would be fulfilled in Christ is 10^{17}. The likelihood that for forty-eight prophecies would be fulfilled in Christ carries a mathematical chance of 10^{157}, which is 157 zeros. One of the many reasons why Scripture is reliable and trustworthy is the fact that God prophesied of future events that have been fulfilled. Therefore, not only do we see the unbelievable foreknowledge and sovereignty of God-fulfilling prophecy, but we also understand how crucial the Holy Scripture is to the gospel and, more specifically as we'll learn, how it declares Jesus Christ. Scripture points to Jesus Christ! The Old Testament predicts Him, the gospels reveal Him, Acts proclaims Him, the Epistles explain Him, and Revelation anticipates Him. The gospel rests on the sturdy foundation of the Old Testament, which points to Jesus Christ.

The Good News – The Person of the Lord Jesus Christ

> *Paul, a servant of Christ Jesus, called to be an apostle, set apart for the gospel of God, which he promised beforehand through his prophets in the holy Scriptures,* **concerning his Son, who was descended from David according to the flesh** *and was declared to be the Son of God in power according to the Spirit of holiness by his resurrection from the dead, Jesus Christ our Lord.* (emphasis added)
>
> —Romans 1:1–3

As we learned from Paul, Scripture points us to the good news of Jesus Christ. The gospel of God is concerned with a person who is God's Son, Jesus Christ. This gospel does not concern the prophet Muhammad of Islam. This gospel does not concern the false god, Allah of Islam. This gospel does not concern Buddha. This gospel does not concern Sun Myung Moon. This gospel does not concern Mary Baker Eddy. This gospel does not concern Ron Hubbard. This gospel does not concern Joseph Smith. This gospel does not concern the false god, Vishnu of Hinduism. This gospel does not concern the false god, Brahman of Hinduism. No, this gospel is all about God's Son, Jesus Christ.

In Romans 1:1–3, notice that Paul claims that Jesus is the Son of God (verse 3), which is a claim to deity, and then he claims that the Son of God was descended from the physical lineage of David according to the flesh. In this verse, Paul makes a very important Christological statement: He declares that the person of Jesus Christ is both God and man. This Christological truth is an essential component of the gospel.

So, what about the person of Jesus should be understood? First, as we already mentioned, Jesus is God as He is the Son of God (Romans 1:3). Peter makes this great confession in Matthew 16:16 where it says, *"Simon Peter replied, 'You are the Christ, the Son of the living God.'"* Paul makes the same claim to Jesus's deity when he says this about Christ in Colossians 1:19: *"For in him all the fullness of God was pleased to dwell."* Later, in Colossians 2:9, Paul explains that Jesus Christ is fully God and fully man when he says, *"For in him the whole fullness of deity dwells bodily."* Likewise, the author of Hebrews says this about Jesus:

> *He is the radiance of the glory of God and the exact imprint of his nature, and he upholds the universe by the word of his power. After making purification for sins, he sat down at the right hand of the Majesty on high.*
>
> —Hebrews 1:3

The author of Hebrews, Paul, Peter, and the Triune God all make the same confession: Jesus Christ is the Son of the Living God and truly God and truly man.

Because Jesus is God, He is also coequal and coeternal with God the Father and God the Holy Spirit. In John 5:17–18, after Jesus healed the invalid, Jesus makes a statement about being equal with the Father:

But Jesus answered them, "My Father is working until now, and I am working." This was why the Jews were seeking all the more to kill Him, because not only was He breaking the Sabbath, but He was even calling God His own Father, making Himself equal with God.

In John 10:30, Jesus makes another statement about being coequal with the Father when He says, "*I and the Father are one.*" Jesus reiterates this same point when He says about the work He is doing in John 10:38, "*But if I do them, even though you do not believe me, believe the works, that you may know and understand that the Father is in me and I am in the Father.*" Thus, we see Jesus make the claim that He is equal with the Father, which is a claim to be coequal and coeternal with the God the Father.

Additionally, we should see that Jesus is the only begotten Son of God (John 3:16). The phrase *only begotten* has been translated from *monogenés*, which means "one-and-only," "one of a kind," "one of a class and the only of its kind." Jesus is the only one of-a-kind Son of God. Jesus is not a created being. We can know that Jesus is not a created being because He is the Son of God, and God is immutable and eternal. God cannot get better, for if He could get better, He would not be

God. God cannot get worse, because if He could get worse, He would be less than God. Jesus is not a created being because God is eternal and immutable. God doesn't become more, and God doesn't become less.

The aseity of God also demonstrates that Jesus is God and not a created being. The aseity of God simply refers to the attribute that God is self-sufficient and exists of and from Himself by His own self and self-will. John 1:4 captures the aseity of Christ where it says, "*In him was life, and the life was the light of men.*" This is simply stating that all created life came from Christ because He is the source of all life, or rather, He is completely self-sufficient and self-existent in and of Himself and needs nothing. The one who is self-sufficient and self-existent in and of Himself cannot be created because He is eternal and is the origin and source of all life. Therefore, Jesus is the coeternal, coequal, and only begotten Son of God. God the Father, God the Son, and God the Holy Spirit have been the Triune God in eternity past and will be the Triune God in eternity future.

The Bible describes the person of Christ in many more ways:

- Jesus is the Anointed One of God, or the Christ, and He proclaims to be the fulfillment of Isaiah's prophecy in Luke 4:18–19.

- Peter declares that Christ is the Prophet that was foretold in Deuteronomy 18 (Acts 3:21–23).

- Paul claims that Jesus is the eternal King and Lord of lords when he says, *"He who is the blessed and only Sovereign, the King of kings and the Lord of lords"* (1 Timothy 6:15).

- The angel declares that Jesus is the Savior, *"For unto you is born this day in the city of David a Savior, who is Christ the Lord"* (Luke 2:11).

- The author of Hebrews says that Jesus is the eternal High Priest, *"But he holds his priesthood permanently, because he continues forever . . . . For it was indeed fitting that we should have such a high priest, holy, innocent, unstained, separated from sinners, and exalted above the heavens"* (Hebrews 7:24, 26).

- Jesus is the Creator and Sustainer of the universe (John 1:1–14, Hebrews 1:1–3, Colossians 1:16–17, 1 Corinthians 8:6).

- Jesus was born of the virgin Mary (Matthew 1:23); He was born from the lineage of David and is the Son of David (Matthew 1:1–16, Luke 3:23–38, Psalm 132:11, Jeremiah 23:5, and 2 Samuel 2:8–17, 27–29).

- Jesus is the God man and only mediator between God and men (1 Timothy 2:5).

- In His person, Jesus is the Christ, the promised Jewish Messiah, Lord and Savior, the baptizer with the Holy Spirit (Matthew 3:11), the Great High Priest, and the only begotten Son of the Living God, which makes Him God and equal with God the Father and God the Holy Spirit.

- He is truly God and truly man.

The Good News –The Work of the Lord Jesus Christ

Paul, a servant of Christ Jesus, called to be an apostle, set apart for the gospel of God, which he promised beforehand through his prophets in the holy Scriptures, concerning his Son, who was descended from David according to the flesh **and was declared to be the Son of God in power according to the Spirit of holiness by his resurrection from the dead, Jesus Christ our Lord.** (emphasis added)

—Romans 1:1–3

So now that we know of the sinful condition of man, the punishment that man deserves, and the person of the Lord Jesus Christ, we run into a divine dilemma. The divine dilemma that sinful man faces is this: How can sinful man be forgiven and reconciled to a just and holy God? How is it possible for God to be a God of justice and punish sin, yet also be the justifier of sinful men? How is it possible for God to punish sinners and yet somehow forgive sinners? Man's sin is incurable. Man cannot earn or merit heaven because sin must be punished. So how can this divine dilemma be solved?

The divine dilemma is solved in the person and work of the Lord Jesus Christ. Christ had to become a man because the wages of sin is death (Romans 6:23), and God cannot die because God is eternal. Therefore, Jesus needed to be a man to die. Jesus needed to be a sinless man to take on the curse of the law, suffer divine punishment, and die in man's place (Galatians 3:13, Romans 8:3). The Son of God needed to become the Son of David to die in our place and make the only atonement for man's sin as it says in Romans 8:3: "*For God has done what the law, weakened by the flesh, could not do. By sending his own Son in the likeness of sinful flesh and for sin, he condemned sin in the flesh.*" The Son of God needed to become the Son of Man to be the mediator between God and man (1 Timothy 2:5). A mediator intervenes to restore peace between two parties. As we saw earlier in this chapter, these two parties are at enmity with each other and were unreconcilable. The mediator must stand in the middle and be equal to both sides. Jesus had to be truly God in order to represent God to man, and He needed to be truly man to represent man to God. No one else could have stood between these two parties. No angel or prophet could have mediated between God and man. Only God could take the wrath of God; Only God could live a sinless life.

So, what is this work of Christ that was powerful to save sinners, justify men, and allow God to forgive transgressors? Paul answers this question in Romans 1:4 where he says that

Jesus *"was declared the Son of God in power according to the Spirit of holiness by his resurrection from the dead, Jesus Christ our Lord."* Thus, we see that the resurrection points us to the redeeming work of Christ.

Jesus's teaching and miracles were impossible to ignore. In His teaching He made several claims to deity such as being Lord of the Sabbath (Matthew 12:8), the Good Shepherd (10:11), the only way to the Father (John 14:6), and more. Jesus's miracles and life validated His claim to be God. Jesus promised that He would be resurrected from the dead, a sign that He was, indeed, the Christ, the Son of the Living God. He promised that He would give them the sign of Jonah, which was a predictive prophecy given in picture rather than in word (Matthew 12:38–42, 16:4; Luke 11:29). As Jonah spent three days and three nights in the belly of the great fish, so Jesus spent three days in the heart of the earth. It looked like the end of Jonah, but it wasn't. It looked like the end of Jesus, but it wasn't. Jonah was in the depths of the sea; Jesus was buried in the depths of the earth in the tomb. Jonah came out, and Jesus came out. Jonah was a picture of Jesus's resurrection. Jesus said in John 2:19, *"Destroy this temple, and in three days I will raise it up."* Jesus was speaking of His death and resurrection. Jesus reasoned with and taught His disciples that He needed to be killed and raised to life on the third day (Matthew 16:21–22, 17:22–23, 20:17–19; Mark 8:31, 9:30–32, 10:32–34; Luke 9:21–22, 9:43–45, 18:31–34). Jesus proclaimed that He had power to lay down His life and resurrect himself (John 10:17–18).

If Jesus could not resurrect Himself, it would prove He was not one with the Father (John 5:17–18). If Jesus could not resurrect Himself, He would be a lying prophet (Matthew 16:21–22, 17:22–23, 20:17–19; Mark 8:31, 9:30–32, 10:32–34; Luke 9:21–22, 9:43–45, 18:31–34). If Jesus could not resurrect Himself, that would be evidence that He was not the Son with whom the Father was well pleased (Matthew 3:17). If Jesus could not resurrect Himself, that would be evidence that He was not anointed by the Holy Spirit (Luke 4:18–21). However, all of Jesus's works, teaching, and life were validated by His resurrection, which proved that He is the Christ, the Son of the Living God. Without the Resurrection, Christ's claims and work would have meant nothing. If Jesus had died and not risen, He would not have been the Resurrection and the Life (John 11:25). If Jesus had not risen, He would have been like any other man who dies and does not come back to life (Psalm 90:1–12, Ecclesiastes 7:2). If Jesus had not risen, all His claims and miracles would have amounted to nothing as even Moses and Elisha were able to perform miracles but could not raise themselves from the dead.

Without the resurrection, Jesus's claims and work would have been invalidated. Without the resurrection, Jesus would not be a conqueror over death. Siddhartha Gautama of Buddhism could not resurrect himself from the dead. Kong Qiu of Confucianism could not resurrect himself from the dead. Lao Tzu of Taoism could not resurrect himself from the dead. Joseph Smith of Mormonism could not resurrect himself from the dead. Muhammed of Islam could not resurrect himself from the dead. Mary Baker Eddy of Christian Science could not resurrect herself from the dead. Charles Taze Russell of the Jehovah's Witnesses could not resurrect himself from the dead. If Christ could not resurrect Himself from the dead, Paul would be exactly right about the Christian faith when he says, *"For if the dead are not raised, not even Christ has been raised. And if Christ has not been raised, your faith is futile and you are still in your sins"* (1 Corinthians 15:16–17).

However, Jesus's work on the cross was accepted. Jesus's resurrection was proof positive that His salvific work was accepted by God. Christ's resurrection was God's apologetic on the sufficiency of Christ's substitutionary suffering and death on the cross for sinners. The resurrection was God's ultimate validation of Jesus's work on the cross. Jesus raised himself from the dead (John 10:17–18), God the Father raised Jesus from the dead (Galatians 1:1), and the Holy Spirit raised Jesus from the dead (Romans 8:11). All three persons of the Godhead raised Jesus from the dead (Acts 2:24)! God approved of Jesus's work by raising Jesus from the dead.

So, what did Jesus's perfect work secure? In Romans 1:3, Paul spoke of Jesus's deity and humanity. In Romans 1:4, he has fast-forwarded to Christ's resurrection. So, what is Paul trying to do by attesting to Jesus's deity and human birth and then going directly to the resurrection? He is capturing the entire life and work of Christ. Paul is saying that this gospel is about the person of Jesus (Romans 1:3) and the work of Jesus (Romans 1:4). Therefore, an essential component to the gospel includes Jesus's work, which include His teaching, miracles, sinless life, substitutionary atonement, resurrection, ascension, present enthronement, and Second Coming. So, how is one to understand Jesus's work that was validated by the Resurrection? Jesus's work can be summed up in eight words: Propitiation, Reconciliation, Redemption, Expiation, Regeneration, Justification, Glorification, and Domination. For the purposes of this book, we will look at Christ's work of propitiation, which brought about reconciliation, expiation, redemption, glorification, justification, and demonstrated Christ's domination.

The word *propitiation* comes from the word *hilastérion*, which means a sin offering, by which the wrath of the deity is appeased by means of propitiation. As we learned earlier, God hates sin and wickedness. God is angry with the wicked every day. God sees sin as filthy and defiling. God sees sin as open hostility toward Him. God considers sin an abomination. God considers sin evil and wicked. God simply hates sin with all His being. Therefore, God needed a way to punish sin; He needed a way to propitiate or appease His righteous wrath toward sin and man. If there's anything that can be learned from the Old Testament Levitical system, it is that the sacrifice of goats, calves, bulls, and heifers, ceremonial washings, and grain and fellowship offerings never brought the Jews into the presence of God (Hebrews 9:9–10). Good works never brought the people into the presence of God. However, we see the God–man, Jesus Christ, who was able to act as a mediator between both parties—God and man—who were at enmity with each other. Neither animals nor angels could step in and mediate. Only one person, the Lord Jesus Christ could be the sinless sacrifice representing man to God and God to man, could mediate between the two parties.

Jesus's work required that He fulfill the law and the prophets by living a sinless life and meeting all the requirements of God's law and prophecy (Matthew 3:15, 5:17). In Matthew 22:36–37, Jesus was asked what the greatest commandment was, and He replied, "*You shall love the Lord your God with all your heart and with all your soul and with all your mind.*" Therefore, we can know that there was not one millisecond when Christ did not fulfill this commandment perfectly. Christ lived His entire life in full and complete obedience of loving the Lord God with all His heart, soul, mind, and strength. On the other hand, we should see that there's not one millisecond when man has ever perfectly obeyed this command. Jesus lived a perfect and sinless life, and the entirety of His life was one of loving the Lord perfectly with all His heart, soul, mind, and strength in complete obedience to God's law. Jesus needed to be sinless in order to offer Himself as a propitiating sacrifice to please God. If Jesus had sinned, He would not have been a pleasing sacrifice to God. If Christ had sinned, He would have been like every other man and could not have presented Himself as a blameless, sinless, and undefiled sacrifice for the sins of mankind.

Second Corinthians 5:21 says, "*For our sake he made him to be sin who knew no sin, so that in him we might become the righteousness of God.*" Here Paul speaks of Christ as a sinless offering—living a sinless life. So, what does it mean that Christ was made to be sin? Does it mean that when Christ was on the cross, He became defiled and corrupted? Does it mean that His nature became something vile, loathsome, and sinful? How did Christ become sin? Before we answer, let's think about how Christ makes sinners righteous when they believe the gospel. The moment a person believes in the gospel and is saved, they do not become a righteous being. That is to say, the moment they believe, they are not so transformed in their nature that they become perfectly righteous and never again sin. We are not infused with a special grace that causes us never to sin. The moment that someone repents and believes in Christ, they are forensically and legally declared righteous before the throne of God. This is a legal declaration before the throne of God that one is declared righteous not based on one's merits or works but righteous based upon the virtue and merit of Jesus Christ, and God treats us as perfectly righteous in Christ.

Therefore, we can understand how God made Christ to be sin. When Jesus Christ was on the cross, His nature did not become polluted. He did not become some vile being. No, what happened was that the sins of His people were imputed or reckoned to Him, and before the throne of God, He was considered and declared guilty, and He was treated by God as a guilty sinner. He always was and will be the spotless Lamb of God. However, on the cross, the sins of His people were imputed to Him. He was legally declared guilty, and then God treated Him as a righteous God should treat the wicked. Upon the cross, the Father treated His Son as the infidel, the sinner, and the lawbreaker.

Galatians 3:13 says that Christ became a curse: *"Christ redeemed us from the curse of the law by becoming a curse for us— for it is written, 'Cursed is everyone who is hanged on a tree.'"* So what does it mean when Jesus became a curse? What is a curse? A curse is the opposite of a blessing. Every curse pronounced in the Bible was to fall on Jesus upon the cross. The divine curse and punishment that is due to sinners in hell, fell upon the beloved Son of God when the Father showed up in judgment and darkness to take His omnipotent, fiery, and vengeful wrath out on His Son (Matthew 27:45–6).

So how did God the Father treat Christ as a cursed sinner? We get a picture of this if we simply look at what it means to be cursed rather than blessed by examining the Beatitudes in Matthew 5:

- Because Christ became a curse, He was punished as one who is refused entrance into the Kingdom of heaven rather than inheriting the kingdom (Matthew 5:3).

- Because Christ became a curse, He was punished and suffered divine wrath rather than comfort (Matthew 5:4).

- Because Christ became a curse, all the goodness of God was taken away, and He suffered and died under the wrath of God as miserable and wretched rather than being satisfied (Matthew 5:6).

- Because Christ became a curse, He received divine justice and punishment rather than divine mercy (Matthew 5:7). Because Christ became a curse, He was cut off from God as one bearing disgrace rather than being called a son of God (Matthew 5:9, Psalm 22:1).

Jesus offered himself up as a sinless offering to God the Father so that God the Father could place all the sins of God's people on Jesus and curse Jesus as if He was the vile sinner. Upon that cross, Jesus suffered the wrath of God for His elect (John 10:11). All those in hell are the only ones who have an idea of what Jesus suffered on the cross and know what it is to be cursed. It wasn't the nails, the flogging, the crown of thorns, the punching, and beatings that Jesus dreaded. Even in the first century there were Christians who were killed by being hung on a tree and being lit on fire, and they went to their deaths singing hymns of praise to God. Jesus wasn't dreading the physical beatings. No, it was the full cup of wrath and the righteous anger of God toward sin that Jesus was dreading (Matthew 26:39). God didn't unload a rifle firing squad on His Son. God didn't unload a nuclear bomb on His Son. God didn't unload the full heat of the sun on His Son. No, God unloaded something far more terrifying than all those combined. God unloaded His full unbridled wrath on His only begotten Son; only the eternal Son of God could take the omnipotent wrath from His Father. Only the Son of God could be presented as a sinless propitiation. Only the eternal Son of God could suffer the eternal punishment we deserve.

To get a picture of this wrath, let's imagine a scenario. Let's imagine a father who has only one son whom he deeply loves. The father decides he's going to show his magnanimous love and put it on display by having his son pay the ransom for twenty serial murderers and rapists so they can be set free and forgiven. As part of the ransom to release the twenty criminals, the punishment that is due to the twenty criminals must be paid. So, here's what the father does. The father chooses to pay the punishment for the twenty criminals by taking the punishment out on his one and only beloved son, and the son agrees to take on the punishment of the twenty criminals. The punishment for these twenty criminals is high and costly, and the twenty criminals deserve the most wrathful punishment. Therefore, the father learns to fly a fighter jet and equips the fighter jet with two nuclear bombs. The father also prepares an area for his son to suffer his wrath, and he surrounds his son with one million nuclear bombs and plans to crash the plane into his son. The father prepares all of this, but first he lets the twenty criminals slap, punch, mock and beat his son until the son's face is no longer recognizable. He then lets the criminals strap his only son whom he loves to the tree surrounded by one million nuclear bombs. The Father then flies the fighter jet directly at his only beloved son, puts the jet on autopilot, and evacuates the plane while it is headed for his son. The jet then crashes into his son; the son is crushed by the plane, and the fire is unleashed by the nuclear bombs consumes his son.

The father then turns his face away in disapproval from his only son and cannot bear to look at his son as he unleashes upon his son the punishment that was due to the twenty criminal serial murders and rapists. The father crushes and curses his only beloved son and is satisfied.

This example falls woefully and pathetically short of describing the wrath of God that was poured out on Christ. God's wrath is far greater and far more terrible than we can imagine. The temperature of a 1-megaton nuclear weapon can produce temperatures of about 100 million degrees Celsius at its center, which is about four to five times hotter than the sun's core. Even in this example, we fall woefully short of the omnipotent fiery wrath of God on sinners. The wrath of God that was taken out on Christ was the propitiation and satisfaction that paid for man's sin. Christ, the sacrificial Lamb bore the sins and punishment of His elect on the cross (Isaiah 53). Therefore, we should never forget and always seek to fathom the incomprehensible worth of Jesus Christ's substitutionary work on the cross for sinners. Not only did He suffer the wrath of God for one man, but He has also suffered the wrath of God for the sins of a great multitude of humanity (Revelation 7:9). Romans 8:1 says, *"There is therefore now no condemnation for those who are in Christ Jesus."* There is no condemnation for those in Christ Jesus because Christ paid the condemnation and punishment for sinners. Every drop of wrath for those whom the Son of God died was satisfied and placated at Calvary. There is not one drop of wrath left for those in Christ Jesus. The wrathful cannon of God has been unloaded and emptied on the Son of God who loved us and gave Himself up for us (Galatians 2:20).

Before yielding up His spirit on the cross, Jesus said, "*It is finished*" (John 19:30). The phrase *It is finished*, is translated from *tetelestai*, which means "to end," "to bring to conclusion," "to accomplish," "to fulfill," or "to finish." Note that Jesus didn't say, "I am finished." No! He said, "*It is finished.*" His perfect propitiating and sin bearing substitutionary work was complete. Jesus paid the full price and penalty for sin. Jesus took the whole wrath of God. There is not one sin of God's people that was not punished at Calvary. There is not one sin of God's people that the Father did not lay on His only begotten Son. God's justice was fully satisfied. In the secular sense, *tetelestai* was used to signify the full payment of a debt. The parchment on which the debt was recorded was stamped with the word *tetelestai*, which meant the debt had been paid in full. Charles Spurgeon shares these insights about this word:

> An ocean of meaning in a drop of language, a mere drop. It would need all the other words that ever were spoken, or ever can be spoken, to explain this one word. It is altogether immeasurable. It is high; I cannot attain to it. It is deep; I cannot fathom it. It is finished is the most charming note in all of Calvary's music. The fire has passed upon the Lamb. He has borne the whole wrath that was due to His people. This is the royal dish of the feast of love.[18]

A. W. Pink said of *tetelestai*, "Eternity will be needed to make manifest all that *tetelestai* contains."[19] A. C. Gaebelein said of *tetelestai*, "Never before and never after was ever spoken one word which contains and means so much. It is the shout of the mighty Victor. And who can measure the depths of this one word!"[20]

This is the propitiation that:

- Brought reconciliation between God and men (Romans 5:10–11).

- Brought about expiation or the forgiveness of sins (Ephesians 1:7, Hebrews 8:12).

- Paid the price of redemption (Galatians 3:13).

- Brought justification or rather, for God to be the just and justifier of men (Romans 3:26).

- Showed forth God's domination over sin, death, and the devil (Colossians 2:13–15).

- Brought about glorification for sinners and glorified the attributes and character of God (1 Corinthians 1:18–25).

Not only does Jesus's work include His resurrection, but it also includes His ascension (24:51) and His second coming and judgment (Revelation 22:12–13, Matthew 25:31–46). This is the work of the Lord Jesus Christ, which secured eternal life and salvation for men. The divine dilemma has been solved through the work of Christ. God did this all because of the great love with which He loved us (Ephesians 2:4).

The Good News – Man's Responsibility to Respond in Repentance and Faith to the Person and Work of the Lord Jesus Christ

We have discussed the objective facts of the person and work of Jesus; now we will seek to understand man's responsibility to respond to the person and work of Jesus Christ. If you know the objective truth about Christ, what good does that do you if you don't know how to respond to Christ? If you know the objective truth about Jesus's person and work, how do you obtain the benefits of what Jesus did? Unfortunately, this is where many churches have lost it. Some churches would teach that you respond to the person and work of Jesus by coming to Him in faith, but you must also bring good works to inherit salvation. Some churches would teach that you must respond to the person and work of Jesus by being baptized to inherit salvation. Some churches would teach that you can respond to the person and work of Jesus by mental assent or believing and agreeing to the objective facts of Jesus, but there is no need to repent to inherit salvation. Some churches would teach that you respond to the person and work of Jesus by becoming a church member to inherit salvation. Some churches would teach that you respond to the person and work of Jesus by praying the sinner's prayer to inherit salvation. Some churches would teach that if you responded to an altar call, you have inherited salvation. Since there is much confusion in Christianity, we will take our time to thoroughly understand Christ's gospel call to follow Him in saving faith. To do this, we will do an exposition of Luke 14:25–33, one of the clearest gospel calls given in the New Testament, which describe repentance and saving faith.

The true pastor must not only explain the person and work of Christ, but they must also compel men to come into the kingdom (Luke 14:23). The true pastor must press men to respond to the gospel call in faith that characterizes the nature of saving faith, which is a repentant, submissive, preeminent loving, humble, and loyal faith in the Lord Jesus Christ. The gospel call in Luke 14:25–33 rang out 2,000 years ago, and it must ring out today. The true pastor is to compel sinners to come into Christ's Banquet, to enter Christ's rest, and make peace with God through Christ. The true pastor is to compel sinners to deny themselves, hate their own life, take up their cross, and follow Jesus wherever He goes. This is where we will pick up Luke 14:25–33.

Luke 14:25 – "*Now great crowds accompanied him, and he turned and said to them.*"

There were many reasons why people followed Jesus. They were interested in His teaching, miracles, physical provisions, and more. At this point in our passage, Jesus turns to the large crowd and declares the cost that was required to follow Him.

This invitation called for supreme loyalty and love toward the Lord Jesus Christ. It is important to note that Jesus turned to the great crowds when He issued this call. This was a call that needed to be heard by those in the crowd who were the committed, the curious, and the counterfeit. It needed to be heard by those that were the faithful, the feigned, and the false. The call needed to be issued to the sincere, the skeptical, and the pseudo. Those who were true disciples needed to be reminded of the cost they committed to when they entered the kingdom of God and the commitment, which was needed to follow the Lord. Those that were false disciples or uncommitted needed to be reminded of the cost of entry into the kingdom of God. Even today, all faithful servants of Christ are to issue this call regardless of church membership or church attendance. The size of the crowd is not what was important; what was important was the message and accepting the invitation to follow the Lord Jesus Christ in faith.

Luke 14:26 – *"If anyone comes to me and does not hate his own father and mother and wife and children and brothers and sisters, yes and even his own life, he cannot be my disciple."*

Notice that the invitation in Luke 14:26 is open to everyone. The invitation is for male and female, Jew and Gentile, barbarian and Scythian, circumcised and uncircumcised, slaves and free, kings and servants, wise and unlearned, poor, and rich, religious and unreligious. The New Testament is a marvelous record of the Lord Jesus Christ saving women (Luke 8:43–48), the ceremonially unclean (Luke 5:12–16), the paralyzed (Luke 5:17–26), despised tax collectors (Luke 5:27–32), prostitutes (Matthew 21:31), Roman Gentiles (Matthew 8:5–13), hardened false teachers such as Paul (Philippians 3:5–9), Samaritans (John 4:39–42), business owners (Acts 16:11–15), physicians (Colossians 4:14), pagan worshippers (1 Thessalonians 1:8–10), slaves (1 Corinthians 7:21), married couples (Acts 18), and more. The invitation is a generous call to all people to come to Christ for salvation.

Christ is inviting everyone to know who He is—both His person and His work. When you come to Christ, it is important to know who Jesus is. No one can be saved by a false Jesus. You could put your faith in an anchor but grasping onto an anchor for salvation will drown you, it will not save you. The object of one's faith needs to be the biblical Jesus Christ. Not only must we know the person of Jesus, but we must also understand His work. Jesus's work is central to the gospel. Jesus is not calling us to decide without getting to know Him or His work. Just as we would take time to get to know someone before we decide to make a marriage commitment, Jesus invites us to get to know Him. Jesus is inviting us to learn about Him and seek Him through the Scriptures. We are told to seek first His kingdom and His righteousness (Matthew 6:33). This is no blind date. This is no quick commitment. Jesus gives the invitation to know His person and work and then commands and demands an answer.

Notice that the one issuing the call in Luke 14:26 sets the

terms. Jesus is the one who sets the terms for what it means to come to Him for salvation. There is no escape clause. There is no redlining and modifying the terms. There is no negotiating with the one who sets the terms. The terms to come and follow Jesus in a salvific way are His terms. As we'll see in this call, there is no redemption without repentance. There is no salvation without submission. There is no salvation without sacrifice. There is no crown without bearing a cross. There is no heaven without holiness. There is no forgiveness without faith. The invitation rings out to everyone, and the call must be answered according to the Lord Jesus Christ's terms. Heaven and earth will pass away, but God's Word will endure forever (Matthew 24:35).

We also see that Jesus is calling for His disciples to have preeminent loving faith toward Him. Jesus's invitation was most likely shocking to the crowd who followed Him. The fact that Jesus talked about someone hating rather than loving would have most certainly caught the crowd's attention. Although Jesus used the word *hate*, He was not calling for His disciples to turn on those they loved and have an evil disposition toward them. In fact, the Lord explained that we should love our enemies and pray for those who persecute us (Matthew 5:43). The Lord stated that the second greatest commandment was to love your neighbor as yourself (Matthew 22:39). The Lord upheld the fourth commandment when He indicted the Pharisees for canceling, voiding, and disregarding the fourth commandment to withhold money that could be used to help their parents (Mark 7:9–13). Therefore, we can see that Christians are called to love and pray for our enemies, love our neighbors as ourselves, and honor our parents.

When Jesus called for hate, He was showing contrast or preference. The Lord used this same method of showing contrast or preference in Matthew 6:24, where He says, *"No one can serve two masters, for either he will hate the one and love the other, or he will be devoted to the one and despise the other. You cannot serve God and money."* In His example about trying to serve both God and money, Jesus is simply saying that both God and money cannot have the same top priority as you will ultimately love one more than the other. If one loves money, they will hate God. To be devoted to money is to despise God. Matthew 10:37 helps us understand as Jesus says, *"The one who loves father or mother more than Me is not worthy of Me; and the one who loves son or daughter more than Me is not worthy of Me"* (NASB2020). Jesus is purposefully creating extremes. He is pitting our affections for our most cherished loved ones against our affections for Him.

It is important to note that He doesn't start with friends, employers, or acquaintances. No, Jesus starts with those who are in your closest concentric circle. If you are a mother, Jesus is calling for your preeminent love and trust over that for your children. If you are a daughter, Jesus is calling for your preeminent love and trust over that for your mother. If you are a happily married husband, Jesus is calling for your preeminent love and trust over that for your wife. Jesus purposefully starts with the people who mean the most to you; He is calling for our preeminent allegiance, love, trust, and affection. Notice that in

Matthew 10:37 if one has greater love and affection for anyone other than Him, He states that they are unworthy of Him.

The one who loves their father, mother, wife, children, brothers, sisters, or anyone else more than the Lord Jesus Christ cannot be His disciple. The word *disciple* comes from the word *mathétés*, which is "a learner, a disciple or a pupil." It was typical in Jewish culture for rabbis to have students or disciples who followed them to learn from them. This word *disciple* has been used earlier in the gospels and included followers who were curious, counterfeit, and committed. However, in this gospel call, Jesus raises the bar, refining and sharpening the definition of what it means to be a true disciple of His. Therefore, we see that this is an evangelistic call on what it means to come to and follow Him in a salvific way or to be a true disciple of the Lord Jesus Christ. What is most shocking is Jesus's statement at the end of verse 26. If anyone comes to Him in a salvific way and has a relationship and love that is greater and takes preeminence over Him, He says, "*He cannot be my disciple.*" Note that Jesus doesn't say, "He may be able to be my disciple." No, Jesus says that such a person cannot be His disciple. *May* is a word of permission; *cannot* is a word of ability.

Those who find a loving relationship greater than Jesus cannot be His disciple. We could paraphrase this condition several ways to emphasize this point:

- If anyone comes to Me for salvation but loves his father, mother, wife children, brothers, or sisters more than me, he is not worthy to be My disciple.

- If anyone comes to Me and desires to enter the kingdom of God but loves his father, mother, wife, children, brothers, or sisters more than Me, He hates Me and cannot be My disciple.

- If anyone comes to Me and desires eternal life but loves his father, mother, wife, children, brothers, or sisters more than Me, he despises Me and is not worthy of Me.

- If anyone comes to Me and desires to enter through the narrow gate, but loves his father, mother, wife, children, brothers, or sisters more than Me, he is not able and is unworthy to be My disciple.

This is all to say that at salvation, Jesus becomes the sum and substance of one's life. Jesus is the priority, and everything else becomes the periphery. This is to say that a person who has decided to follow Christ will live a life that loves Jesus to the extent that, by comparison, it appears as hate toward others. This is to say that the true disciple of Christ cares more about what Christ thinks than what their most cherished loved ones think. The disciple of Christ will still love all those in his close concentric circle, but it will become clear to them that the true disciple's allegiance, loyalty, and love are given to the Lord Jesus Christ.

Finally, in Luke 14:26, we see that one who loves his own life more than Christ cannot be His disciple. It is as if Jesus is just pushing down His foot on the accelerator. If there was ever a chance to lighten His terms of discipleship, it would seem appropriate to do so now. However, Jesus only intensi-fies His call. Not only does Jesus call for hating one's father, mother, wife, brothers, sisters, and children, but He also calls for them to hate their own life. In fact, the word *life* comes from the original word *psuché*, which can mean "the human soul," "the soul as the seat of affections and will," "the self," or "a human person, an individual." Jesus certainly isn't call-ing for self-mutilation, suicide, or anything of the sort. So, what does it mean for one to hate their own life or their own soul?

Once again, Jesus is purposefully creating extremes. He is pitting the affections of one's own life and soul against their affections for Him. Jesus says this about hating one's life in John 12:25: "*Whoever loves his life loses it, and whoever hates his life in the world will keep it for eternal life.*" This could easily be paraphrased to say, "Whoever loves his soul and becomes the lord of his life loses it for all eternity, and whoever hates his soul for My sake in the world will keep it for eternal life." As we noted earlier, the one who hates his own soul and forsakes it for the sake of Jesus is the one who saves it. You could sim-ply love your own soul and be the lord of your own life but, in the end, you lose it for all eternity. This is a call to absolute devotion and love for the Lord Jesus Christ. It is not only hard to love Jesus above one's most loved ones, but now Jesus is calling for one's love and devotion to Him to be greater than the love for one's own life. This call demands a spiritual evaluation of one's life and whether one's personal interests, hobbies, sins, ambitions, and pursuits will take precedence, priority, and preeminence over Christ. It is a call to assess whether one loves their own lordship over their life or loves Christ preeminently. To love Christ preeminently is to say that Jesus's will for your life is the driving force and not your own pursuits. The Lord Jesus Christ may choose to give His true disciples abundance and great wealth. However, He may also call for one to give everything, perhaps one's own life, for the sake of Him and His gospel.

Jesus reiterates this very same message in Matthew 10:39 where He says, "*Whoever finds his life will lose it, and whoever loses his life for my sake will find it.*" To love one's own life more than Christ is to despise Christ. To love one's own life more than Christ is to hate Christ. The one who loves their own life more than Christ will never deny themselves, pick up their cross, and come after Christ because they love their life too much to deny themselves. To love one's life more than Christ is to worship the unholy trinity of me, myself, and I. We could paraphrase Christ's call to hate one's own life this way:

- If anyone comes to Me for salvation but loves being the lord of his life more than they love Me is not worthy to be My disciple.

- If anyone comes to Me and desires to enter the kingdom of God but loves his life more than they love Me and will not deny himself shows his hate for Me and cannot be My disciple.

- If anyone comes to Me and desires eternal life but loves his life more than they love Me, despises Me and is not worthy of Me.

- If anyone comes to Me and desires to enter through the narrow gate but loves his own soul and selfish desires more than they love Me is not able and is unworthy to be My disciple.

This call to hate your life also carries with it the call and command to repent. John the Baptist's message of repentance was described as making straight paths for the Lord by filling in every valley, making every hill low, and making the crooked road straight and the rough ways smooth (Luke 3:4–6). John the Baptist was calling for heart-searching repentance. This is not a road construction project; this is cleaning out the spiritual closet of the heart. Every valley being filled in is taking the debased sins in your life, elevating, and raising them before the Lord, and confessing them to the Lord and turning from them. The sins of the valley of one's heart need to be exposed, confessed, and rejected. Every mountain being filled in is bringing low every righteous act and every self-exalting accomplishment. There is no room for confidence in circumcision. There is no boasting of confidence before the Lord in ceremonial washings and water baptisms. There is no room for confidence in Sabbath observance-keeping. Your sins must be elevated, all your good deeds and religious accomplishments brought low, and every other obstacle in your life must be dealt with and removed. The Lord dwells in a high and holy place, but He also dwells with the contrite and lowly in spirit who are broken over their sin (Isaiah 57:15). The Lord does not dwell with the proud, arrogant, and self-righteous. There is blessedness when there is brokenness over sin (Matthew 5:3). There is comfort for the contrite (Matthew 5:4). There is no room for religious exaltation, only room for soul-searching repentance and humility and a heart readiness to accept the Messiah as Lord and Savior. This is the one who hates their own life.

Repentance comes from the word *metanoia*, which means "a change of mind." Repentance is certainly a change of mind, but when this change of mind occurs, it is radical. When this change of mind occurs or when there is true repentance, the person realizes they've been wrong about sin. This change of mind leads one to realize they have been wrong about God, wrong about salvation, wrong about sin, wrong about their standing before God, wrong about Jesus, wrong about their worldview, and much more.

Biblical repentance is always characterized as a violent act. In fact, Jesus describes the kingdom of heaven being taken by violence and the violent claiming it (Matthew 11:12). Paul speaks of the violence of entering the kingdom of heaven when he says that those who belong to Christ Jesus have crucified the flesh with is passions and desires (Galatians 5:24). Jesus pictures repentance as the gouging out of eyes and the cutting off of hands (Matthew 5:29–30). In Matthew 16:24, Jesus describes repentance as denying yourself and refusing to associate with your sinful desires, self-righteousness, and self-will

(Matthew 16:24). In Luke 18:9–13, Jesus pictures repentance as seeing your own sin and crying to God for propitiation of your sin. In 2 Corinthians 7:11, Paul pictures true repentance as an eagerness to turn from sin, having holy indignation and anger with your personal sin, having fear of bringing shame to God's name and God's glory, longing for godliness, and having zeal for holiness (2 Corinthians 7:11). In Ephesians 4:22, Paul pictures repentance as taking off and laying down your sinful former manner of life. Therefore, we see how the Bible speaks of the violent and zealous nature of repentance in which an individual is radical in dealing with their own sin. The individual who has true repentance is pictured as taking sin in their life and violently killing it and maiming it. True repentance pictures an individual deliberately shunning and refusing to associate with their sin. True repentance pictures an individual hating their life of sin and turning from it. True repentance pictures the violent and aggressive attitude of killing, maiming, denying, shunning, and turning from sin in one's life and a continual turning to Christ.

To come to Christ and not hate yourself or give Christ your preeminent love is self-love that will not repent of sins; say goodbye to worldly desires, pride, self-will, self-righteousness; will not deny self; and will not take Christ's yoke and learn from Him. To love the unholy trinity of me, myself, and I is to hate the Lord Jesus Christ. Once again, these are absolute terms. Christ will not take second place. Christ the Creator will not share preeminent love and loyalty with anything or anyone else for He is a jealous God (Exodus 34:14).

Luke 14:27 – "*Whoever does not carry his own cross and come after Me cannot be My disciple*" (NASB2020).

From this passage, we see that the one who does not pick up his own cross, or rather, die to himself and come after Christ, cannot be His disciple. So, not only does Jesus call for the preeminent love over every other relation, including the love of one's own life, Christ now calls for His true disciples to carry their own cross. To take up one's cross is a command to make a final decision to not only deny yourself and hate yourself, but to also die to yourself. Notice that this is not cross-wearing; it is cross-bearing. Bearing a cross 2,000 years ago had a very specific meaning; it meant strapping an instrument of death on your back. It was a walk of death that included disgrace, shame, pain, and persecution. Disgrace was guaranteed. It was the mode of execution reserved for the worst of criminals. Shame was promised. Pain was a certainty. Persecution was inevitable. Jesus is calling for a self-denying, self-hating, cross-bearing, Christ-identifying walk of life where a person would so identify with Him that they would do so even to the point of death. Notice in Luke's account that Christ says this cross-bearing would be daily (Luke 9:23). A cross-bearing death to self and life to Christ was to be the walk and manner of one's life. Cross-bearing was not glorious.

To come after Christ is the same thing as following Him (Matthew 16:24, Mark 8:34, Luke 9:23). To come after Christ is to listen to the Good Shepherd and follow Him (John 10:3–4). To come after Christ is to hear His words and practice them (Matthew 7:24–27, Luke 6:46–49). To come after Christ is to hear His words and keep them (Luke 11:28). To come after Christ is to listen to His commands and obey them (John 14:23, 15:10). To come after Christ is to be a slave of Christ, which is where the slave has no life of his own, no will of his own, no purpose of his own, and no plan of his own. All things are subject to his master. Every thought, breath, and effort are subject to the will of his master. The existence of the slave was for the will and purpose of his master and nothing else. To come after Christ is to follow Christ with a submissive, self-denying, obedient, loving, and repentant faith.

This statement by Jesus would have been shocking. Just as one was to deny themselves, they were also called to repent and die to worldly desires, die to pride, die to self-will, die to self-sufficiency, die to self-wishes, die to self-righteousness, and die to themselves. They were to live for Christ's yoke, Christ's will, and Christ's rule over their life. This is a step of self-humiliation and of self-renunciation. Taking up one's cross is to die to self and surrender to the King of heaven, the Lord Jesus Christ. Is it possible to be a true disciple and follow Christ without a faith that is submissive and obedient and that gives preeminent love to the Lord? Jesus does not think so. In fact, Jesus knows it is not possible; He says that such a person *"cannot be my disciple."* To put it another way, Jesus said it this way in Matthew 10:38, *"And whoever does not take his cross and follow me is not worthy of me."*

In Matthew 10:38 and Luke 14:27, we see that Jesus is

making a claim to deity—a claim to be God. There is nothing or no one in all creation that should have this kind of love and devotion other than God (Mark 12:28–34, 22:34–39, Deuteronomy 6:4–5). For Jesus Christ to turn to the crowd and call the crowd to love Him more than anyone else was a claim to deity, and the people should have known this.

Jesus spoke about this kind of love and inexpressible joy in coming to Him in saving faith in two parables: the Hidden Treasure and the Pearl of Great Value. In Matthew 13:44, He says, "*The kingdom of heaven is like treasure hidden in a field. When a man found it, he hid it again, and then in his joy went and sold all he had and bought that field*" (NIV). This is speaking of a man who finds Jesus Christ, the forgiveness of sins, eternal life, and reconciliation and a relationship with the Living God. The man is filled with joy inexpressible and sells everything to buy the field. This more specifically talks about the joy and price people are willing to pay to enter the kingdom of God. This is the most valuable possession in the world that is worth the cost of a personal cross, denying yourself, and submitting and trusting in Christ. In Matthew 13:45–46, Jesus says, "*Again, the kingdom of heaven is like a merchant looking for fine pearls. When he found one of great value, he went away and sold everything he had and bought it*" (NIV). These parables have some differences, but the underlying theme is that those who have found the forgiveness of sins, Jesus Christ, and eternal life will pay the price because what they have found is so much more valuable than anything else in this life.

Luke 14:28–30 – *"For which of you, desiring to build a tower, does not first sit down and count the cost, whether he has enough to complete it? Otherwise, when he has laid a foundation and is not able to finish, all who see it begin to mock him, saying, 'This man began to build and was not able to finish.'"*

In this passage, we see Jesus calling people to count the cost to follow Him. He has laid down His terms for being His disciple. He is calling everyone to stop and consider the cost. He does not want a quick decision. He does not want to coerce anyone. He is not guaranteeing what will happen in the next five, ten, or twenty years. He is simply stating that you will need to carefully consider whether you're willing to commit to Him. In an ultimate shame and honor society, such as the Jewish culture, they would have understood this parable. They would know that it would be foolish to start to build a building without first determining whether they could finish. The one who had not carefully counted the costs and decided to build without considering the costs could ultimately face great shame. Is it worth losing your life to gain Jesus? Is hating your own soul, denying yourself, dying to yourself, taking up your own cross, and following Jesus worth it? Christ is calling for a serious spiritual assessment. Consider whether you can truly relate to what Paul says in Acts 20:24:

But I do not account my life of any value nor as precious to myself, if only I may finish my course and the ministry that I received from the Lord Jesus, to testify to the gospel of the grace of God.

All those who have been justified by faith can relate to such self-denying, self-hating, cross-bearing faith in Christ.

Luke 14:31–32 – *"Or what king, going out to encounter another king in war, will not sit down and deliberate whether he is able with ten thousand to meet him who comes against him with twenty thousand? And if not, while the other is yet a great way off, he sends a delegation and asks for terms of peace."*

We should see that the King will return one day and that He will not be coming as the Suffering Servant but as the conquering King. This King will come to judge and wage war (Revelation 19:11). This King will come with His armies (Revelation 19:14). This King will strike down nations with His Word (Revelation 19:15). This King will tread upon His enemies with the wrath of God (Revelation 19:15). This King will kill and destroy His enemies (Revelation 19:21). This King will come with a wrath so horrible that people will cry for mountains and rocks to fall on them rather than suffer the wrath of the Lamb (Revelation 6:16–17). This is the King who is coming, and He has made terms of peace. Jesus is saying that the king with twenty thousand men should see that he is outnumbered and outmatched against the king with twenty thousand men. This King will either say, "*Well done, good and faithful servant*"

(Luke 19:17) or "*Bring them here and slaughter them before me*" (Luke 19:27). This King will either say, "*Enter into the joy of your master*" (Matthew 25:23) or "*Cast that worthless servant into outer darkness. In that place there will be weeping and gnashing of teeth*" (Matthew 25:30). The King will either say, "*Come, you who are blessed by my Father, inherit the kingdom prepared for you from the foundation of the world*" (Matthew 25:34) or "*Depart from Me, you cursed, into the eternal fire prepared for the devil and his angels*" (Matthew 25:41). The King will either say, "*Well done, good and faithful servant*" (Luke 19:17) or "*Cut him in pieces and put him with the unfaithful*" (Luke 12:46). This King will either say, "*Well done, good and faithful servant*" (Luke 19:17) or "*I never knew you, depart from Me you worker of lawlessness*" (Matthew 7:23).

In Luke 14:31–32 Jesus is saying that the king with ten thousand men should request terms of peace from the king with twenty thousand men. Psalm 2 pictures this beautifully as the nations are seen raging against the Lord and against the One enthroned in heaven. At the end of Psalm 2, in verse 12, the psalmist says, "*Kiss the Son, lest he be angry, and you perish in the way, for his wrath is quickly kindled. Blessed are all who take refuge in him.*" Psalm 2:12 is a picture of someone coming to the throne and submitting to the Lord. The psalmist is picturing a dignitary receiving the humble kiss of an inferior submitting and pledging allegiance. In this same way, the Lord Jesus Christ has given an invitation to submit and pledge allegiance to Him. The great banquet invitation has been issued. The terms of this invitation have been defined by the King of heaven for all mankind. You don't want to meet this King without agreeing to His terms of repentance and faith. You don't want to meet this King if you've created your own terms of peace. You don't want to meet this King relying on water baptism, confirmation, money given to the church, church membership, the Lord's Supper, good works, or any of the like for salvation.

There is still time to come to terms with this King, for He is a good, gracious, kind, compassionate, forgiving, loving, and merciful King. If you come to this King on His terms of faith, He will forgive your sins and give you His righteousness. The transaction will be swift and instantaneous. This gracious King says, "*Come now, let us reason together, says the Lord: though your sins are like scarlet, they shall be as white as snow; though they are red like crimson, they shall become like wool*" (Isaiah 1:18). Come to this King and accept His invitation and you will find rest for your soul (Matthew 11:28–30) and grace in your time of need (Hebrews 4:16). Come to this King and receive His invitation into the kingdom of God, and He will remember your sins no more (Hebrews 8:12).

Luke 14:33 – "*So therefore, any one of you who does not renounce all that he has cannot be my disciple.*"

Finally, we should see that those who do not renounce all they have cannot be Christ's disciple. The word *renounce* comes from the original word *apotassó*, which means to "withdraw from," "renounce," or "send away." *Apotassó* means "to say goodbye and depart from or to bid farewell, forsake, or send away." When Jesus calls for the renouncing of all one has, He is calling for a repentant, submissive, preeminent loving, and humble faith in Him. As mentioned previously, He may not ask you to give up everything, but you must be willing to give up everything if He calls you. In fact, in this life, He may give you an abundance or more than you need. However, He may require everything of you. Regardless of what He decides, are you willing to give up everything for Him? As we learned earlier, Jesus promises that for those who follow Him, there will be persecution and a narrow road to walk (Matthew 5:10–12, 7:14). Therefore, Jesus Christ is calling you to become an owner of nothing and a steward of everything. He is calling for total allegiance and trust with your personal relationships, life, and possessions. This is the invitation to the great banquet. This is a gospel call for a submissive, preeminent loving faith in the Lord Jesus Christ and a relationship with Him. As in the parable of the Great Banquet, Christ calls for an evaluation: Will you lovingly submit to and trust in Him above land (Luke 14:18), possessions (Luke 14:19), and relationships (Luke 14:20)?

It is true that God is sovereign over salvation (Psalm 3:8). It is true that all those that the Father has given Christ will come to Him and He will lose none of them (John 6:37). It is true that no one can come to Christ unless the Father draws them (John 6:44). It is true that only God can regenerate and give new life (John 3:1–10). However, it is also true that Christ calls all men to repent and put their faith in Him (Mark 1:15). It is true that those who reject Christ and the gospel have judged themselves unworthy of eternal life (Acts 13:46).

This is the gospel message that the true pastor is committed to preach without compromise. All true pastors have the necessity, compulsion, and obligation to preach this gospel. The true pastor does not shy away from preaching about hell, for he knows that men's souls are at stake. The true pastor exalts the person and work of Christ and what Christ accomplished. The true pastor preaches true repentance and saving faith. Many will find the gospel foolish (1 Corinthians 1:18), and they will hate and persecute the pastor on account of the gospel because it confronts the sin and life they love (Matthew 10:24–25). However, the true pastor can say the same words as Paul said, *"For necessity is laid upon me. Woe to me if I do not preach the gospel"* (1 Corinthians 9:16)! The grace of God has been poured out on the life of the true pastor to fervently and unashamedly preach the gospel with all authority, conviction, urgency, zeal, compassion, and love. How is the true pastor able to do such a thing? Because the true pastor is made, commissioned, and equipped by God (Ephesians 4:11–16).

Chapter 4

A Man Who Has the Grace of God Poured Out on His Life to Teach, Preach, and Love God's Word

Do your best to present yourself to God as one approved, a worker who has no need to be ashamed, rightly handling the word of truth.

—2 Timothy 2:15

In this chapter, we will see how the grace of God is poured out on the true pastor to be skilled in teaching Scripture as well as preaching the Word. Just as the pastor is to have the moral character that we find in 1 Timothy 3:1–8, Titus 1:5–9, and other portions of Scripture, he is also required to be skilled in teaching God's Word. Far too often, men are put into the position of pastor or elder because they are successful in running businesses, are likable and friendly in the church, and have a charismatic personality, but they are not skilled in teaching Scripture, and they fail to preach the Word. Let's remember that God gives His church pastors who are skilled in teaching and preaching the Word to equip the saints for the work of ministry, for building up the body of Christ, for attaining unity of the faith and the knowledge of Christ to become Christlike and mature (Ephesians 4:12–13). Therefore, we will seek to understand this important qualification of the pastor and understand what it means to be a pastor who is skilled in teaching and preaching the Word of God.

He Must be Skilled in Teaching God's Word

In 1 Timothy 3:2, we see that being skilled in teaching is a nonnegotiable requirement for a pastor as Paul says, "*Therefore an overseer must be above reproach, the husband of one wife, sober-minded, self-controlled, respectable, hospitable, able to teach.*" The phrase "able to teach" comes from *didaktikos*, which means "apt to teach" or "instructive." This word *didaktikos* is used to describe someone who is skilled or apt in teaching. It not only implies the ability to convey knowledge effectively but also the possession of the wisdom and patience necessary to instruct others. It has been said that heresy flourishes where sound Christian teaching lags. As we've mentioned earlier, biblical Christianity contains hard sayings and truths that may appear harsh, and it is the duty of the pastor to deliver these truths with unwavering conviction and boldness while remaining compassionate and kind.

Notice in the beginning of 1 Timothy 3:2 that Paul uses the word *must*, which comes from the original word *dei*, which means "necessary" or "must happen." It is not an option or a recommendation that the pastor or elder be skilled in teaching. It is an absolute necessity that the pastor be skilled in teaching.

A pastor who is not skilled in teaching is a pastor who is unqualified. If we look back to the previous exposition of Ephesians 4:11–16, we see that the office of the pastor, evangelist, and teacher are given to the church to build the church up in the knowledge of the Son of God and to bring about maturity so that the church is not blown about by false doctrine and the cunning and crafty schemes of the world and of false teachers. Warren Wiersbe quotes Phillips Brooks (prominent American theologian) who said this of being apt to teach, "A pastor must be a careful student of the Word of God, and of all that assists him in knowing and teaching that word. The pastor who is lazy in his study is a disgrace in the pulpit."[21] Phillips Brooks is exactly right. The pastor who is sloppy in studying God's Word is dishonorable. The pastor who is lax in his study of God's Word is a reproach to the office of the pastor. The pastor who is shallow with God's Word is a defilement to the church. The man who is unskilled in handling the Word of God is like a surgeon performing open heart surgery with a rusty chainsaw. A man who positions himself as a pastor and speaks from the Bible but has spent little time understanding Scripture is a man who can do great damage.

James warns of the great damage that teachers can do to the church when he warns that not many should become teachers because they will be judged with greater strictness (James 3:1). James then goes on to give illustrations of how damaging the tongue can be; his first illustration comes in James 3:3 where he says, "*If we put bits into the mouths of horses so that they obey us, we guide their whole bodies as well.*" In this example James speaks of how a tiny instrument such as a horse's bridle is used to guide a large horse. When you consider the size of a bridle compared to the size of the horse, it is amazing that such a small instrument can control a horse. So, it is with the pastor. His teaching can have a great impact. For example, in Iain Murray's biography of A. W. Pink, Pink recalls his time serving in Australia in a church on Belvoir Street. A. W. Pink described the unbalanced problem he saw with pastors in teaching, handling Scripture, and the inability of spiritual leaders in the church to balance the doctrine of human responsibility and the sovereignty of God:

> Pastors had for so long given emphasis to divine sovereignty that it was virtually believed that man has practically no part or duty in his conversion . . . The sad thing is that almost everywhere today there is just one feature of truth being disproportionately emphasized. There are Arminians who have presented the "free will" of man in such a way as to virtually dethrone God, and I have no sympathy whatever with their system. On the other hand, there have been some Calvinists

who have presented a kind of fatalism (I know not what else to term it) reducing man to nothing more than a block of wood, exonerating him of all blame and excusing him for his unbelief. But they are both equally wrong, and I scarcely know which is the more mischievous of the two.[22]

Here, we see how the unbalanced teaching of doctrine can become dangerous and lead to devastating consequences. Yes, it's true that God is sovereign in election, predestination, and salvation. Yes, it's true that man is responsible for his sin and responding to Christ in repentance and faith. However, if one truth becomes dominant, it leads to the obscuration of other truths as it did in A. W. Pink's observations about the improper handling of divine sovereignty and human responsibility. In this case, Pink ultimately left the church when he discovered that the "Articles of Faith" used in the Ryde and Smithfield churches was going to be applied to the Belvoir Street church he was pastoring because the "Articles" explicitly and emphatically denied human responsibility and categorically repudiated "duty-repentance" and "duty-faith." Thus, we see how the tongue and teaching, though they may seem small, have large consequences.

James gives a second illustration to show how the tongue, which is small, can be used to move or control large things in proportion to its size when he says this in James 3:4, *"Look at the ships also: though they are so large and are driven by strong winds, they are guided by a very small rudder wherever the will of the pilot directs.*" Here James illustrates how a rudder, which is tiny in size when compared to a big ship, can control the direction of the ship. Even though the size of the rudder is miniscule in size compared to the rest of the ship, it has the power to direct the course of the ship. Once again, James wants us to understand how what the teacher teaches can have significant impact on big things. James gives a third illustration of how something small can build and do much damage in James 3:5, "*So also the tongue is a small member, yet it boasts of great things. How great a forest is set ablaze by such a small fire!*" Here, James wants us to see how a tiny spark in a forest, which is miniscule in size compared to the forest, can build and ultimately destroy an entire forest.

Therefore, we can understand the devastating impact a pastor who is not skilled in teaching can have. The words and teaching of a pastor can have both positive and negative impacts on a local church body and beyond. Of course, we have examples of how powerful speech has been used negatively in history. Speeches have been powerful tools to lead nations into devastation and wickedness as well as prosperity. Germany and the Nazi party stand as the abhorrent example of a nation being plunged into wickedness led by Adolf Hitler. There are also modern-day examples of the tongue having both a positive and extremely negative impact in Christianity. For example, think of the veneration of Martin Luther five hundred years after the Reformation; he has been honored because of his positive impact on the Reformation and his belief in *sola scriptura, sola fide,* and *solus Christus.* However,

Martin Luther was also a staunch believer and advocate for baptismal regeneration, which teaches that one is born again, given saving faith, and united with Christ in a water baptism. This is a false gospel that Luther could not escape from when he came out of the shadows of Roman Catholicism. Because Martin Luther is so honored in the Reformation and protestant circles, very few people will address the fact that Luther aggressively taught this false gospel, which persists in the Lutheran church and many other protestant churches because such a critique appears as an attack and sleight against Luther. Therefore, because Martin Luther is still honored and venerated by many protestant churches and is rarely criticized for his errant doctrine, the devastating false gospel of baptismal regeneration still exists in Lutheran churches five hundred years later! Here, we see how words and teaching can have both a powerfully positive and disastrously negative impact. Though the tongue is small, it can move things much larger than itself.

Therefore, the pastor is to be a man who is skilled in teaching. He must understand the responsibility and the accountability that are on his shoulders. Many people are critical of the church and say that the pastor has too much authority. However, another way to understand this is that with the authority God has bestowed upon this position comes much accountability to the Lord and a stricter judgment. The true pastor knows that the authority of his teaching ministry is simply given to him by the Lord to whom he will give an account on the day of judgment (Hebrews 13:17).

He Must Be Diligent and Zealous to Present Himself to God as Approved, Rightly Handling the Word of Truth

Do your best to present yourself to God as one approved, a worker who has no need to be ashamed, rightly handling the word of truth.

—2 Timothy 2:15

Now that we understand that the Bible requires the pastor to be skilled in teaching and we understand the impact he can have through his teaching ministry, let's look at how the pastor is to teach. We will use 2 Timothy 2:15 as our text to examine how the true pastor is to be skilled in handling the Word of God. First, we see that the pastor is to be diligent (2 Timothy 2:15). The word for "diligent" is translated differently in various Bible translations. For example, the NIV translates it as "*Do your best.*" The NKJV translates it as "*Be diligent.*" The phrase "be diligent" comes from *spoudazó*, which means to "make every effort," "to hasten," "to be eager," or "be zealous." *Spoudazó* conveys the sense of earnestness and diligence and implies a concerted effort or striving toward a goal with urgency and commitment. It conveys a call to action with dedication and seriousness and applying oneself fully and wholeheartedly. It speaks of intensity of purpose followed by intensity of effort with careful unremitting attention and persistent application. The command to "be diligent" is to give maximum effort, spare no effort, and do your best. Let's also note that *spoudazó* is written in the imperative mood, which means that it's a command, and it is in the active voice meaning that Timothy and the true pastor are the ones responsible for obeying this command. Paul is not giving a suggestion or a recommendation that Timothy must be diligent. No, this is a command. Timothy and the true pastor are to be diligent, zealous, and wholehearted in teaching and handling the Word of God.

The true pastor is not to be one who is apathetic, indifferent, passive, or uninterested. If a man has the position of pastor and is apathetic and uninterested in teaching the church, that man would do well to take himself out of this office. Examples of men being apathetic, indifferent, and passive include men buying sermons online and copycatting these sermons in the pulpit. This includes men who step in as a transition pastor and do not teach the elders, deacons, or men of leadership in the church. This includes men who are satisfied with fifteen-minute shallow and superficial sermons that do not feed, guide, or guard the flock. This includes men who teach from a catechism with questions and answers but cannot and are not skilled in teaching from Scripture. This includes men who do not wrestle with Scripture to understand the true meaning of a text and will not put forth the mental and physical exertion to mine the truth out of God's Word. This includes men who prioritize meetings, administrative tasks, church events, but do not prioritize reading, understanding, and meditating upon Scripture. Men who exhibit these behaviors are not diligent; they need to repent or step down from the office of being a pastor.

The true pastor is to be diligent to present himself to God. He is not to seek the approval of the choir, the congregation, the deacons, the elders, the administrative committee, the financial team, the denomination or Synod, or his online followers. He is to be a man who presents himself to God. It has been said that if a man pleases God, it does not matter who the man displeases. Though the pastor is to conduct his ministry with all godliness, he must realize that he is to teach the Word of God while continually presenting himself before God. Paul explains how he conducted his ministry in 1 Corinthians 4:2–5:

> *Moreover, it is required of stewards that they be found faithful. But with me it is a very small thing that I should be judged by you or by any human court. In fact, I do not even judge myself. For I am not aware of anything against myself, but I am not thereby acquitted. It is the Lord who judges me. Therefore do not pronounce judgment before the time, before the Lord comes, who will bring to light the things now hidden in darkness and will disclose the purposes of the heart. Then each one will receive his commendation from God.*

Paul was saying that his ministry needed to be carried out faithfully before God and that it was the Lord, and not man, who was judging him. Just like Paul, the true pastor should carry out his teaching ministry faithfully and with diligence before God, and not man. The true pastor is to be aware that one day God will judge his life and ministry (Romans 2:16). So what will God be looking at? Paul says in Romans 2:16 that *"God judges the secrets of men by Christ Jesus."* And in 1 Corinthians 4:5, we learn that He will disclose the purposes of the heart. The following are examples of what God will be judging. God will judge whether the man was looking for praise from men or praise from the Lord. God will judge how the man prepared in his study of the Word. God will judge how the man meditated on the Word. God will judge whether the man was diligent and resourceful in his study of the Word. God will judge whether the man applied the teaching of the Word to his own life. God will judge whether the man was scripturally balanced in his teaching. God will judge whether the man used big and exotic words to sound impressive or simple words so that the listeners could learn and be built up. God will judge whether the man was insincerely emotional to illicit a fleshly response or whether he was emotional out of godly affections. God will judge whether the man relied on his charisma and persona rather than on teaching the Word of God. This is what it means for the true pastor to present himself before God. The Lord watches over the way of the righteous and all things are open and laid bare before Him, including the thoughts, conduct, words, and intentions of the heart (Psalm 1:6, Hebrews 4:13). Nothing is hidden from His sight. The true pastor must understand that he is always to present himself before the watchful, discerning, and loving eyes of the Lord.

The true pastor is to present himself as approved before God. The word *approved* comes from *dokimos*, which means "tested," "tried," or "genuine." This word is used to describe something that has been tested and found to be genuine, reliable, or approved. It often carries the idea of having passed a test or trial and thus prove its worth or authenticity. This word was used to describe the process for purifying metals such as gold or silver, which had been purified to remove various alloys. Kenneth Wuest explained that being approved "means to put to the test for the purpose of being approved, and having met specifications, having the stamp of approval placed upon one."[23] The true pastor is to zealously and diligently pursue being a teacher who is approved by God.

So how would a man be approved by God? This brings us to our fourth point, which is that the man must be diligent to be approved before God by rightly handling the word of truth. The true pastor is to be one who can rightly handle and divide the Word of God. The phrase *rightly handle* comes from *orthotomeó*, which means to "cut straight." This term is used to describe someone who accurately, correctly, and precisely handles God's Word; it implies a precise and careful approach to teaching and understanding Scripture to avoid distortion or error. The man must be able to approach the Word of God as a skilled laborer. He must be equipped to study God's Word. Such careful study of Scripture means the pastor must be able to understand the authorial intent of a book of the Bible along with its cultural and geographical setting, understand the context of a verse, perform word studies, utilize cross references (Scripture analogia), find the doctrine in the text, understand whether the text is prescriptive or descriptive, ensure his interpretation does not clash with other Scripture, parse verbs, understand structural syntax, and more. The man is not to take a chainsaw when studying and teaching; he is to take a scalpel. He is to be careful in his handling of Scripture.

The true pastor is also to ensure that the whole of Scripture is sound and fits together by having a sound hermeneutics and systematic theology. He must have sound soteriology because there is a defined way of salvation and a way that brings condemnation. He must have sound Christology because Scripture defines the person and work of the Lord Jesus Christ. He must understand the purpose for the Word of God, which includes sanctifying, reproving, rebuking, and exhorting (John 17:17, 2 Timothy 3:16). He must understand that there is a defined plan of God for the family and seek to understand and teach it. He must understand that there is a defined plan of God on how to work. There is a defined plan of God for submitting to the government. There is a defined plan of God for how He is to be worshipped. There is a defined plan of God in the Old Testament. There is a defined plan of God for the Levitical system. There is a defined plan of God for the structure and layout of the Tabernacle and Temple in the Old Testament. There is a defined plan of God for understanding the Abrahamic Covenant, Mosaic Covenant, Davidic Covenant, and the New Covenant. God has defined what sin is, how He views sin, and how He deals with sin. There is a defined plan for how the saved sinner is to walk in sanctification. God gives us special revelation of Himself through Scripture and the true pastor must not distort this picture of the true and Living God.

The New International Dictionary of New Testament Theology and Exegesis defines "handling the Word of Truth" this way:

> The image of *orthotomeo* is that of laying out a road. The teacher is to lay out a clearly marked pathway for others to walk. This effort requires study. Teachers are those who have been gifted by the Spirit and have devoted their minds to God so that they might impart His wisdom to His people. The Word of God however can be abused as well as used. It is always in danger of being distorted by teachers who handle it casually. The only effective way to prevent distortion of the Word of truth is diligent preparation at the study desk.[24]

Let us note that God's Word is called the "Word of Truth." Psalm 12:6 gives a picture of the pure, undefiled, and perfect Word of God when David says, "*The words of the Lord are pure words, like silver refined in a furnace on the ground, purified seven times.*" Note that God's Word is always true, perfect, and undefiled; it is man who twists, corrupts, and perverts the Word of God (2 Peter 3:16). The pastor does not have an issue with God's Word being the source of error; rather, it is the true pastor who can become the source of error by wrongly handling the Word of Truth. No man is perfect or has perfect knowledge. Just because the true pastor is a man gifted by

God does not mean he should be casual when dealing with the Word of Truth. There are several warnings throughout Scripture of scribes, prophets, and religious false teachers who corrupted the Word of God with their pens and changed it into a lie (Jeremiah 8:8), delivered self-willed messages (Jeremiah 23:16), distorted and perverted the Word of God (Jeremiah 23:36), and threw away the key of knowledge through misinterpretation (Luke 11:52). To mishandle the Word is to bring disgrace and reproach on God who spoke the Word. To mishandle the Word and be casual with it is to esteem it as insignificant. To be casual with the Word is to think casually upon God to whom the Word belongs, which shows an immense lack of reverence. This is not how the true pastor is to approach the Word; he is to be a man who is careful. Just like the skilled carpenter who measures twice and cuts once, so the true pastor is one who studies diligently, prays fervently, and then speaks to His congregation. The true pastor is guarded in what he says. Like the prophet Ezekiel, he is a man who eats the Word of God, internalizes the Word of God, and then speaks the Word of God (Ezekiel 3:1–11). The true pastor is like the psalmist in Psalm 119. He is a man who delights in the testimonies of the Lord (v. 14), meditates on the Lord's precepts (v. 15), prays to the Lord so that he may behold wondrous things from the law (v. 18), inclines his heart to God's Word (v. 36), and looks for good judgment and knowledge in God's Word (v. 66). The true pastor is a Spirit-empowered man who loves God's Word because it reflects God's character and will; thus, the pastor seeks to handle the Word of Truth with diligence, zeal, great care, and responsibility as one standing before God.

The way a man handles the Word of God speaks volumes of what he thinks about God. God is the divine author of Scripture; therefore, there is a direct relationship between God's Word and the God who spoke the Word. To handle God's Word with shallow study is to think shallowly of God. To handle God's Word with no care is to have no or little care for the God who spoke the Word. To bend or twist God's Word and alter it is to defy the God who gave His Word. To misinterpret God's Word is to give a skewed and false picture of God. To be a man who is not controlled by God's Word is to be a man who is insubordinate unto God. To be a man who does not love God's Word is to be a man who does not love the God who revealed Himself through His Word. To esteem God's Word lightly is to esteem God lightly.

Therefore, a man who rightly handles the Word of Truth is a man who loves the God who gave the truth, and he would not dare to misrepresent the God whom he serves. It has been said that the Word of Truth flows from under the throne, mirrors heaven, is undefiled through the ages, and nourishes holiness as it flows. The true pastor knows that handling the Word of Truth is directly tied to what he thinks of the Author of the truth.

We see in 2 Timothy 2:15 that the true pastor is to be hardworking. The word *worker* comes from the original word *ergatés*, which can mean a "field-laborer," "laborer," or "general workman." Paul wanted Timothy to carry out the ministry as one who labored and worked hard. In 2 Timothy 2:4–6, Paul gives Timothy a picture of how he was to carry out his ministry. In 2 Timothy 2:4, Paul says, "*No soldier gets entangled in civilian pursuits, since his aim is to please the one who enlisted him.*" Notice that Paul does not want Timothy to have several pursuits, but rather, one pursuit. Just as the aim of the soldier is to please the commanding officer, so Timothy and the true pastor are to seek to please the Lord. Just like a soldier is not to pursue civilian affairs while he is enlisted, so Timothy and the true pastor are not to pursue and get entangled in other pursuits. Just as the soldier is submissive, obedient, and in a state of readiness to obey, so Timothy and the true pastor must be submissive, obedient, and girded for spiritual battle. Just as the soldier is ready for battle at any moment while enlisted and willing to face the dangers that come with war, so the true pastor must be ready for spiritual battle and quick obedience to his Lord (Ephesians 6:10–20).

Paul also tells Timothy that he must be like an athlete: "*An athlete is not crowned unless he competes according to the rules*" (2 Timothy 2:5). Here we see that Paul wants Timothy to be like an athlete in training, discipline, and following the rules. Timothy would readily understand the training of an athlete as he would likely have been familiar with the Olympic Games in Greece, which started around 700 BC. Olympic athletes were to prepare for competition in order to win; they would train their body and put themselves through rigorous exercise. The athlete would not let their body dictate the discipline; rather the athlete would be disciplined and train their body and make it their slave. Paul gives this very analogy in 1 Corinthians 9:24–27, where he talks about beating his body and making it his slave, training with purpose, and training to win. In the same way, Timothy was to envision the winner's podium with the goal of being crowned by the Lord, the Righteous Judge (2 Timothy 4:8). He was to train, be disciplined, and compete according to the rules in the Word of God, so that he would not be disqualified. He was to give maximum effort in his ministry and work with purpose under the will of God just as an athlete would give full physical effort. Thus, the true pastor is to carry out his ministry like a hard-working, disciplined, rule-competing, and race-winning athlete.

In 2 Timothy 2:6, Paul tells Timothy that he must be like a farmer in one respect: *"It is the hard-working farmer who ought to have the first share of the crops."* This phrase *hard-working* comes from *kopiaó*, which means "to labor," "to grow weary," or "to toil." This word conveys the act of laboring to the point of exhaustion with diligent effort and perseverance. This implies not just the act of working, but the accompanying fatigue and weariness that result from the exertion. The term does not stress the amount of work, but rather the effort. A farmer plows, sows, tends, reaps, and harvests the crop through inclement weather, problematic insects, crop-killing weeds, and other difficult conditions before he can enjoy the spoils of his work. One day Timothy will be able to enjoy the spoils of his toils, but first he must labor intensely. Not only this, but Timothy is also to wait patiently. Just as a farmer waits patiently for the results of his hard work so Timothy must be patient while he works hard. The true pastor must have this same mindset of the farmer. He is to be a patient, hardworking, and hopeful pastor. He may not see immediate results, but he knows that his labor for the Lord is not in vain (1 Corinthians 15:58). When Paul tells Timothy to be a workman, this is the type of workman that he has in mind.

Finally in 2 Timothy 2:15, we see the true pastor is to be a man who is unashamed. The word *unashamed* comes from *anepaischuntos*, which means "having no cause to be ashamed." This word describes a state of being without shame because of one's integrity and conduct. So how would the true pastor be unashamed? Simply put, the true pastor would be diligent and zealous to rightly handle the Word of Truth as a hardworking farmer, self-disciplined athlete, and subordinate soldier while working tirelessly and hopefully with the aim of pleasing the Lord. The true pastor is not ashamed because he is not sloppy with the Word. He presents himself and lives before the face of God. He is diligent and sincere in his study of the Word, and he seeks to please the Lord. As we close this brief exposition of 2 Timothy 2:15, we can see that the true pastor is to be skilled in teaching the Word as well as how the pastor is to teach the Word. This is how the true pastor is to conduct his teaching ministry. God has equipped and made men who are able to carry out this task of teaching His Word and building up the church.

He Must Preach the Word

In this section, we will examine how the grace of God is poured out on the true pastor to preach the Word. In modern Christianity, many pastors give speeches in the pulpit but do not preach the Word. Many pastors give lectures, but they fail to herald the Word. Many pastors speak about the Word, but they do not proclaim the Word. Not only are there many pastors who fail to preach, but there are also many men who act as cowards and purposefully choose to avoid certain doctrines and hard verses or to dilute and water down the Word. The true pastor is a man who is called to preach the whole Word and counsel of God. We will perform an exposition of 2 Timothy 4:1–8 to understand the call from God to every pastor to preach the Word.

In the very last letter ever written by the apostle Paul, he gives Timothy, his son in the faith, instructions for completing the ministry with which he has been entrusted. While Paul waits for his inevitable execution, he gives Timothy a series of nine commands that come quickly in verses one through five of 2 Timothy 4, and then he closes with the reason and hope for Timothy to fulfill his ministry in verses six through eight. These instructions provide lasting instruction and hope for every true pastor who has been commissioned by God as he seeks to be a preaching pastor who proclaims the Word.

> **2 Timothy 4:1** – *"I charge you in the presence of God and of Christ Jesus, who is to judge the living and the dead, and by his appearing and his kingdom."*

The first point we should see is that Paul gives Timothy a solemn charge. This word *charge* comes from the original word *diamarturomai*, which means "to testify earnestly" or "declare solemnly." This word is used to convey the act of solemnly testifying or earnestly charging someone with a truth or command. It often implies serious or emphatic full and clear testimony. Not only is this charge serious, but we also find that it is a continuous charge. *Diamarturomai* is written in the present tense and indicative mood meaning that this solemn charge stands until Timothy and the true pastor die. It is a charge to be carried out when times are good, when times are bad, when he is abandoned, when he is betrayed, when he has much, when he has little, when he is being persecuted, and even if and when someone puts a sword to his neck and threatens to take his life.

Note that this solemn charge to Timothy comes from Paul. Some may ask, "Why is it important that this charge comes from Paul?" Paul was the model of a faithful pastor to Timothy. Paul was a model of suffering for the gospel, and he commanded Timothy not to be ashamed of the testimony of the Lord or of him, but rather, to suffer for the sake of the gospel (2 Timothy 1:8). Paul was a model of proclaiming the good news of Jesus Christ with all boldness and no hindrance (Acts 28:31). Paul was a model of remaining faithful and relying on the Lord even when he was abandoned by all (2 Timothy 4:16–18). Paul was a model of one who suffered tremendous persecution, the threat of death, having very little sustenance, and being in danger from false brothers and

Gentiles (2 Corinthians 11:16–33). Paul was no hypocrite, and he was a model of what it means to be a true pastor. This solemn charge carries special weight because it comes from the apostle Paul who was charged and commissioned by God as an apostle, pastor, and teacher.

Not only is this solemn charge from Paul who was a model of the faithful pastor, but this charge must be done in the presence of the Living God. The phrase *in the presence* comes from the original word *enópios*, which is a compound word with *en* meaning "in" and *ops* meaning "face" or "sight." Literally, *enópios* means "before the face of" or "in the eyes of." In this context, this means that this charge and the imperative commands that Paul will give are to be carried out diligently, faithfully, unashamedly, and zealously before the face of the Living God. This charge applies not just to external acts that are before the face of God, but also to internal motives, intents, desires, thoughts, and affections that are before the face of God. As we learned earlier, God cares how the true pastor studies. God cares about the pastor's diligence in studying His Word, which no one else sees. God cares whether a man manipulates a congregation or crowd to get a reaction or whether the man is relying on the Word of God in the power of the Holy Spirit. It is God who performs the final evaluation of a man's ministry. Paul does not make this solemn charge in the presence of elders, deacons, an assembly of men with theological doctorates in divinity, or God's holy angels. No, Paul charges Timothy before the face of the omniscient, imminent, transcendent, eternal, all-wise, and Holy God. God will evaluate whether Timothy builds on the foundation, which is Jesus Christ, with gold, silver, and precious stones, which will last or wood, hay, and straw, which will be worthless and burned up (2 Corinthians 3:10–15). God will determine what works had eternal value and what had no value. God will determine what Timothy did out of a good conscience, a pure heart, and a sincere faith and what Timothy did in the power of the flesh. Paul and Timothy had to give an account of their ministries and so too will every true pastor. Thus, every true pastor must understand that this charge to preach the Word, is to be done with the understanding that God is evaluating and will evaluate the man's faithfulness and work.

It is noteworthy that this solemn charge and the following imperative commands to preach the Word are to be obeyed with the understanding that God is about to judge and is judging the living and the dead. When we parse the two verbs in the phrase "is to judge," we can get a better sense of what Paul is saying. The phrase *is to* comes from the original word *melló*, which conveys a sense of immanence or inevitability that something will happen. This word *melló* is also written in the present tense and participle mood, which means that Christ Jesus is "being about or on the verge of judging." The word *judge* is also written in the present tense, which gives the idea that not only is judgment about to take place, but it's also taking place even now because people are dying and going to heaven or hell.

When you put this phrase together, it could also be rendered this way: "I solemnly charge you before the face of God and of Christ Jesus **who is going to and is presently judging** the living and the dead." This phrase pictures the imminence of Christ's judgment, but as we know, men are dying now and entering heaven or being cast into hell. Men are dying and being told, "Well done good and faithful slave," or "Cast that worthless slave into the outer darkness." Thus, it is true that Christ is on the verge of judging men's souls, and He is judging men when they die for it is appointed for man to die once, and after that comes judgment (Hebrews 9:27).

The next question that must be answered is, "Who are the living and the dead in 2 Timothy 4:1?" Some theologians believe that the living are those who will be alive at the time when Christ returns and that the dead are those who have died and will face God in judgment as pictured in Revelation 20:11–15. I think there's a good case and rationale for this reasoning. However, I believe Paul is speaking of something different. In a more general sense, I believe Paul is stating that Christ Jesus is going to judge and is judging those who are spiritually alive and those who are spiritually dead. Jesus speaks of the spiritually alive and spiritually dead in John 5:25 where he says, "*Truly, truly, I say to you, an hour is coming, and is now here, when the dead* [nekros] *will hear the voice of the Son of God, and those who hear will live* [zaó]." In the context of John 5, Jesus is saying that those who are spiritually dead will hear the words of the Son of God and be made spiritually alive or born again and believe in Him. In John 5:25, to be dead is to be spiritually dead and apart from Christ, and to live is to believe in Christ. Thus, Timothy is to see the seriousness of this charge to preach the Word. There are those who are spiritually dead, perishing, being judged, and thrown into eternal hell. There are also those who are spiritually alive and saved who will give a final account to the Lord for the service they rendered (Matthew 25:20–23). Some who are spiritually dead have not yet heard the gospel of their salvation. And others are spiritually alive and must continue in faith. The command to preach the Word is to be understood in this context. The command to preach the Word has serious responsibility. Men are either being condemned or being commended by the Lord. Men are either entering heaven or being thrown into hell. Thus, we see that this solemn charge to preach the Word must be done in light of this reality. Richard Baxter captures the heart of this with this comment about preaching the Word: "I preached as never sure to preach again, and as a dying man to dying men."[25]

We see that this solemn charge and the following imperative commands to preach the Word should be done considering Christ's Second Coming. The Lord has stated that no one knows the day or hour when He will return (Matthew 24:36). The Lord also exhorted and commanded that we must be ready for His coming because He will return at an hour when we do not expect it (Matthew 24:44). So not only is Timothy to preach in the reality that Christ is about to judge and is presently judging, but also with the hopeful expectation that he will be found faithful and unashamed when Christ returns to render His final judgment and establish His eternal kingdom (Matthew 24:45–46). This is to be the sober reality and hope of every pastor. True pastors are to understand the realities of

Christ's judgment with the eager expectation, hope, and anticipation of the day of His return, which will be one of great despair and sorrow for unbelievers, but one of great joy for true believers.

2 Timothy 4:2 – "*Preach the word; be ready in season and out of season; reprove, rebuke, and exhort, with complete patience and teaching.*"

Now that Paul has solemnly charged Timothy before God, he gives Timothy the first of nine commands. The first command is the primary command, and the other eight commands are how Timothy and the true pastor are to conduct the first and primary command. The first and primary command is that Timothy must preach the Word. We looked at what it meant to preach in the previous chapter, but it is helpful to summarize what preaching is. In ancient times, a herald or proclaimer would go before a king and announce the king's message. The herald was to have certain qualities and attributes to carry out this important role. First, he had to have a voice of certainty. In fact, auditions were often held to ensure that the herald had a powerful voice and had an honest disposition to protect against tampering or exaggerating the message. He was not to announce the king's message with words such as *perhaps, maybe,* or *probably.* His voice, posture, and delivery were to match the seriousness of the message he was delivering. The herald also needed to be accurate, precise, and faithful to the message he proclaimed. In fact, the herald was allowed to ask the king questions to ensure he understood the message as well as the intention of the message, so he could proclaim the message with the same spirit and attitude of the king.

Additionally, when delivering his message from the king, there were things that the herald was not allowed to do. He was not allowed to enter debates, discussions, or chats; he was not to enter into negotiations. The herald would come with the king's message and whether it was an order for the nation's surrender or an edict from the king, the herald would go throughout the towns and villages and announce the king's message. The herald would not be quiet. The herald would bring forth the message with conviction and the full authority of the king. The herald did not dare to misrepresent the king's message, add to the king's message, leave anything out from the king's message, or announce the message quietly. In fact, the herald was to announce the message with a gravity and authority that required the listeners to obey. The herald would boldly, loudly, and clearly articulate the message of the king to all the people with conviction; tampering with the message meant being unfaithful.

This is what Timothy is commanded to do. He is not to chat the Word, discuss the Word, debate the Word, or whisper the Word. He is to preach the Word with the full authority and conviction of Christ the King. He is not to change the Word or water it down and soften it to suit the ears of carnal men. No! He is to proclaim and herald this message as if Christ were delivering the Word.

Second, the true pastor is commanded to preach the Word. He is not commanded to preach about politics, scholastics, philosophy, or science. He is commanded to preach the all-sufficient, infallible, inerrant, and inspired Word of God. He is to preach on the Old Testament and New Testament. He is to preach on the hard verses as well as the easier verses; nothing is off the table when it comes to preaching the Word. Let's just examine some of the many doctrines the man is commanded to preach even though they are unpopular:

- Preach from the Word against the false health and wealth prosperity gospel and show that the God of the Bible says the way to life is narrow, constricted, and one of persecution (Matthew 7:14).

- Preach the Word against false Christianity in Roman Catholicism and show that praying to Mary is detestable to God and that only the Living God is to be prayed to and worshipped (Deuteronomy 18:11–13, Isaiah 45:5).

- Preach from the Word that there are many people in churches who are religious but lost and on the broad road to destruction, and that there are few that find eternal life (Matthew 7:13–14).

- Preach from the Word against damning sacramentalism in Roman Catholicism and in Protestant churches such as Lutheranism, Anglicanism, and even liberal reformed churches (Galatians 1:8, 2:21, 5:1–12).

- Preach from the Word against those who declare that God loves everyone while ignoring the attributes of God and His holy indignation against sin.

- Preach from the Word against easy-believism and antinomian (anti-law) false Christianity and preach on true repentance, true saving faith, and true biblical assurance of salvation.

- Preach from the Word about allowing women to be pastors in the church and that men who allow this are unspiritual, ignorant, and not true pastors (1 Corinthians 14:38).

- Preach from the Word on Christian living and God's plan for the family. The true pastor is called to preach the Word and the whole counsel of God (Acts 20:27).

Third, note that the second command describes when the true pastor is to preach. The phrase *be ready* comes from *ephistémi,* which means "to be present" or "be at hand." It conveys the idea of standing by and being prepared. Not only is Timothy to be ready to preach the word, but he must be ready to preach it in season and out of season. The phrase *in season* comes from *eukairós,* which means "an opportune time" or "favorable time;" it conveys the idea of an event being well-timed or appropriate. *Out of season* comes from the word *akairós,* which means "an inopportune time" or "untimely;" it conveys the idea of something happening at an inopportune time and often implies a lack of readiness or suitability. Thus, when Paul says that Timothy must be ready to preach in season and out of season, he is simply stating that Timothy must be prepared in every circumstance to preach the Word.

Every true pastor is to be ready to preach the Word in the good times and the bad times. They are to preach the Word when they are loved by their congregation and when they are despised by their congregation. They are to preach the Word when the giving of offerings is good and when the giving of offerings is poor. They are to preach the Word when the topics of sin and hell are unpopular and when they are accepted. They are to preach the Word when they feel like it and when they don't feel like it. They are to preach the Word when they are depressed and when they are joyful. They are to preach the Word in times of revival and in times of rejection. They are to preach the Word among unbelievers as well as unbelievers. They are to preach the gospel when they are called to preside over a funeral of a known unbeliever as well as the funeral of a believer. The true pastor is called to always be ready to preach the Word under every type of circumstance.

Fourth, note that the third command tells us that one of the purposes of preaching the Word is to convict. This word *convict* comes to us from the original word *elegchó*, which means to "reprove," "refute," or "correct;" it conveys the idea of convincing someone of their sin, error, or wrongdoing with the aim of leading them to repentance and truth. To refute, carries the idea of convincing with solid, compelling, biblical evidence. Therefore, we can understand that the true pastor will have a ministry that includes refuting and confronting sin, error, and falsehood. It has been said that to be biblical is simply to understand reality. The pastor is to preach the Word for the purposes of correction and refutation to bring about a biblical reality; he preaches the Word to convict his listeners of sin and error, which can lead to restoration, repentance, and godliness (2 Corinthians 7:10–11).

However, convicting someone of sin and error can lead to conflict, hostility, and a sword of division (Matthew 10:34–36). The sovereignty of God in salvation will be offensive to those who believe in "free-will." The doctrine of human responsibility for repentance and faith will be offensive to hyper-Calvinists. Both the doctrine of the sovereignty of God in salvation and human responsibility are true, and the pastor is to refute error and sin through the preaching of the Word. It has been said that a man who does not convict of sin and error is not a man who is led by the Holy Spirit. Jesus said that the Holy Spirit would convict the world concerning sin, righteousness, and judgment (John 16:8). Therefore, a man who does not convict of sin and error through the preaching of the Word is a man who is disobedient to God, and it is questionable whether he is a true pastor if this is his walk and manner of life and ministry.

Fifth, note that the fourth command also tells us the purpose of preaching the Word, which is to rebuke. The word *rebuke* comes from *epitimaó*, and it means to "charge," "warn," or "admonish." In this context, rebuke conveys the idea of warning to prevent something from going wrong. Here, we see the stepwise progression in the preaching of the Word. First, we see that the Word convicts. Now, we see that the Word is preached to rebuke with the goal of re-directing. Not only must the listener understand that they are wrong and why they are wrong, but they must also understand the consequences and impending penalty that will happen if they do not repent. It is not enough to simply convict, for if someone is convicted of sin and error, they must understand the seriousness and consequence of their sin and error. Steven Cole has this helpful observation about rebuking:

> A preacher must make an appeal to the conscience of the hearers: "Rebuke." This moral aspect of preaching says, "You are wrong; you need to repent!" We tend not to like that sort of thing, but it is desperately needed in our day of watered-down, feel-good Christianity.[26]

Additionally, William Barclay has this critique of the pastor who will not rebuke: "Any teacher . . . whose teaching tends to make men think less of sin is a menace to Christianity and to mankind."[27] Proverbs 27:5 reinforces the biblical wisdom in rebuking to turn one away from sin where it says, "*Better is open rebuke than hidden love.*" This verse is essentially saying that it is better to turn someone away from sin than to let them persist in sin because that is not showing genuine love. The true pastor is commanded to rebuke when preaching the Word.

Sixth, note that the fifth command tells us the purpose

of preaching the Word, which is to exhort. To exhort in this context carries a positive connotation whereby the sinner has been shown to be wrong and shown the seriousness and consequences of their sin and error; now, they are being called to change course. The call of exhortation is to be one of encouragement. The pastor is called to encourage and exhort the listeners to obedience unto Christ. Barclay clarifies the importance of the pastor's exhortation: "The function of the true Christian preacher and teacher is not to drive a man to despair, but to lift him up to hope."[28] Without exhortation and encouragement, there is only conviction of sin and the rebuke and awareness of the penalty of remaining in sin but no hope and no encouragement. An excellent example of exhortation is found in Paul's second letter to Timothy where Timothy seems to be showing signs of acting cowardly. Rather than rebuking Timothy and being harsh with him, Paul encourages Timothy by telling him that he was in his prayers and that he is convinced that Timothy has sincere faith, a gift that he must fan into flame. Though the evidence suggests that Timothy was becoming cowardly, Paul exhorted and encouraged Timothy while also reminding him that God does not give us a spirit of fear (2 Timothy 1:4–7). In this example, we see how Paul encouraged his son in the faith. So it is with the true pastor that he must not only convict and rebuke, but he must also exhort and encourage.

Seventh, note that Paul explains that preaching the Word must be done with complete patience and instruction. Timothy is to preach the Word while convicting, rebuking, encouraging, and being long-suffering. This phrase *complete patience* comes from *makrothumia*, which means "forbearance" or "long-suffering" and conveys the idea of being patient and showing self-restraint that does not retaliate or punish especially when wronged. It literally means "long-temper." It is the capacity to be wronged and not retaliate. Charles Spurgeon comments on the importance of long-suffering, "Continue to put up with others, remembering the Lord's longsuffering with you."[29] The true pastor is not to seek revenge, retaliate with word battles, or fight to get the last word in. Rather, he is to be one who can take the ill-treatment and forgive others from the heart and not hold grudges (Matthew 18:35). Additionally, he is to preach the Word with all instruction; all preaching stands on the sturdy foundation of teaching. Teaching and instruction are the bedrock, which undergirds preaching. As we learned earlier in this chapter, the true pastor is to be one who is skilled in teaching, and all the pastor's preaching must be grounded in the sound pattern of teaching (2 Timothy 1:13).

2 Timothy 4:3–4 – *For the time is coming when people will not endure sound teaching, but having itching ears they will accumulate for themselves teachers to suit their own passions and will turn away from listening to the truth and wander off into myths.*

In these next two verses, we see the reason why the pastor is to continue preaching the Word with all patience and instruction. First, there is coming, and to some extent exists already, a time when people will not endure or tolerate sound teaching. One may ask, "What is sound teaching?" The word *sound* comes from *hugiainó*, which is where the English word *hygiene* comes from. This word means "healthy." It conveys the idea of spiritual health and integrity, which adhere to true and wholesome teaching. Thus, sound teaching is that which is true teaching from the Word of God, which glorifies God and leads to salvation and godliness (2 Timothy 1:13–14). Conversely, the opposite of sound teaching would be myths, false teachings, or misinterpretations of Scripture that do damage to the listeners, lead to ungodliness, and do not glorify God. Paul wants Timothy to know that there is coming a time when people will no longer tolerate, sit under, or endure sound teaching.

We also see that people will turn to teachers who will tell them what they want to hear. Paul does not want Timothy to be unaware of the apostasy and hardship that he'll endure. He doesn't want Timothy to think that by preaching the Word, he will be well-liked, well-received, and honored. Rather, Paul tells Timothy that as he preaches the Word and gives sound teaching and instruction, there will be those who will stockpile pastors and teachers for themselves to suit their own passions and desires. In fact, the word *accumulate* comes from *episóreuó*, which conveys the idea of amassing in piles. Rather than hearing sound words, apostates and unbelievers will accumulate pastors and teachers in false religion and false Christian denominations that will tell them what is pleasing to their ears rather than what is true. For example, for those who love self-righteousness and earning or meriting salvation through a false Christ, there are cardinals, bishops, priests, and popes in Roman Catholicism who will tell self-passion pursuers what they want to hear. For those who choose to adhere to a sacramental salvation by baptism and communion, there are a plethora of Lutheran pastors who will tell them what their itching ears want to hear. For those who choose to turn away to the health, wealth, and prosperity gospel, there are stockpiles of men and women pastors who will scratch their ears and feed their desires. For those who want a false gospel of easy-believism where the definition of true repentance is stripped from its biblical meaning and the definition of saving faith is plundered, there are mounds of pastors who will suit their passions. For those who want a mystical experience and esoteric Christianity, there is charismatic Christianity, which promotes being drunk in the Spirit, holy laughter, being slain in the Spirit, and being seized by the fire of the Holy Ghost, speaking in unknown languages without interpretation, private revelation, and more. This is the hardship that awaits the true pastor.

We also see that there will be a turning away from true Christianity and growing apostasy toward false religion and false Christianity. Paul says that these men will no longer listen to the truth and sound doctrine, but they will turn away from the truth. The phrase *turn away* comes from *apostrephó*, which means "to turn back" or to "reject." It conveys the idea of departing from a previous point. Also note that the verb *apostrephō* is written in the active voice, which means that these apostates who previously seemed to hold firm to the truth will now actively pursue myths and false doctrine. These apostates have personally chosen to swerve from and reject the truth. Additionally, Paul says they will also wander off into myths. *Wander off* comes from *ektrepó*, which means "to deviate" or "to turn aside." In the medical sense, this word is used to describe limbs being put out of joint and dislocated. Just as someone who moves too quickly and throws their bones out of joint, so too will these apostates swerve quickly from the truth. Additionally, the verb *ektrepó* is written in the passive voice, which means that these apostates will be turned aside or yanked out of joint by an outside force. Of course, this would be false teachers who are under the influence of demons (1 Timothy 4:1). Timothy will need to endure this. While Timothy is faithfully preaching the Word in the presence of God and Christ Jesus, there will come times of devastation where people will turn away from the truth and will amass many false teachers and abandon Timothy and God. Every true pastor must know this. No matter how godly the man, this is part and parcel of being a true pastor and preaching the Word. Every pastor will endure the heartache of seeing friends, colleagues, supposed co-laborers, and family who once professed the faith, turn away from the true faith. Thus, Paul does not want this to come to Timothy as a surprise; he wants Timothy and every true pastor to be prepared for this aspect of ministry.

2 Timothy 4:5 – *As for you, always be sober-minded, endure suffering, do the work of an evangelist, fulfill your ministry.*

Here, we come to the last four commands for how Timothy is to faithfully preach the Word. The sixth command is to remain sober among such hardship. This word *sober* comes from *néphó*, and in this context, it means to be free from the influence of outside forces. Timothy is to think biblically about apostasy and the hardships of ministry rather than despair about what he is seeing. He is to remember that there is a soil that will fall away during a time of testing (Luke 8:13)—a soil where plants will be choked out by the deceitfulness of riches and life's worries (Luke 8:14). He is to remember that the Lord had many disciples fall away when He gave hard sayings in the Bread of Life discourse (John 6:66). He is to remember that there are many false teachers and that they will attack from outside of the church as well as inside the church (1 John 4:1, Acts 20:29–31). To remain sober is to understand these events from a biblical perspective and deal with these hardships in a godly and biblical manner.

Paul's seventh command is to endure hardship. This phrase *endure suffering* comes from *kakopatheó*, which literally means "to endure evil." All Christians are called to endure the suffering of evil caused by the atrocity and apostasy of men as well as persecution. Paul commanded Timothy to suffer with him for the sake of the gospel (2 Timothy 1:8). Likewise, James told his listeners to count it all joy when they face all kinds of trials because trials produce steadfastness (James 1:3–4). Paul told the Romans to rejoice in sufferings because they produce endurance, character, and hope; and hope does not fail (Romans 5:3–5). Paul told the Philippians that they had been graced to suffer for the sake of Christ (Philippians 1:29). Timothy had Paul as a model of what it meant to endure suffering. However, the greatest example of someone suffering evil though they did no wrong was Christ (1 Peter 2:21–23). Paul's command to endure hardships was a command to Timothy and is a command to the true pastor to joyfully endure suffering for the sake of the Word, the gospel, and Christ.

The eighth command is to do the work of an evangelist. Back in the first chapter, we established that an evangelist is the one who proclaims the gospel message. Evangelists proclaim the fallen condition of man and the eternal torments and punishment of hell that man justly earns. They also pronounce the good news of Jesus Christ as found in Scripture—who Jesus is and what He did. They explain the propitiating, reconciling, expiating, redeeming, justifying, regenerating, sanctifying, and glorifying work of Christ. They also exhort and call men to Christ by commanding that all men repent and come to Christ in saving faith. The evangelist is a bold proclaimer of Christ. They have an unusual love for the lost and preach the gospel with conviction and urgency. They seek to reach the lost in the world as well as the lost in the church. They are unwavering in proclaiming the gospel message, which they dare not pervert, twist, alter, or modify. Timothy is to have the same mindset of

Paul as stated in 1 Corinthians 9:16: "*For necessity is laid upon me. Woe to me if I do not preach the gospel.*" Just as Timothy was commanded to be an evangelist, so too is the true pastor.

The ninth command to Timothy is to fulfill his ministry. This is essentially a command to fulfill the obligation and duty of a pastor. Timothy is to do the whole work of a pastor and nothing less. As we learned earlier, he is to do this with diligence, steadfastness, godliness, integrity, and careful study of Scripture all while being "in the face of God and Christ Jesus." Just as Timothy is commanded to fulfill his ministry, so too is the true pastor.

2 Timothy 4:6 – *For I am already being poured out as a drink offering, and the time of my departure has come.*

Paul transitions into reason and hope for fulfilling his ministry. First, let's notice that Paul sees his whole life as a sacrificial offering to the Lord. He certainly spoke this way when he exhorted the Romans to offer themselves as a living sacrifice, holy and acceptable to God as their logical act of worship (Romans 12:1). Peter says that the believer is offering up spiritual sacrifices to God through Christ (1 Peter 2:5). The author of Hebrews says that we are to offer up a sacrifice of praise to God (Hebrews 13:15). The pastor is to live his whole life as a holy and acceptable sacrifice to the Lord. Note that in the sacrificial system, the drink offering was the last offering given following the burnt offering and grain offering (Numbers 15:1–16). The last sacrifice that Paul would offer up was his death. Essentially, Paul was saying that Timothy must fulfill his pastoral duty with all faithfulness even if he is put to death for Christ. Timothy was not being called to retreat, but to entreat himself to the Lord even if it costs him his life.

Paul is looking forward to his death as he sees that the time of his departure has come. Notice the language that Paul uses when speaking of martyrdom. Paul calls his death a departure. The word *departure* comes from *analusis*, which was a nautical term used when a ship is released from its moorings, and it is also used in agriculture when an animal is unyoked from a plow. Paul saw his impending death as a release from this life; it will be a release from the body of death (Romans 7:24). To Paul, death is the reality of departing to be with Christ, which was far better than to remain on the earth (Philippians 1:21–23). Regarding the hope of seeing the Lord, it has been said that Martin Luther made the following comment, "I have two days on my calendar: this day and that Day.[30]"

2 Timothy 4:7 – *"I have fought the good fight, I have finished the race, I have kept the faith."*

There is something in this text that does not come through in the English translations. The syntax of the original language could also render the verse this way:

The good fight, I have fought,
The race, I have finished,
The faith, I have kept.

Note that in the original language, Paul states that there is *the* good fight, *the* race, and *the* faith. Note the emphatic position of definite article of *the*. The Christian faith is comprised of many definite articles. Jesus Christ is *the* Way, *the* Truth, and *the* Life (John 14:6). There is *the* narrow gate and *the* narrow way that leads to life (Matthew 7:13-14). There is *the* good fight, *the* race, and *the* faith (2 Timothy 4:7). Men will choose to fight many battles; however, the greatest fight one can fight is for the King of heaven. Many races and marathons are run; however, the greatest race one can run is the race of faith (Hebrews 12:1–3). There is false religion and false Christianity that produce false faith; however, the greatest faith is the faith in the Lord Jesus Christ.

This statement is Paul's testimony and is the testimony that every true pastor should strive for. It is the testimony of a life well spent, a noble fight that has been fought, a race that has been run, a faith that has been kept, and a master who has been served. It is a picture of the soldier who was called to arms and valiantly went to warfare for his king, and now it is time for the man to lay down his sword and shield and rest from his service. It is the picture of an athlete who trained and disciplined himself, competed according to the rules, crossed the finish line, and will now receive his prize (2 Timothy 4:8). It is the picture of a man holding onto and laying ahold of eternal life (1 Timothy 6:12). *The* good fight, *the* race, and *the* faith are what every true pastor is to fight for, race for, and keep.

2 Timothy 4:8 – *"Henceforth there is laid up for me the crown of righteousness, which the Lord, the righteous judge, will award to me on that day, and not only to me but also to all who have loved his appearing."*

Notice that Paul knew there was a crown of righteousness that would be given to him. So how is one to understand what this crown of righteousness is? I believe this should be understood in three ways. First, Paul will now attain the hope of eternal life and crown of glory that will never fade away (2 Timothy 4:8, 1 Peter 5:4). Second, Paul will attain the hope of glorification and becoming like Christ (Romans 8:30). Third, Paul will attain the hope of knowing Christ and seeing Him face to face (1 Corinthians 13:10–12). This is the award that Paul was looking forward to.

Paul is certain of this crown of righteousness. The hope that he had when he was born again and converted to Christ is going to be realized and awarded to him by the Righteous Judge. Christ is not some corrupt or double-minded judge. No, Christ is faithful and will reward Paul. All the promises of God are Yes and Amen in Christ (2 Corinthians 1:20). Paul has full confidence in the promise of eternal life in Christ, which will be awarded to him by the Righteous Judge.

All true believers and every true pastor are longing for and loving Christ's appearance. This is the hope and reason for Timothy and every true pastor to preach the Word before the face of the Living God. The true pastor and true believer render service to God out of love for God and Christ. This is one of the strongest marks of being a Christian. It's not church attendance or church activity or the amount of money donated. No, the love of Christ and faithful submission and obedience mark the true Christian.

As we close this chapter, we've learned much about how the true pastor is equipped to teach and preach the Word. The task of the pastor is daunting. Who is sufficient for such things? We discussed the answer to this question in the first chapter: It is God who equips and commissions men to make them sufficient for such things (2 Corinthians 2:16–17). The man is to be skilled in teaching and preaching of God's Word to equip the saints for the work of ministry, for building up the body of Christ, and for attaining unity of the faith and knowledge of Christ to become Christlike. This is why the pastor must be skilled in teaching and preaching and have a love for the Word of God.

Chapter 5

A Man Who Has the Grace of God Poured Out on His Life to Stand Firm Against False Teachers

He must hold firm to the trustworthy word as taught, so that he may be able to give instruction in sound doctrine and also to rebuke those who contradict it.

—Titus 1:9

In this chapter, we will see how the grace of God is poured out on the true pastor to stand firm against false teachers. In chapter 1, we saw that God gives pastors, teachers, and evangelists to the church so that the church can become mature and not be like children tossed to and fro by the waves and carried about by false doctrine propagated by the cunning and craftiness of men and their deceitful schemes (Ephesians 4:14). To this end, God has given men to the church who are skilled in teaching and preaching the Word and who can and will stand against false teachers.

Pastors are given by Christ to the church to not only guide and feed the flock, but also to guard and protect the flock. It is essential that the pastor be able to stand against false teachers who come from inside the church and from outside the church. The New Testament writers speak in unison on the deceptiveness and danger of the damning doctrines of false teachers. One cannot read the New Testament without seeing how false teachers are an ever-present threat to the church. In this chapter, we will see how the true pastor is to warn of, identify, and deal with false teachers. Before we dive into this chapter to describe how the true pastor is to stand against the false teacher, we will first define what a false teacher is and then survey the Old Testament to see how false teachers are portrayed and how that matches the New Testament's profile of a false teacher.

A false teacher is one who unrepentantly and persistently holds to, teaches, and preaches a false gospel that damns men's souls by attacking, twisting, misinterpreting, adding to, or leaving out the essential components of the gospel or essential components of the bad news of sin, death, and hell. A false teacher could also be one who teaches the true gospel but lives a life in contradiction and opposition to the gospel and thus, blasphemes the gospel through their life (Galatians 1:6–9; Matthew 15:14, 23:13–15; 2 Peter 2:1–22, 3:16; Luke 11:52; Jude 4; Titus 1:16).

Jeremiah's Portrait of a False Teacher

"From prophet to priest, everyone deals falsely. They have healed the wound of my people lightly, saying, 'Peace, peace,' when there is no peace. Were they ashamed when they committed abomination? No, they were not at all ashamed; they did not know how to blush. Therefore they shall fall among those who fall; at the time that I punish them, they shall be overthrown," says the Lord.

—Jeremiah 6:13–15

Jeremiah had a difficult ministry, which was mostly directed at the people of Judah. His ministry was to call Judah to repent and avoid the impending judgment of God, which would be carried out by the Babylonians. Jeremiah prophesied calamity and judgment against Judah for idolatry and running after other false gods (Jeremiah 1:16). Jeremiah called Israel and Judah to repent and to turn from idolatry to the Lord (Jeremiah 4:1–4); he announced judgment against Judah if the people would not repent. This judgment included Babylonian destruction that would come from the north, which would ravage and destroy the nation (Jeremiah 4:6). Although Jeremiah prophesied of impending judgment, he was met with resistance from the false prophets who opposed and resisted his message.

First, we see that the false prophets dealt falsely and addressed Judah's sin superficially. The religious leaders of Jeremiah's time did not convict the nation of her idolatrous sin and wicked offense against God. In fact, Jeremiah accused the people of being fools who did not know the Lord; rather they were skilled in doing evil and not knowing how to do good (Jeremiah 4:22). The religious leaders and false teachers led the nation into sin and rebellion against God, and they did not address the sin as a serious issue, nor did they warn the people to repent.

Second, we see that the false prophets gave a false gospel. Rather than warn the people of impending judgment and doom, they prophesied, "*Peace, peace.*" Repeating the word *peace* twice indicates that the false prophets doubled down and strongly emphasized that there was no judgment coming. They proclaimed that the nation was at peace with God, so the people had no fear of impending judgment.

Ezekiel faced the same thing with the false prophets giving false messages of hope to the people. In Ezekiel 13:10, he says, "*Precisely because they have misled my people, saying, 'Peace,' when there is no peace, and because, when the people build a wall, these prophets smear it with whitewash.*" Thus, for both Ezekiel and Jeremiah the false prophets gave a false message of hope, a false gospel, and false, unfounded assurance of security with God.

Third, we see that this false gospel was an abomination to the Lord. This sin of leading the nation into idolatry and giving a false gospel was not something minor or arbitrary. No! The Lord saw this as an abomination, detestable, loathsome, obscene, outrageous, and an atrocity. To stand in the place as a spokesman for God and lead people into sin and give a false gospel is an absolute abomination to the Living God.

Fourth, we see that the false prophets were not repentant. We understand that they were unashamed and unrepentant when we read that *"they did not know how to blush"* (Jeremiah 6:15). They had no sensitivity and no spiritual bashfulness about leading the covenant people of God into idolatry and continuing to give them a false message of peace. They were not repentant. They were not sorrowful. They were not ashamed. They were not broken and contrite in spirit. No, they didn't even know how to blush. Thus, we see that they had a conscience that was absolutely seared, and they had a spiritual awareness that can only be described as blind.

Fifth, we see that they were to be condemned. We see this when the Lord says that they will fall, be punished, and be overthrown (Jeremiah 6:15). The end for the false prophet is not heaven and honor. Rather, it is disgrace, condemnation, and everlasting contempt.

Jeremiah 5:12–13 – *"They have spoken falsely of the Lord and have said, 'He will do nothing; no disaster will come upon us, nor shall we see sword or famine. The prophets will become wind; the word is not in them. Thus shall it be done to them!'"*

In this portion of Scripture, we see Jeremiah once again giving a message from the Lord concerning the false prophets. First, we learn that the false prophets give a false gospel and speak falsely of the Lord. Rather than warning the nation of destruction, famine, and sword, the false prophets prophesy that "*God will do nothing*" and that "*no disaster will come upon us.*" The false prophets led the people into false security and assurance with God although God was actually angry with their sin and promising destruction, not peace.

Second, we see that the false prophets pretended to speak for the Lord, but they did not carry the Lord's true message. Jeremiah makes this abundantly clear when he says, "*the word is not in them.*" Though the false prophet and false teacher pretend to act and speak on behalf of God, they do not proclaim the truth of His Word. In fact, we see in Jeremiah 5:30–31 that the false prophets only speak lies and do so by their own authority and self-will: "*An appalling and horrible thing has happened in the land: the prophets prophesy falsely, and the priests rule at their direction; my people love to have it so, but what will you do when the end comes?*" Thus, we see the false teacher and false prophet are marked by standing in the place of God's spokesman, but they lie and speak on their own authority.

Third, we see that they will be condemned. We see this in Jeremiah 5:14 where it says, "*Therefore thus says the Lord, the God of hosts: 'Because you have spoken this word, behold, I am making my words in your mouth a fire, and this people wood, and the fire shall consume them.'*" The false teachers do not have favor with God; they will be judged and condemned, and the words they speak will only damn their listeners. Jesus makes this very point in Matthew 23:13 where He speaks to the Pharisees about their damning religion: *"But woe to you, scribes and Pharisees, hypocrites! For you shut the kingdom of heaven in people's faces. For you neither enter yourselves nor allow those who would enter to go in."* Just like the Pharisees of Jesus's time, the false prophets in Jeremiah's time damned the people with their lies, and they damned their own souls. Their message kept others and themselves out of the kingdom of heaven.

Jeremiah 8:8 – *"How can you say, 'We are wise, and the law of the Lord is with us'? But behold, the lying pen of the scribes has made it into a lie."*

Jeremiah also confronted the trickery and deception of the religious leaders in how they perverted and corrupted God's Word. First, in Jeremiah 8:8, we see that the scribes who were responsible for rightly handling the Word of God had twisted it into a lie. Although it is not clear what portion of Scripture was corrupted, it is clear that the scribes had changed the Word of God into something that was false.

Second, we see that the people or religious leaders thought they were safe because they had the Scriptures or the *"law of the Lord."* However, because the Scripture had been corrupted by the scribes, it did them no good. Jesus denounces the lawyers for this very same thing in Luke 11:52 where He says, *"Woe to you lawyers! For you have taken away the key of knowledge. You did not enter yourselves, and you hindered those who were entering."* Here, Jesus denounces them because they have taken away the correct interpretation of Scripture, which is *"the key of knowledge."* The lawyers hindered people by causing them to have a wrong understanding of the Messiah, a wrong understanding of salvation, a wrong understanding of sin, and a wrong understanding of God. The lawyers hindered the people by causing them to have a wrong understanding of how man was saved and by polluting the way of salvation with their works-righteousness system. Just as Jesus denounced the scribes for corrupting the Word of God and taking away the correct interpretation of Scripture, so Jeremiah denounces the lying pen of the scribes.

Third, we see that the lying pen of the scribes was most likely a false gospel. We see this in Jeremiah 8:11:

> *They have healed the wound of my people lightly, saying, "Peace, peace," when there is no peace. Were they ashamed when they committed abomination? No, they were not at all ashamed; they did not know how to blush. Therefore they shall fall among the fallen; when I punish them, they shall be overthrown, says the Lord.*

The lying pen of the scribes most likely had to do with a false gospel and false message of peace. Just like the false prophets, they proclaimed peace with God when there was actually enmity with God. They dealt with sin superficially. Rather than being faithful to God, their message and actions were an abomination to God. They were not repentant, and they were not broken over the role in leading the nation of Israel astray. Rather, they did not even know how to blush.

Therefore, God determined to bring judgment and destruction on them.

Jeremiah 23:16–19 *–Thus says the Lord of hosts: "Do not listen to the words of the prophets who prophesy to you, filling you with vain hopes. They speak visions of their own minds, not from the mouth of the Lord. They say continually to those who despise the word of the Lord, 'It shall be well with you'; and to everyone who stubbornly follows his own heart, they say, 'No disaster shall come upon you.'" For who among them has stood in the council of the Lord to see and to hear his word, or who has paid attention to his word and listened? Behold, the storm of the Lord! Wrath has gone forth, a whirling tempest; it will burst upon the head of the wicked.*

In these verses, Jeremiah prophesies against the false prophets again. First, we see that the Lord rebukes the false prophets for giving a false gospel, when He says that they are *"filling you* [Israel] *with vain hopes"* and saying, *"It shall be well with you,"* and *"No disaster shall come upon you."* Rather than warn of destruction and judgment, the false prophets were prophesying lies that assured the people that no harm would come to them. Rather than turning people from their sins, the false prophets kept the people in their sins.

Second, we see that the words they speak are not the words of the Lord, but rather, their own self-willed messages. Though they stand up and pretend to be spokesmen for the Lord, they do not speak the words of the Lord. Rather, they speak visions of their own minds and tell the people what they want to hear. Additionally, we see that they do not stand in the council of the Lord to hear His Word; they don't seek the Lord or seek to understand His will.

Third, we see that the false prophets speak false gospels to people who despise the Word of the Lord. Not only do the false prophets show their insubordination and hatred for the Word of God by giving their own self-willed messages, but they also speak to people who also despise God's word. Jeremiah indicts the religious leaders and the people for their hatred of God's Word in Jeremiah 5:31: "*The prophets prophesy falsely, and the priests rule at their direction; my people love to have it so, but what will you do when the end comes?*" It's not just the false prophets who loved lies; it was also the people who loved it when the false prophets gave comforting messages rather than God's Word. Thus, the false prophets give a false gospel to false believers who love the false message, who despise God's Word, and who love to heap up for themselves teachers who will tickle their ears to suit their own passions so they can turn from the truth (2 Timothy 4:3–4).

Fourth, we see that the false prophets are condemned. Do the false prophets escape from God's judgment? No, they will suffer the wrath of God; they will have judgment and wrath burst upon their head. Peter confirms the same judgment in 2 Peter 2:3: "*And in their greed they will exploit you with false words. Their condemnation from long ago is not idle, and their destruction is not asleep.*"

Jeremiah 23:1–2 – *"Woe to the shepherds who destroy and scatter the sheep of my pasture!" declares the Lord. Therefore thus says the Lord, the God of Israel, concerning the shepherds who care for my people: "You have scattered my flock and have driven them away, and you have not attended to them. Behold, I will attend to you for your evil deeds, declares the Lord."*

As we learned earlier, the role of the pastor is to feed, guide, and guard the flock of God. It is a serious task and responsibility of the pastor to feed the sheep the truth of God's Word, build the sheep up in the truth, and defend them from error. However, we see that the Lord was denouncing the false prophets in Jeremiah's time for failing to fulfill the role of a spiritual shepherd. First, we see that the shepherds and religious leaders did not guide, feed, and guard the sheep. Rather, they destroyed and scattered the sheep. They did the very opposite of what a shepherd is called to do. The shepherds had destroyed the sheep, scattered the sheep, driven the sheep away, and not attended to the sheep. Thus, the shepherds of the nation had neglected their God-given duty.

Second, we see that the Lord promised to attend to the shepherds for their evil deeds. Of course, this meant judgment for the unrepentant shepherds. As we read a little further in Jeremiah 23, we find that they were ungodly (v. 11), evil (v. 11), walking in lies (v. 14), strengthening the hands of evildoers (v. 14), and not calling for repentance (v. 14). The way of the false prophet is never glory. Rather, the way of the false prophet is condemnation and shame. Jeremiah sums up the devastation and ruin of the false prophet in Jeremiah 23:40: *"And I will bring upon you everlasting reproach and perpetual shame, which shall not be forgotten."*

Isaiah's Portrait of a False Watchman

All you beasts of the field, come to devour— all you beasts in the forest. His watchmen are blind; they are all without knowledge; they are all silent dogs; they cannot bark, dreaming, lying down, loving to slumber. The dogs have a mighty appetite; they never have enough. But they are shepherds who have no understanding; they have all turned to their own way, each to his own gain, one and all. "Come," they say, "let me get wine; let us fill ourselves with strong drink; and tomorrow will be like this day, great beyond measure."

—Isaiah 56:9–12

Isaiah also had a ministry of prophesying during a time of apostasy and dead religion in the divided kingdom of Israel and Judah. He condemned empty ritualism (Isaiah 1:10–15) and idolatry (Isaiah 40:18–20). Isaiah also foresaw and warned of the coming Babylonian captivity and destruction of Judah (Isaiah 39:6–7). In Isaiah 56:9–12, Isaiah gives a detailed portrait of a false watchman or false prophet.

First, Isaiah calls the spiritual leaders blind watchmen. A watchman was responsible for keeping watch and vigil; he was to be on the lookout for approaching danger. Though the religious leaders weren't physically blind, they were spiritually blind. They were blind to God's anger against sin, spiritual adultery, and dead and empty religion. Rather than turning the people to a singleness of heart and devotion to the Lord and warning the people of judgement, they did not warn the people because they were spiritually blind. Jesus also spoke this way of the Pharisees when he warned that the blind will lead the blind into a pit (Matthew 15:14). Thus, these watchmen were spiritually blind when it came to sin, salvation, and the Savior.

Second, we see that the spiritual leaders of Isaiah's day were without knowledge. These blind watchmen were without the knowledge of God. Isaiah says in Isaiah 1:3, "*The ox knows its owner, and the donkey its master's crib, but Israel does not know, my people do not understand.*" The people had forsaken the Lord and did not know Him. The people called evil good and good evil, put darkness for light and light for darkness, and put bitter for sweet and sweet for bitter (Isaiah 5:20). They did not savingly know the Lord. The spiritual leaders did not know God and led the people into sin because they lacked the knowledge and fear of the Lord.

Third, we see that the spiritual leaders were silent dogs. A watchman is supposed to warn the people of impending danger. However, the spiritual leaders were like mute dogs who don't even bark to warn of imminent danger. A dog's job would be to bark and warn. Not so with these false watchmen. They did not bark. They did not warn. They did not admonish. They did not cry out. They did not do their job as watchmen.

Third, we see that they were the opposite of faithful watchmen. The picture of the watchman is one who stays vigilant. However, false watchmen are pictured as lazy and even sleeping! Rather than having a clear mind, they are dreaming. Rather than being knowledgeable, they are ignorant. Rather than standing up, they are lying down. Rather than staying awake, they are sleeping. Rather than watching out for the safety of others, they are concerned with their own appetite and needing more. Rather than following the way of the Lord, they turn to their own way. Thus, instead of being vigilant over the spiritual welfare of the nation, the false watchman is one who is stupid, ignorant, lying down, sleeping, and dreaming with a blindfold on, and thinking about his own selfish desires and indulgent pleasure. What a picture the Lord draws of a false watchman, a false teacher, and a false pastor!

We see from the Old Testament that the portrait of a false teacher lines up with how the New Testament describes a false teacher. The Old Testament and the New Testament agree that the definition of a **false teacher, false prophet,** and **false pastor** describes one who unrepentantly, and persistently holds to, teaches, and preaches a false gospel (Galatians 1:8–9, Jeremiah 6:14–15, Matthew 15:14, 23:13–15) that damns men's souls by attacking, twisting (Jeremiah 23:36, 2 Peter 3:16), misinterpreting (Jeremiah 8:8, Luke 11:52), adding to (Galatians 5:3–4), or leaving out the essential components of the gospel or essential components of the bad news of sin, death, and hell (Jeremiah 8:11). A false teacher could also be one who teaches the true gospel but lives a life in contradiction and opposition to the gospel and thus, blasphemes the gospel through their life (2 Peter 2:2, Jude 4, Titus 1:16).

It is important to distinguish between a false teacher and those under the false teacher. The Bible clearly teaches that we are to love our enemies (Matthew 5:43–48). However, the Bible also makes a distinction that false teachers who lead people astray hold more responsibility and, thus, will be judged with greater strictness (James 3:1) as more people are affected (1 Timothy 4:16), and teachers are to be spiritual models of Christ (1 Timothy 4:12). Therefore, there should be a clear distinction between a false teacher and those in false religious systems who are not false teachers. **False teachers are to be treated differently from those in false systems.** Let's remember this definition of a false teacher as we seek to understand who the true pastor is to stand firm against and oppose, the false teacher.

Know the Gospel, Know Your Salvation, Know Scripture

In Peter's second letter he wants his listeners to know their salvation (1:3–11), to know the Scriptures (1:12–21) and, thus, know their adversaries (2:1–22). Peter knows that unless one knows the gospel, is saved, and knows Scripture, they are vulnerable to being swept away by false doctrines. Being knowledgeable in the gospel and Scripture is essential for the true pastor. If he does not know the truth, he will not be able to detect error. For example, it is a sad, painful, and unfortunate thing to watch a Lutheran and a Roman Catholic argue over justification by faith alone when they both believe a false gospel of baptismal regeneration; that is, being born again and saved through water baptism. Thus, the true pastor must know the gospel, know his salvation, and know Scripture. This is a basic and elementary step if a man is to ever even identify a false teacher.

Watch, Beware, and Test for False Teachers

Beware of false prophets, who come to you in sheep's clothing but inwardly are ravenous wolves. You will recognize them by their fruits. Are grapes gathered from thornbushes, or figs from thistles? So, every healthy tree bears good fruit, but the diseased tree bears bad fruit. Every tree that does not bear good fruit is cut down and thrown into the fire. Thus you will recognize them by their fruits.

—Matthew 7:15–20

It is also important that the true pastor must be vigilant and test what another man teaches and compare it to Scripture. Sometimes, the false teaching or false teacher will be known immediately or in due time by the fruit of their doctrine or life (1 Timothy 5:24). However, when the error is not obvious, you must continue to listen, discern, and compare the teaching to Scripture. It is a dangerous and foolish to rush in and claim someone is a false teacher without testing the spirits and examining their doctrine and their life. In this section, we will do a brief exposition of Matthew 7:15–20 to see how we are to watch for, beware of, and test for false teachers.

Let's note that Jesus wants us to beware of false prophets and false teachers. The word *beware* comes to us from *prosechó*, which conveys the act of paying close and full attention or giving heed to something. *Prosechó* implies a sense of caution or alertness. In 2 Peter 2:1, Peter says that just as false prophets arose among the people in previous times, false teachers will also be among believers in the church. For the purposes of this book, the terms *false prophet* and *false teacher* will be used interchangeably as both terms refer to individuals who come and claim to be teachers of God's Word but instead teach falsehood, which deceives others, distorts the gospel, and leads others astray.

Paul issues a similar warning to be aware of false teaching Judaizers. Though Paul's warning applies specifically to Judaizers, it is also true for every false teacher; Paul says, "*Look out for the dogs, look out for the evildoers, look out for those who mutilate the flesh*" (Philippians 3:2). Here, Paul tells the Philippians that they are to beware or watch out for false teachers. The phrase *watch out* comes from *blepó*, which conveys the idea of perceiving or understanding something either in the physical, literal, or spiritual realm. Christians are to continually be watchful of what they are observing and being taught. They are not to let down their guard. Also notice that Paul uses the word *blepó* three times; this threefold use of "look out" or "watch out" is repeated to give a strong warning. When Paul tells the Philippians to watch out three times, it's as if he's adding three exclamation points to emphasize the warning. Also, the word *blepó* is written in the present tense and imperative mood, meaning that this is an ongoing command to watch out and remain vigilant.

Additionally, Paul uses derogatory words to describe these false teachers. He calls them dogs because they are scavengers, they carry spiritual disease, and they are dirty and unclean just like the dogs of ancient times. He calls them evildoers rather than co-laborers because they are enemies of God and oppose God's message. He calls them the false circumcision because they are unregenerate, have not had a circumcision of the heart, have never been born again, and teach a ritual-ceremonial based salvation. Just as Jesus commanded believers to beware, so Paul commands that believers be aware and attentive for false teachers.

Note also that there will be many false teachers and many false prophets. The apostle John helps us understand this when he says, *"Beloved, do not believe every spirit, but test the spirits to see whether they are from God, for many false prophets have gone out into the world"* (1 John 4:1). Notice that many false prophets go out into the world. John and Jesus want believers to be aware that they will be among a large multitude of false teachers. The question is not whether you will ever encounter a false teacher. The question is, "When have you encountered a false teacher?" Given the vast number of them in the world, there is a high likelihood that you have met one or heard one.

Thus, because there are so many false teachers in the world, the believer and the true pastor must be on guard.

Moreover, false teachers will come disguised as true pastors, teachers, and evangelists. When Jesus says they will come in sheep's clothing, He is warning that they will come dressed in the shepherd's attire. In Jesus's day, the shepherd would wrap himself in a large cloak of sheepskin or thick material woven of wool or goat hair. False teachers will look, dress, and act the part of pastors, teachers, and evangelists. They will hold Bibles. They will come from seminaries. They will be called "pastor" or "reverend." Not only this, but they will come in unnoticed (Jude 4).

In Jude's letter, he states that certain people have crept in unnoticed (Jude 4). The phrase *crept in unnoticed* comes from *pareisduó*, which means "to come in by stealth," "coming in a secret manner," or "entering under pretense." Likewise, Peter also warns that they will secretly bring in destructive heresies (2 Peter 2:1). Not only do they enter by stealth, but Peter says they will exploit you with false words (2 Peter 2:2). The phrase *false words* comes from *plastos*, which means "formed," "molded," or "false." *Plastos* conveys the idea of something being artificially derived or formed and not the real thing. These men will come in and use words that Jesus used such as, *grace, faith, love, mercy*, and *God*. Although they will use the same words, they will use a different dictionary and change the biblical meanings. Grace is corrupted into licentiousness. Faith is corrupted into intellectual assent. Jesus is turned into a man who preached nothing but love and forgiveness but never judgment and hell. These men will quote Scripture, but they will give false meanings and false interpretations of these words and doctrines. This is why Jesus, Jude, Peter, and Paul warn of this threat because false teachers come disguised as true teachers and pastors, and they come by stealth.

Scripture warns that false teachers are ravenous wolves. When Jesus calls them ravenous, he means to say that they are inwardly are rapacious, robbers, and extortioners. They kill and steal by unjust means. For example, let's think of the Pharisees. Jesus described the Pharisees and religious leaders as those who spiritually skinned, flayed, and cast down the people of Israel (Matthew 9:36). Not only were they ravenous, but they were also described as wolves, which are predators. They are those who shut the kingdom of heaven in men's faces, and they are kingdom obstructionists (Matthew 23:13). They teach destructive heresies that damn men's souls (2 Peter 2:1–3). They throw away the key of knowledge and give false interpretations of Scripture and hinder those who are trying to enter heaven (Luke 11:52). They give a false message of peace, deal with sin lightly, and are unrepentant (Jeremiah 6:14–15). They are ravenous, rapacious, soul-killing wolves.

The Lord promises that we will know these false teachers by their fruits. So, what fruits should the believer examine? To put it simply, this would be the fruit of their teaching and the fruit of their lives. When we examine the fruit of a teacher's life and doctrine, Jesus tells us that we will be able to recognize them. The word *recognize* comes from *epiginóskó*, which speaks of knowledge through personal relationship or experiential knowing. Thus, Jesus promises that we will be able to recognize them by what they teach regarding the doctrines of sin, hell, the authority of Scripture, the person of Christ, the work of Christ, the gospel, the attributes of God, and the right response to Christ of repentance and faith. We will be able to recognize the fruit of their character and contrast that with the character of a true pastor. Thus, we will recognize them by their fruits.

Note that Jesus gives an illustration of how believers will experientially recognize false teachers. Jesus gives a picture of someone gathering grapes from thornbushes or figs from thistles. One could simply ask these questions:

- Do believers continue to go to a thornbush to find grapes?

- Do believers continue to go to thistles to find figs?

- Do believers continue to go to false teachers for spiritual food?

- Do believers continue to go to harmful thornbushes and thistles that cut, prick, and cause pain?

- Do believers continue to go to harmful teachers to look for fruit when there continues to be no fruit?

Additionally, thornbushes and thistles were seen as a curse (Genesis 3:18), and Jesus uses the imagery of thornbushes and thistles as a picture of false teachers. Regarding false teachers and how true believers should respond to them, Jesus says, *"A stranger they will not follow, but they will flee from him, for they do not know the voice of strangers"* (John 10:5). In other words, Jesus is promising that true believers will know a false teacher by their fruits and will flee from them. True believers will not continue to seek nourishment and spiritual food from these heretics; rather, true believers will flee for their life because they do not recognize them as true teachers and pastors.

Let's see that there are only two types of trees: good trees that bear good fruit and diseased trees that bear evil fruit. Here, the word *good* comes from *agathos*, which speaks of that which is beneficial, virtuous, and intrinsically good; good in nature; and that which aligns with God's will. Additionally, the fruit that the good tree produces is characterized as *kalos*, which means "good," "beautiful," and "noble," something outwardly beautiful as a result of the inner good. The bad tree is described as *sapros*, which means "rotten," "corrupt," "bad," "worthless," and "depraved." *Sapros* speaks of that which is spoiled because of moral corruption. The type of fruit that the bad tree produces is described as *ponéros*, which means "evil," "wicked," or "bad." A true and regenerated pastor will produce good fruit because the Lord has made him into a good tree. This is not to say that the true pastor is sinless, but it is to say that the pastor produces visibly good fruit of doctrine and that his life and character reflect this. The false teacher will produce evil and wicked fruit; it is impossible for a diseased tree to produce good fruit. Though false teachers may appear to be religious, they will continue producing either bad fruit of doctrine, bad fruit of an immoral character, or both.

False teachers will be cut down and thrown into the fire; this is exactly why the true pastor warns the flock about false teachers. They are blind guides and lead the blind into a pit of destruction (Matthew 15:14); they are dangerous, and they damn themselves and their followers. This is why the true pastor is to beware and watch out for these false teachers.

Identify the Type of False Teacher

And have mercy on those who doubt; save others by snatching them out of the fire; to others show mercy with fear, hating even the garment stained by flesh.

—Jude 22–23

Once the true pastor has identified that someone is a false teacher, it is important to identify the type of false teacher and the error they are propagating. Jude gives us helpful instruction when thinking about various false teachers and how to distinguish the error and danger they present. Jude notes that there is a group who are the doubters who should be treated with mercy. He also notes that there is a group of false teachers who are dangerous and should be dealt with cautiously and swiftly as if snatching someone out of the fire. Finally, Jude warns that there is another group of false teachers who are the full-fledged, committed false teachers that should be treated with mercy, fear, and a hatred toward the false teaching they propagate. Thus, Jude categorizes false teachers in three groups: confused, convinced, and committed.[31]

First, some false teachers are confused; they are "*those who doubt*" (verse 22). The word *doubt* comes from *diakrinó*, and it means to "distinguish," "discern," "doubt," or "hesitate." In this context, it refers to false teachers who are examining their teaching and are going back and forth and questioning or vacillating over their doctrine. For such people who are in a false religion and have legitimate questions and concerns, Jude commands that they be shown mercy.

The true pastor is commanded to love and show mercy to false teachers who doubt. True love is self-sacrificing love, which means doing what is in the other person's best interest; compassion flows out of this kind of love and moves one with empathy and feelings toward another's felt needs. Love and compassion for another move us in showing mercy to alleviate the other person's suffering or condition. Why make this point? Because if you don't love people, you will never show mercy. To deal rightly with false teachers, the true pastor shows mercy; he is able to see false teachers' pitiable condition, love them, and act on this love and compassion with mercy. If you never love people, you will never show mercy. There are those who love debating, arguing, and showing their elevated knowledge. However, this is not to be the way the true pastor addresses false teachers because this is done out of pride and love of self rather than love and concern for the false teacher.

Note that some false teachers are dangerous and must be dealt with cautiously; we could categorize these people as the convinced. This appears to refer to those who have been convinced that what they believe and teach is true. They're not doubting or confused, and they are convinced that what they are teaching is the gospel truth. This word *snatching* comes from *harpazó*; it conveys an idea of taking something away forcefully and quickly. When somebody in a false religious system is convinced that they are right, you must not turn your back on them or push them away or shun them. However, you don't embrace them in true fellowship either because they are still damning false teachers. Instead, you confront the error bluntly; you remind them that the Bible has severe warnings, promises of judgment, devastation, and hell for false teachers. For example, there were rulers in Israel who believed in Jesus but were afraid to come to Him in a saving way because of the threat of excommunication from the synagogue and because they loved the approval of people rather than the approval of God (John 12:42–43). Sometimes, those who are convinced false teachers may see the truth of the gospel and Christ but still be convinced that they must stay in their damning false religion. Discernment is needed to understand how you can "snatch" them out of the fire.

Note that some false teachers are even more dangerous than those in the first two categories; we could call these the committed. Dealing with them should only be done with mercy and great fear. These are people who know the system and know their false gospel. They are more than convinced; they are committed and are very deceptive, sneaky, and misleading. Jude gives us a vivid picture of the danger and the disgusting nature of dealing with these false teachers by using an analogy of the ancient modern wardrobe, which included a *chitón* or undergarment, and there was *himation*, which was a cloak or robe. Jude says that we should be "*hating the garment stained by the flesh.*" Getting close to false religion is defiling and should be done with caution. In Jewish terms, this would have been like saying, "If you get too close to this false religion or false gospel, you will ceremonially defile yourself, so make sure you have a healthy dose of fear as well as mercy."

False gospels damn the men that teach it and damn the listeners who embrace it. These teachings are demonic and deceitful. Notice here that it says to hate the false gospel or system, but there is no directive to hate the false teacher. We are commanded to think about these individuals with mercy and fear even as we hate the false gospel they propagate. Therefore, Jude is telling us to be careful around these types of false teachers. This is not to suggest that we necessarily go and address the false teacher, but this certainly calls someone to give heed to the dangers of addressing a committed false teacher.

Not only must we understand the types of false teachers, but we must also understand the error they're teaching. The apostles were constantly fighting the spread of false gospels and false teachings. At the Jerusalem Council, we see them contend with the heresy and false gospel that advocated that one needed to be circumcised and adhere to the Mosaic law to be saved (Acts 15). In the book of First John, we read about the gnostic belief that denied the humanity of Christ and His suffering and death. Not only must the true pastor discern the error, but he must also be able to counter with the truth. He must not attack the fruit; he must attack the root of the false teaching. For example, some people want to argue and debate against the Roman Catholic understanding of the Lord's Supper. However, what they don't realize is that doing so would be attacking the fruit rather than the root. Rather than trying to refute the Roman Catholic teaching on the Lord's Supper, they would do much better to teach on the doctrine of substitutionary atonement and propitiation and explain what happened at the cross and how the wrath of God was poured out on Christ for the sins of those who would believe in Him. Thus, the pastor must be equipped to both identify the type of false teacher, identify the false doctrine, and refute the error with the truth of Scripture.

Command Them to Stop Teaching False Doctrine

As I urged you when I was going to Macedonia, remain at Ephesus so that you may charge certain persons not to teach any different doctrine.

—1 Timothy 1:3

In Paul's first letter to Timothy, he tells Timothy to stay in Ephesus for many purposes, one of which is to deal with false teachers. Once we know that someone is teaching a false gospel, our only option is to command them to stop. Paul instructs Timothy to charge the teachers in Ephesus to stop teaching anything that is not in accordance with the truth. The word *charge* comes from *paraggelló*, which means "to command" or "entreat solemnly." This word conveys a directive that is meant to be followed as in a hierarchical relationship between one who gives the command and one who receives it. This is a military term that conveys the idea of a commanding officer giving a charge that must be obeyed by the subordinates.

Thus, the true pastor is charged to command false teachers to stop teaching false doctrine; this is not a suggestion, and it's not an option. The pastor has the authority from God to command that heretics and false teachers stop preaching another gospel or a different doctrine that swerves or deviates from the truth (Galatians 1:8–9, 1 Timothy 1:3). How can we know that the true pastor has such authority? We take our authority from Ephesians 4:11–16 where the pastor is given to the church to feed, guide, and guard the church, and part of the pastor's office in guarding the flock is to command false teachers to stop teaching false doctrine because this throws the church into confusion and distorts the truth (Ephesians 4:14, Galatians 2:1–11, Galatians 5:9). When error thrives in the church, the flock suffers, and God is dishonored.

Second, note that the pastor is to command false teachers not to teach different doctrine. The phrase *different doctrine* comes from *heterodidaskaleó*, which means "different teaching." This word implies teachings that are contrary to the core message of the gospel and the Christian faith—teaching that disrupt the unity and purity of the church. At a minimum, a *heterodidaskaleó* would include a different gospel, but this could also include other teachings that disrupt the unity of the church. False teachings that disrupt the unity of the church and break God's law but don't attack the gospel could include things such as allowing women to be pastors, allowing the speaking in tongues without an interpreter, advocating that women can take authority over men in the church, and more. To keep the purity and unity of the church, the true pastor is called to command false teachers not to teach false gospels or different doctrines.

Rebuke Them Sharply

He must hold firm to the trustworthy word as taught, so that he may be able to give instruction in sound doctrine and also to rebuke those who contradict it.

—Titus 1:9

One of the qualifications of a pastor is that he must not only hold onto to sound doctrine, but he must also rebuke those who contradict sound doctrine. First, let's notice that the true pastor must hold to the faithful Word they have been taught. The phrase *hold firm* comes from *antechó*, which means to "hold fast" or "be devoted to." This word conveys the idea of holding firmly and standing one's ground in the face of opposition. The true pastor is not to be casual in their study and conviction of Scripture. No! The true pastor is to be a man who is devoted to Scripture for the purposes of giving sound doctrine to the church. A pastor with no biblical convictions is a disgrace. G. K. Chesterton made this observation about the lack of conviction, "Tolerance is the virtue of the man without convictions." A man with no conviction will allow and tolerate all sorts of error and folly in the church. Therefore, we see that the true pastor must hold firm, stand strong, and have biblical convictions.

Another reason why a pastor must hold firm to Scripture is to be able to rebuke those who contradict sound doctrine. As we learned earlier, the verb *convict* conveys the idea of convincing someone of their sin, error, or wrongdoing with the aim of leading them to repentance and truth. To convict, carries the idea of convincing with solid, compelling, biblical evidence. The purpose of convicting is not to win a debate or argument or to show one's intellectual prowess. No, it is to win someone over to Christ or to make one sound in the faith (Titus 1:13). The true pastor does not have the option to be passive, apathetic, or indifferent; nor can he purposefully avoid conflict. No, the pastor is commanded to convict those who contradict sound doctrine. The pastor must be able to bring the one contradicting the truth to Scripture and show them their error. A pastor who is not able to refute error is an unqualified man, and he proves he is not able to guard the flock against ravenous wolves.

The pastor must sharply rebuke the insubordinate, empty

talkers, and deceivers (Titus 1:10–13). Paul gives this charge to Titus, "*This testimony is true. Therefore, rebuke them sharply, that they may be sound in the faith, not devoting themselves to Jewish myths and the commands of people who turn away from the truth*" (Titus 1:13). Paul wanted Titus to know that those insubordinate, empty talking, deceiving, and truth-rejecting false teachers needed to be rebuked sharply. The word *sharply* comes from *apotomós*, which means "severely." This word is used to describe something that is sharp or harsh in nature either in speech or action. This word also conveys the idea of putting an end to something immediately in a way that leaves no room for discussion, debate, or denial. When the truth is being perverted, the gospel distorted, and people are being led astray, the pastor is to act swiftly. He is not to walk around the issue, suggest reading books that tiptoe around the false doctrine, or downplay the error. No! He is to put an end to the false doctrine immediately, swiftly, and in such a way that he leaves no room for debate. He is to attack the root of the error, not the fruit of the error. He is to strike a death blow to the heresy. He is to so thoroughly step on the throat of the false doctrine that it can no longer breathe. He must attack the false doctrine and prove it to be erroneous so that the flock is protected and built up. Hopefully, the false teacher becomes sound in faith as well. Thus, we see why the pastor is to hold firmly to the Word. It is for the purpose of instruction and building up of the church and rebuking and guarding the flock.

Warn Them

As for a person who stirs up division, after warning him once and then twice, have nothing more to do with him, knowing that such a person is warped and sinful; he is self-condemned.

—Titus 3:10–11

In Paul's closing words to Titus, he gives instructions for dealing with false teachers and heretics. Note that those who contradict the truth and sound doctrine are heretics who "*stir up division.*" This phrase comes from *hairetikos*, which means "heretical" or "factious." This word refers to a person who chooses to follow self-willed opinions or doctrines, and it implies a deliberate choice to deviate from accepted teachings or practices. Of course, this is where we get the word *heresy*, which would refer to teachings that strike at the heart of the Christian faith and gospel. A heretical person is one who has a self-willed teaching, interpretation, or doctrine that strikes at the heart of the gospel and the Christian faith.

Paul commands Titus to warn them. The word *warn* comes from *nouthesia*, and it means "instruction," "warning," or "admonition." This word conveys the idea of providing guidance, correction, or instruction with the intent of restoring or improving one's spiritual understanding or behavior. It is often used in the context of a loving and caring relationship to guide someone from error. This word also implies a gentle yet firm approach to correction and emphasizes the importance of wisdom. When a heretic is discovered, it is true that he must be commanded to stop teaching and rebuked sharply, but it is also true that the admonition is done with wisdom and with the goal of restoration. This is not to say that the true pastor compromises his convictions, but rather, he demonstrates the biblical conviction and truth in a way that seeks to win that person(s) to Christ or make them sound in the faith.

Then, if the false teacher rejects the pastor's command, warning, and admonition, they are to be avoided and shunned. We'll talk about this more later, but for now, we'll just say that the reason for shunning is that the false teacher is corrupt, perverted, and self-condemned. Thus, they are to be excluded, shunned, and kept away from the flock and left to their own demise as a self-condemned heretic.

Silence Them

> *They must be silenced, since they are upsetting whole families by teaching for shameful gain what they ought not to teach.*

> —Titus 1:11

In Paul's letter to Titus, he gives more instructions on how to deal with those who contradict sound doctrine and the truth. Paul tells Titus that the false teacher must be silenced. The word *must* comes from *dei* and means "necessary." It is important to note that this is not an option or a recommendation; silencing the false teachers is a necessity. Additionally, the word *must* is written in the present tense, which means that the action must be continually done; *must* is written in the indicative mood, which means it is a true statement. The true pastor has no option when it comes to those who contradict sound doctrine; they must be silenced.

Let's look more closely at the word *silenced*. This word comes from the word *epistomizó*, which means "to muzzle" or "stop the mouth." This word conveys the idea of stopping someone from speaking and implies a forceful and authoritative action to prevent further speech. So, how does one muzzle the false teacher? The answer is simple: The true pastor refutes the false teacher with sound doctrine and refutes them sharply to put an end to the false teaching. Additionally, the false teacher is to be taken out of the pulpit, pulled from their teaching ministry, and rebuked before the whole congregation, so that they may stand in fear and not repeat this sin and error (1 Timothy 5:20).

If a false teacher is not silenced and allowed to continue teaching, they end up overturning, overthrowing, subverting, and corrupting the church. To allow a false teacher to stand in the pulpit after teaching erroneous doctrine or even a false gospel is to bring disunity to the church, upset the flock, and dishonor God. The true pastor cannot let this happen, and they are to shut the mouth of the false teacher.

Teach Them if Possible but Mixed with Fear

And the Lord's servant must not be quarrelsome but kind to everyone, able to teach, patiently enduring evil, correcting his opponents with gentleness. God may perhaps grant them repentance leading to a knowledge of the truth, and they may come to their senses and escape from the snare of the devil, after being captured by him to do his will.

—2 Timothy 2:24–26

In Paul's second letter to Timothy, he instructs Timothy and the true pastor to be able to teach opponents with gentleness while enduring evil. We see that the pastor must be skilled in teaching and must correct with gentleness. The word for *gentleness* comes from *épios*, which means to be "mild." This word conveys the idea of a sense of tenderness and care. Essentially, the pastor is to have the gentleness of Christ. Though Christ was firm, unwavering, and even angry with the Pharisees (Mark 3, Matthew 23:1–36), He was and is the perfect model of how one is to deal with false teachers. Christ could both instruct Nicodemus (John 3:1–21), call the Pharisees blind guides and vain worshippers of the Living God (Matthew 15:1–14), and call them adulterous and evil for demanding a sign when great evidence had been given to them validating His claims to deity (Matthew 16:1–4). Thus, the pastor must look to Christ for how to be gentle when teaching and dealing with false teachers and not quarrelsome.

The pastor must be able to endure evil. As we learned earlier, the pastor is not to be quick-tempered, a brawler, or quarrelsome. He must be a man who is long-tempered and can endure evil. The phrase *endure evil* comes from *anexikakos*, and it means "enduring evil" or "patient of evil." This word is used to describe someone who can face provocation or adversity with Christlikeness while being wronged. In ministry, it is certain that the pastor will endure apostasy, betrayal, duplicity, empty words with no actions, gossip, slander, provocation, and more. The pastor is not to teach an opponent with a combative or retaliatory spirit. Rather, he is to be understanding and gently teach opponents and seek their highest good. Even with patient instruction, false teachers may not receive the instruction, turn from the instruction, betray him, lie about him, or do slanderous harm to his character. Thus, the pastor must be able to endure evil when instructing opponents.

Ultimately, the pastor's goal is to teach with the hope that God will lead the false teacher and opponents to repentance and a knowledge of the truth. As we learned earlier in Titus, the goal of refutation and sound instruction is restoration, being sound in the faith, and even the hope of God leading one to salvation. The pastor knows that it is God who grants salvation, and so the pastor will labor with gentleness and enduring evil in the hopes that God grants salvation and a knowledge of the truth to the false teacher (Philippians 1:29–30).

The true pastor must understand that the false teacher is trapped. Paul says that the opponents are captured by the devil, caught in a snare, don't have their senses, and are doing the will of the devil. Thus, the pastor understands the spiritual war-fare that is taking place. The pastor gives sound instruction in all Christlikeness and depends on teaching his opponents the Word of God in the power of the Holy Spirit and with all prayer in hopes that God delivers the false teacher who is doing the will of the devil. When possible, the pastor must be prepared to instruct opponents in this manner with the hopes of rescuing the false teachers as snatching a branch from the fire (Jude 23).

Do Not Give Them a Greeting, Do Not Welcome Them, Avoid Them, Shun Them

2 John 9–11 – *"Everyone who goes on ahead and does not abide in the teaching of Christ, does not have God. Whoever abides in the teaching has both the Father and the Son. If anyone comes to you and does not bring this teaching, do not receive him into your house or give him any greeting, for whoever greets him takes part in his wicked works."*

When a false teacher gives evidence that they will not be taught and that they remain unrepentant, stubborn, obsti-nate, recalcitrant, and proud, the pastor and all true believers are called to deal with these false teachers in accordance with God's Word. Of course, this is not the default position a pas-tor or a believer should take, but it is what God calls for when mercy has been exhausted, the command to stop teaching has been ignored, when gentle teaching has been disregarded, and stubbornness and pride remain. Although it may seem harsh and unloving, this is what God commands.

John's second letter is written to a lady who has most likely been doing her best to exercise Christian hospitality to traveling teachers but has inadvertently or unwisely given hospitality and aid to false teachers. John may have feared that false teachers would attempt to take advantage of her kindness. But John warns his readers about showing such hospitality to deceivers. Although his exhortation may to be harsh or unloving, the damning false gospels that false teachers propagate warrant these actions, especially as they threaten the very foundations of faith.

Not only are Christians to adhere to the fundamentals of the faith, but the gracious hospitality that is commanded of them must be discriminating (Romans 12:13). The basis of hospitality must be common love of or interest in the truth, and Christians must share their love within the confines of that truth. They are not called to universal acceptance of anyone who claims to be a believer but is really a false teacher. Love must be discerning; hospitality and kindness must be focused on those who are adhering to the fundamentals of the faith and gospel. Otherwise, Christians may aid those who are destroying the basic truths of the faith and the gospel. Sound doctrine and the gospel must serve as the test of fellowship (1).

Truth must always guide the exercise of love (Ephesians 4:15) love and truth are inseparable in Christianity. Love must stand the test of truth. The main lesson of 2 John is that truth determines the bounds of love, and, consequently, of unity. Therefore, truth must exist before love can unite, for truth generates love (1 Peter 1:22). When the truth is compromised, true Christian love and unity are destroyed. Only a shallow sentimentalism exists where the truth is not the foundation of unity.

Let's first notice in 2 John 9 that those who go beyond the teaching of Christ and no longer abide in Christ's teaching do not have God: "*Everyone who goes on ahead and does not abide in the teaching of Christ, does not have God. Whoever abides in the teaching has both the Father and the Son.*" The definition we developed of a false teacher helps us understand that someone who has deviated from the truth of the gospel and whose teaching strikes at the heart of the gospel is a heretic. The false teacher is one who:

- Shuts the kingdom of heaven in men's faces and does not enter himself (Matthew 23:13).

- Teaches destructive heresies and is condemned (2 Peter 2:1–3).

- Teaches another gospel and is accursed (Galatians 1:8–9).

- Follows their sensuality and blasphemes the way of truth (2 Peter 2:2).

Thus, a false teacher is one who has deviated from the truth of the gospel and is condemned. The false teacher has not made some minor error such as having a certain view of song choices, order of worship, preferred method of Bible study, time of worship on Sunday, or other minor matters. No, this person has deviated from the gospel and the heart of the Christian faith. They do not have God because they do not have the Holy Spirit and do not belong to God and Christ. As Romans 8:9 says, "*You, however, are not in the flesh but in the Spirit, if in fact the Spirit of God dwells in you. Anyone who does not have the Spirit of Christ does not belong to him.*" To not have the Holy Spirit means that one is unconverted, unregenerate, and has not come to Christ in saving faith and received the Holy Spirit or been converted.

Second, John makes a distinction between the false teacher and a true believer. The true believer abides in the teaching of Christ. How do we know what the teaching of Christ is? Quite simply the teaching of Christ is the teaching from Christ, which is also the teaching about Christ, which is also the truth that is taught by the apostles about Christ. At a minimum, this teaching includes the gospel because only those who are in Christ, remain in Christ (John 15:1–11). Who are those who have Christ? Paul says that they are those that have put their faith in Christ, have been united with Christ, and have received the Holy Spirit; thus, they have a relationship with the Father (Galatians 3:24–4:6). These are the true believers who abide in the teaching of Christ and have both the Father and the Son.

Third, John gives an imperative command that anyone who brings a teaching that has deviated from the gospel and the heart of the Christian faith gives evidence that they are a false teacher and should not be welcomed into one's home or aided. As we noted earlier, traveling teachers were common when John's letters were written, and it was dangerous for travelers to stay in inns. Therefore, it was safer for them to stay in the home of a Christian. But John tells the lady that this false teacher must not be accepted into her home (2 John 10). What would the reason be for this? John is warning that providing care and hospitality to a false teacher would be equivalent to showing support and endorsing their false teaching. Therefore, disassociation is commanded. Note that John writes this command in the present tense, which represents an ongoing action and in the imperative mood, which makes it a command. This is a command to not give support or assistance to false teachers because they disguise themselves as true teachers but inwardly are ravenous wolves and damn men's souls. It is also a command to be followed because the true pastor and true Christian are not to in any way affirm the false teacher's teaching or doctrine.

Fourth, John gives another imperative command that the lady is not to give a false teacher a greeting. The word *greeting* comes from *chairó*, which means "to rejoice," to be glad" or "be joyful." This was essentially a Christian greeting. The true pastor or any Christian is not even to give a false teacher a Christian greeting and acknowledge them as a Christian. Once again, John writes this command in the present tense and imperative mood, which means this is a command that must be obeyed continually. To disobey this command is to bring confusion to the gospel message, disobey God, and help the enemy. John's commands may seem harsh, but he is not the only New Testament writer that affirmed shunning and refusing to acknowledge and fellowship with false teachers.

In Romans 16:17, Paul writes this regarding false teachers: *"I appeal to you, brothers, to watch out for those who cause divisions and create obstacles contrary to the doctrine that you have been taught; avoid them."* The word *avoid* comes from *ekklinó*, which means "to turn away" or "shun." This word implies the deliberate choice to steer clear and avoid a situation or behavior. Notice that it is those that teach contrary doctrines who are to be avoided and shunned. Just like John, Paul writes this command in the present tense and imperative mood meaning that the command to shun a false teacher is to be continually obeyed.

In 2 Timothy 3:5, Paul says this regarding apostates and false teachers: *"Having the appearance of godliness, but denying its power. Avoid such people."* Apostates and false teachers who appear to be religious but are unregenerate are to be avoided. In this instance, the word *avoid* comes from *apotrepó*, which means to "turn away" or "shun." When Paul commands Timothy to turn away from such people, he gives this command in the present tense and imperative mood which, once again, is a command that is to be obeyed continually. Timothy is to continually shun and turn away from such people.

In Titus 3:10–11, Paul tells Titus how to handle heretics and false teachers: *"As for a person who stirs up division, after warning him once and then twice, have nothing more to*

do with him, knowing that such a person is warped and sinful;
he is self-condemned." The phrase *have nothing more to do with*
him comes from the original word *paraiteomai*, which means
to "refuse," "reject," "shun," or "avoid." This word speaks of
the purposeful rejection and shunning of certain behaviors
and teachings that are contrary to God's Word. When Paul
commands Titus to reject heretics, he gives this command in
the present tense and imperative mood which, once again, is a
command that is to be obeyed continually. To not obey this
command is to act in defiance against God's command for how
a false teacher is to be dealt with.

Fifth, we see that to even give a false teacher a greeting is
wicked; John says that to give a false teacher a greeting is to fellowship in his wicked works. This phrase *takes part* comes from
koinóneó, which means "to partake" or "have fellowship." This
word conveys the idea of having common part or fellowship
and possession. This is a serious warning from the apostle John.
To give a false teacher a Christian greeting is to fellowship in
their wicked works. To give a false teacher a greeting is wicked,
perverse, and malicious. To give a false teacher a greeting is
to give heed and fellowship in the perverse and wicked false
teaching that they are propagating. It is a serious matter for a
true pastor or any Christian to give a Christian greeting to a
false teacher because this is fellowshipping with evil, partaking
in deception, and partnering with damning lies. Thus, the true
pastor must not fellowship or even acknowledge false teachers
as Christians.

As we close this chapter, we see the uncomfortable and

challenging job of the true pastor. The true pastor must know the gospel, know his salvation, know the Scriptures, beware of false teachers, identify false teachers, command false teachers to stop teaching damning doctrines and errant teachings, refute them, warn them, silence them, teach them if possible, and shun them when they remain unrepentant. The true pastor will surely be hated by the world and hated by false religious Christian churches. However, if all the world and all of false Christianity is against the true pastor, God is for the pastor. The man with God on his side is more than a conqueror through Him who loves him, and all things work together for his good (Romans 8:28–37). Though this is hard work, let us remember the importance of opposing and standing firm against the false teacher. Consider this statement from Paul Dowling on the danger of false teachers:

> The worst enemies of the true church of Christ are not the pagans or the heathen. The worst enemies of the true church of Christ are not the Muslims, or the Hindus, or even the satanists. The worst enemies of the church of Christ are not the perverts or the amoral politicians that we have. But the worst enemies of the true church of Christ throughout the entirety of Scripture history up to the present day are the religious. Those that say they are Christians when they are not. They make a profession that they are God's people, but they don't believe God's Word, nor do they obey it. That has always been the worst enemy of the true church. These

types of people have to be the church's worst enemy throughout the ages. They claim to be Christians but they're blind. They claim to be Christians but they're ignorant. They don't give warnings. They don't believe in punishment for the lost. They're self-centered, pleasure seeking, and notice what God says, they mock, and they malign the true preachers and prophets. They criticize those that really hold to the truth. And those who do this appear to be in the visible church. They appear to be leaders in the visible church, but they hate the truth. And when you come to the passage that you want them to preach on, you know what they say? "It doesn't mean that." And they give a wee explanation telling you that it means just the opposite of what it says on all the controversial issues in the Bible. That's what they do. They hate God's truth. They hate God's prophets and preachers because they are false prophets. They are watchmen who do not watch and they're the worst enemies the church has ever had.[32]

Chapter 6

A Man Who Has the Grace of God Poured Out on Him to Endure Persecution, Suffering, and Hardship

Therefore do not be ashamed of the testimony about our Lord, nor of me his prisoner, but share in suffering for the gospel by the power of God.

—2 Timothy 1:8

In this chapter, we will see how the grace of God is poured out on the true pastor to endure persecution, suffering, and hardship. Not only are suffering and persecution promised for the pastor, but they are also promised for every true believer. Standing for Christ is standing against the world. Standing for God's Word is to be at enmity with the world. Standing for the Lord is resisting the devil. Therefore, it is important to understand that the true pastor whom the Lord has called to serve Him will suffer persecution at some point in his ministry. However, the Lord will give grace to the pastor, so he is able to endure it.

As we begin this chapter, we'll look at how persecution is a sign of blessing. We will then see how persecution will come from false Christianity and the secular world and consider that Jesus promises hostility and hatred. Then we will examine Paul's suffering as an apostle and pastor, which included being considered filth and offscouring, enduring hardship, enduring betrayal, and enduring revile and slander. Nevertheless, Paul continued to be joyful in Christ. Though the true pastor will experience persecution, he will also experience joy and blessing. Whatever persecution that may come to the true pastor, God will make the man ready and able to endure it.

Blessed Persecution

Blessed are those who are persecuted for righteousness' sake, for theirs is the kingdom of heaven. Blessed are you when others revile you and persecute you and utter all kinds of evil against you falsely on my account. Rejoice and be glad, for your reward is great in heaven, for so they persecuted the prophets who were before you.

—Matthew 5:10–12

In the Sermon on the Mount (Matthew 5), the Lord begins with the attitudes of those who are in the kingdom of heaven. He pronounces blessing on those who are contrite and broken over sin (v. 3), those who are mourning over sin (v. 4), those who are meek and submissive unto the Lord (v. 5), those who hunger and thirst for a positional and practical righteousness they do not possess (v. 6), those who are merciful (v. 7), those who are pure in heart and have undivided devotion to the Lord (v. 8), and those who are peacemakers through the gospel and seek peace in their relationships (v. 9). When we transition into verse ten, there is an abrupt change; the final blessing the Lord pronounces doesn't describe the attitude of the true believer, but rather blessing as a result of possessing kingdom attitudes.

Before transitioning into verse ten, we should explore what it means to be blessed. The word *blessed* comes from *makarios*, which is translated to "blessed" or "happy" in English. The reason for happiness is because these individuals have divine favor or God's grace. Essentially, Jesus provides an upside-down picture of what divine blessing looks like when compared to the world's perspective. In His kingdom, the blessed aren't those who are rich in money, but who are poor and broken in spirit over their sin. The blessed aren't those who are continually happy and joyful, but rather those who are mourning over their sin. The blessed aren't those who are self-willed and self-made successful people of the world, but rather those who are self-denying and submissive unto the Lord. The blessed aren't those who have all their worldly needs met, but those who are hungering and thirsting for righteousness. Thus, the picture of the divinely blessed man stands in opposition to what the world considers blessed. Let's keep these distinctions in mind as we transition into Matthew 5:10–12 as this divine principle of suffering and persecution will be key in understanding blessing.

First, we see that those who are persecuted for righteousness' sake are blessed. The word *persecuted* comes from *diókó*, which means "to pursue" or "to chase." This word is often used in connection with persecution where individuals are pursued with the intent to oppress or harm. Although *diókó* can mean a pursuit of righteous things, in this context, it means to be pursued for persecution. This word speaks of an intensity of effort to chase, harass, vex, and pressure. It gives us the picture of hunting something down. It is also important to note that *diókó* is written in the perfect tense and participle mood, which means that the persecution has happened in the past and continues in the present. Jesus is not saying that persecution will be a one-time event. Not at all. Rather, He is stating that the true Christian and the true pastor will continue to experience persecution from the time they enter the Christian faith to the time they depart to be with the Lord. Thus, the true pastor should not be surprised that persecution awaits him as he enters ministry.

Why does the true believer face persecution? The reason that believers experience persecution is not because they are being unruly, cannot control their tongue, or continually perform poorly at work. Peter says that it is of no credit to the believer if they suffer for sin rather than good (1 Peter 2:20). No, the true believer is blessed because they are persecuted for righteousness' sake. They are persecuted because of their view of sin (Matthew 5:3–4), their view of the Lord (Matthew 5:5), their view of salvation and righteousness (Matthew 5:6), their devotion to the Lord (Matthew 5:8), and the gospel and peaceful lives they live (Matthew 5:9). The suffering that receives blessing is suffering that is for Christ, the gospel, and righteousness' sake.

We also see that those who are persecuted belong to the kingdom of heaven. The Lord opens the Beatitudes with a promise that the poor in spirit are possessors of the kingdom of heaven, and He closes the Beatitudes with a promise that those who are persecuted for righteousness are possessors of the kingdom of heaven. Is this persecution and suffering for righteousness' sake useless? Not at all because those who are persecuted for righteousness' sake possess the kingdom of heaven, will be comforted, inherit a new heaven and a new earth, be satisfied, receive mercy, see God, and be called sons of God. Therefore, the true pastor and every Christian should be assured that when persecution comes for the sake of Christ, they are divinely blessed and possess more than all the accumulated wealth of the world; for they have Christ and Christ is all.

Second, there is divine blessing when the pastor and true Christian are reviled, persecuted, and slandered on account of Christ. Once again, Christ reminds the believer that though they are hated, mistreated, and persecuted for His sake, they have God's favor. So, what kind of treatment can the true pastor expect? Jesus says that they will revile him. The word *revile* comes from *oneidizó*, and it means to "reproach," "insult," or "upbraid." This word carries the connotation of casting blame or shame upon another, typically in a public or humiliating manner; it depicts both verbal attacks and contempt and conveys the act of disgracing and casting blame upon someone. The Christian should not be surprised that when they come to faith in Christ, they become an enemy of the devil rather than his slave. Jesus acknowledges this this reality in Luke's account of the Beatitudes, *"Blessed are you when people hate you, when they exclude you, and insult you and reject your name as evil, because of the Son of Man"* (Luke 6:22). The Christian will be mocked and scorned if they try to fit in a dead church with unregenerate church members who don't understand their zeal for Scripture and the Lord. The Christian will offend the antinomians for their biblical belief about sanctification and holiness. The Christian will be reviled by the LGBTQ community for his stance that marriage is between a man and a woman. The Christian will be insulted, hated, cast out, and regarded as evil when they stand against sacramental salvation in Roman Catholicism and protestant Lutheranism. Rejection, exclusion, and hatred are the natural man's responses to the Christian and the true pastor.

Jesus also says that people will say all kinds of evil against the Christian falsely. It won't matter if the Christian or pastor speaks the truth in love and conviction with a gentle voice; the world and false Christianity will still slander the Christian. It won't matter if the Christian uses Scripture to show that the world to be wrong or even false Christianity to be wrong. The world will ignore them and hold the Bible in contempt, and false Christians will act like the Pharisees and justify themselves before men, rather than humble themselves before the Lord (Luke 16:15). It is not something the true pastor or the true Christian can avoid. When they stand firm in the truth and in Christ, people will speak all kinds of evil against them.

Not only this, but the world and false Christianity will speak lies about the Christian. If we look at Jesus and the false teaching Pharisees, we can understand how the Christian and the true pastor will be treated. Jesus healed a man with a withered hand on the Sabbath, which was not breaking the Mosaic law. However, the Pharisees had created burdensome manmade Sabbath laws, and when Jesus publicly humiliated them with a question of whether it was lawful to do good or do to harm, to save a life or to kill on the Sabbath, the Pharisees went out with the Herodians to plan how to kill Him (Mark 3:1–6). Though Jesus had done no wrong, the Pharisees had hardened their hearts and were plotting a way to kill Him, and they continued to label Him as a Sabbath day lawbreaker (John 9:16). On another occasion when Jesus healed a demon-possessed man who was blind and mute, the Pharisees said that He was doing this work by Beelzebul rather than by God (Matthew 12:22–28). The Christian and the true pastor can expect the same kinds of lies and false accusations on account of living a godly life and standing firm in Christ. Though they be pure in heart, peacemakers, broken over their sin, and merciful, the world and false Christianity will speak evil of them and tell lies.

Third, the proper response to persecution, false accusations, and slander is to rejoice and be glad. The phrase *be glad* comes from *agalliaó*, which means "to be exceedingly glad" or "exult." This word conveys a sense of exuberant joy and gladness, which is often expressed physically or emotionally. Such joy is not merely an emotional response but a profound spiritual state of being that reflects the believer's relationship with God and hope in Him. It describes a jubilant exultation, a quality of joy that remains unhindered and unchanged by what happens. It's also important to note that the verbs *rejoice* and *be glad* are written in the present tense and imperative mood, which means that to rejoice and be glad are commands to be continually obeyed when the believer is persecuted.

It is true that persecution can bring despair and sadness, but faith looks to the Lord, and the Lord commands joy and gladness. So, why should the believer be joyful? Jesus immediately gives the answer. It is because the believer's reward in heaven is great. From the previous chapter and Paul's last letter to Timothy, recall why Paul was looking forward to "that day." He was about to attain the hope of eternal life and the crown of glory that will never fade away (2 Timothy 4:8, 1 Peter 5:4). He was about to attain the hope of glorification and becoming like Christ (Romans 8:30). He was about to attain the hope of knowing Christ and seeing Him face to face (1 Corinthians 13:10–12). After one trillion years of being with Christ, this will be just a drop in the ocean for the believer as they continue to live in the presence of God and have unhindered communion with the King of glory. William Penn put the persecution that comes before the prize in perspective: "No pain, no palm; no thorns, no throne; no gall, no glory; no cross, no crown."[33] Thomas Brooks wrote this about the great exultation and expectation that encourage the believer when facing persecution: "A tearless Heaven will make amends for all!"[34]

Fourth, Christ affirms that the prophets who came before were also persecuted. The Old Testament records the persecution of Elijah (1 Kings 19:1–8), Elisha (2 Kings 6:31), Moses (Numbers 16:1–4), and more. It has always been the way of false religion, false Christianity, and the world to attack and persecute those who belong to the Lord. They hate the message and the prophet who brings the divine truth.

Fifth, in Luke's account of the Beatitudes, Jesus pronounces judgment and condemnation for those who are spoken well of. In Luke 6:26, He says, *"Woe to you when everyone speaks well of you, for that is how their ancestors treated the false prophets"* (NIV). *Woe* is translated from *ouai,* which can be said as "alas!" or "woe" and uttered in grief or denunciation. It is an onomatopoeic word (an imitation of the sound), which serves as an interjection or a cry of intense distress, displeasure, or horror. It can also be an announcement of doom. In this context, Jesus in pronouncing doom for those who are spoken well of. How could this be? The false prophets in the Old Testament prophesied false messages of hope. They dealt with sin lightly, gave a false gospel message of hope, and cried "Peace, peace" when there was no peace with God (Jeremiah 6:14). They continued to cry "Peace, peace" when there was no peace, and they covered Israel's sin with false visions (Ezekiel 13:1–16). The false teacher in false Christianity will have a message that is watered down and appeases many, and they will be acclaimed. However, they have received their temporary reward, which is the applause of men, but they will receive their eternal punishment and eternal disapproval from the Lord when they are cast into hell (2 Peter 2:3). Thus, the true pastor understands that persecution is to be expected when living a godly life and preaching divine truth. Though persecution comes, the true pastor is to exult and be glad for his reward in heaven is great.

You Will Be Hated and Suffer Religious and Secular Persecution

"If the world hates you, know that it has hated me before it hated you. If you were of the world, the world would love you as its own; but because you are not of the world, but I chose you out of the world, therefore the world hates you. Remember the word that I said to you: 'A servant is not greater than his master.' If they persecuted me, they will also persecute you. If they kept my word, they will also keep yours."

—John 15:18–20

As Jesus is on His way to be betrayed by Judas, He continues to teach His disciples regarding the importance of remaining in Him (John 15:1–17), and He also reminds them that when they remain in Him, they will be hated by the world. Therefore, the first point we should see is that just as Christ was hated, so too will all true believers and true pastors be hated. The word *hate* comes from *miseó* and in this specific context, it means "to hate," "to detest," or to "abhor." *Miseó* indicates a strong aversion or rejection and can denote personal animosity. The disciples had firsthand knowledge of what Jesus was speaking about when He said that the world "hated" Him. They saw the Pharisees claim that He did His works by the power of Beelzebul (Matthew 12:24); they hunted Him down and tried to trap Him in His speech and teachings (Luke 11:53–54); they sought to kill Him after He healed the invalid and claimed to be equal with the Father (John 5:18); they could not bear His word and sought to kill Him (John 8:43–44); they tried to trap Him with questions (Matthew 22:15–22); and eventually they crucified Him on a cross and scorned Him (Acts 2:23). Just as Jesus was slandered and called a worker of Beelzebul, attacked with questions, and targeted for death by the Pharisees, so the disciples could expect this very same treatment. In fact, Jesus reminds them that the world hated Him first before they hated them.

Second, we should see the contrast of how the world deals with those who are of the world and those who belong to Christ. The world is full of false ideologies, including atheism, agnosticism, nihilism, relativism, pluralism, and more. The world is full of false religion, including Buddhism, Taoism, Confucianism, Hinduism, Islam, Zoroastrianism, and more. The world is full of false Christianity, including Roman Catholicism, anti-trinitarianism, Mormonism, Jehovah's Witnesses, Christian Science, sacramental Protestantism, and more. The true pastor will stand up against the false ideology of the world and false Christianity because these are not from Christ but come from the prince of the power of the air, the spirit that is now at work in the sons of disobedience—the god of this world who has blinded the minds of the unbelievers from seeing the light of the gospel of the glory of Christ (Ephesians 2:2, 2 Corinthians 4:4). False Christianity can tolerate false Christianity. The pope of Roman Catholicism can declare along with Lutherans that they agree on the false salvific work of water baptism. So-called reformed churches will cave to allow "gifted" women to be pastors because the world wants equality. False Christianity will look for common points of agreement rather than standing firm in the truth (1 Corinthians 16:13).

This is not so with the true pastor and man of God. God chose the true pastor and regenerated him, gave him a new heart, gave him a new spirit, and put the Spirit of God in him (Ezekiel 36:25–27). The true pastor has been made by God, gifted by God, and equipped by God to stand for Him and not for the world. He has been chosen out of the world by Christ. The true pastor does not love the world nor the things of the world, but desires to do the will of God (1 John 2:15–17). Thus, the world can love false prophets because they are from the world and speak from the world (1 John 4:5). However, the true pastor is not loved by the world because he is from God and has the Spirit of truth, not the spirit of error (1 John 4:6).

Third, we should see that Jesus reminds the disciples that

a servant is not greater than their master and that they will suffer persecution. Jesus reminds His disciples of what He said when He sent out the Twelve in Matthew 10. He told His disciples that they would be delivered over to courts and flogged in synagogues, which speaks of both secular and religious persecution (Matthew 10:17–18). In Matthew 10:21–22 He reminds them that they will be betrayed by those closest to them:

> *"Brother will deliver brother over to death, and the father his child, and children will rise against parents and have them put to death, and you will be hated by all for my name's sake. But the one who endures to the end will be saved."*

Family members and loved ones will betray believers because of Christ. Persecution will come from false religion as well as false Christianity. Though the true pastor and Christian truly belong to Christ, they will be called Beelzebul and wicked. How did Jesus teach His disciples to overcome and deal with such animus and hostility? The answer is in Matthew 10:26, 28:

> *So have no fear of them, for nothing is covered that will not be revealed, or hidden that will not be known. . . . And do not fear those who kill the body but cannot kill the soul. Rather fear him who can destroy both soul and body in hell.*

The Christian and true pastor is not to fear man. He is to fear and obey the Lord. Though he be hated by men, he is known by God. Though false religion and the world would seek to cut off the true pastor's head, the Lord shall give the man a new body and a new head, put a crown on the man's head, and then the man will immediately cast the crown down at the feet of the Lord (2 Timothy 4:8, Revelation 4:10). The true pastor does not fear man; he fears the Lord and serves Him only (Deuteronomy 10:12).

Considered the Refuse, Offscouring, and Filth of the World

1 Corinthians 4:12–13 – *"And we labor, working with our own hands. When reviled, we bless; when persecuted, we endure; when slandered, we entreat. We have become, and are still, like the scum of the world, the refuse of all things."*

In this passage Paul gives a description of the required humility of the pastor as compared to the pride of the Corinthians as they were becoming proud and puffed up (1 Corinthians 4:6–8). Amid speaking of this humility, Paul describes the persecution that he and the apostles endure; this gives us a picture of how the true pastor will suffer persecution and how they are to deal with it. We will take a brief look at 1 Corinthians 4:12–13 to understand this persecution. First, we see that the apostles were reviled. The word *reviled* comes from *loidoreó,* meaning "to abuse" or "to insult." This word describes the act of reviling or insulting someone and conveys a sense of verbal abuse or harsh criticism; it is often associated with unjust or malicious speech, which reflects a spirit of disdain. In contrast to words that build up, the apostles were verbally abused and maligned. However, notice the godly reaction of the apostles, which was to bless. Rather than take revenge or seek retaliation, they invoked God to bless and bestow favor upon those who reviled them.

Second, the apostles were persecuted. As we learned earlier, this word *diókó* is often used in connection with persecution where individuals are pursued with the intent to oppress or harm. Although *diókó* can mean a pursuit of righteous things, in this context, it means to be pursued for persecution. Paul gives us an idea of how Christians were persecuted. Before Paul was converted, he persecuted Christians by punishing them in the synagogues and trying to get them to blaspheme; he even chased them to foreign cities (Acts 26:9–11). He ravaged the church and dragged off men and women and threw them into prison (Acts 8:3). He approved the stoning of Stephen. This is how the early Christians were treated. However, notice the godly reaction of the apostles to persecution: They were to endure it. The word *endure* comes from *anechó*, which means "to suffer," "to bear with," or "persist." The apostles didn't quit, forfeit, or give up. Rather, they endured these difficulties and did so in faith and love.

Third, the apostles were slandered. The word *slandered* comes from *dusphemia*, which means "to slander," "to defame," or "speak evil." This word refers to speech that is harmful, slanderous, or defamatory with the intent of damaging someone's reputation or character through false or malicious statements. However, notice the godly reaction of the apostles to slander, which is to entreat or encourage. Rather than tearing down, they encouraged and built up. They did the very opposite of what a false teacher does, which is to give false doctrine and malign the character of the true teacher.

Fourth, the world considered the apostles as scum, refuse, and offscouring. The word *scum* comes from *perikatharma*, which means "refuse," "offscouring," or "filth." This word is used to describe something or someone who is considered as the lowest or most despised person or criminal. It conveys the idea of being treated as the refuse, scum, rubbish, and offscouring of society and humanity. Additionally, the word *refuse* comes from *peripséma*, which means "scrapings" or "wiped off filth." This word conveys the idea of something that is rubbed off or the off-scrapings and worthless. John MacArthur commented on how these words were used describe the apostles:

> They were religious scum and dregs, and no better than the criminals like whom they were often treated. It is not hard for believers to get along in the world as long as they keep the gospel to themselves. But if they preach, teach, and live God's full Word, the world takes great offense.[35]

Thus, we see that the true pastor will be slandered, maligned, reviled, and considered as scum by the world and false Christianity. Though the true pastor be mistreated by the world, he knows he is a servant of Christ and precious to the Lord (1 Corinthians 4:1, Psalm 116:15).

Danger, Hardship, Struck Down, Often Near Death, Yet Possessing Everything

2 Corinthians 11:23 – *"Are they servants of Christ? I am a better one—I am talking like a madman—with far greater labors, far more imprisonments, with countless beatings, and often near death."*

In this section, we'll see the type of suffering and persecution that Paul endured by doing an exposition of 2 Corinthians 11:23–29 and the account of Paul's persecutions in 2 Corinthians 6:3–10. Though the true pastor may not experience all the persecution that Paul faced, he will face many difficulties and persecution if he is standing firm for Christ, His gospel, and the Word.

From the text, we see that Paul does not boast in his sufferings or persecutions for the sake of vain glory or for the approval of men. Prior to listing the hardships that he had encountered, he says "*I am talking like a madman*" or "as if insane" because of his disdain for human boasting. Paul didn't want to boast of his labors and work in the Lord, but he was being attacked by false apostles and false teachers who were trying to discredit him by attacking his character. Paul knew that their attack on his character was an attack on the gospel message he was proclaiming. If the false teachers and false apostles could attack Paul's character, it would discredit the message he was proclaiming. Though Paul disdained boasting, he notes that he must act contrary to sound thinking by "boasting" or listing the persecutions he's endured for the sake of Christ.

Notice that Paul endured imprisonments. We get a picture of what these imprisonments looked like in Acts 16:22–24 where it says that Paul and Silas were beaten with many or numerous blows from rods. Both Paul and Silas were put into the stocks in the inner prison. The stocks used in this era had a series of holes that got wider; the idea was to spread the prisoner's legs so they would cramp up, causing excruciating pain. Having been beaten with rods, Paul would likely have had broken bones, tissue damage, and possibly internal bleeding. Not only this, but the prisons were dirty, dark, and poorly ventilated. So we can picture Paul beaten, stretched in the stocks to the point of cramping while suffering from bruising, potentially having broken bones, and bleeding all while locked in a dirty, dark prison. This is what imprisonment looked like for Paul.

Paul also endured countless beatings. The word *beatings* comes from *plégé* and gives us the picture of someone being wounded or receiving punishing blows. Not only was Paul beaten as we read in the account of his imprisonment above, but 2 Corinthians 11:23 tells us that he endured countless beatings. The word *countless* comes from *huperballontós*, meaning "beyond measure" or "surpassingly." Paul had lost count of the number of times he had been beaten. Paul was not one to lie; so for him to say that he endured so many beatings that he had lost count speaks of how wretchedly he was treated. In fact, Paul says this in Colossians 1:24 regarding his beatings: *"Now I rejoice in my sufferings for your sake, and in my flesh I am filling up what is lacking in Christ's afflictions for the sake of his body, that is, the church."* In this verse, Paul isn't saying that Christ's suffering was insufficient or that Christ's substitutionary atonement was inadequate. No, he is saying that just as they persecuted Christ, so they persecuted him. Because Christ was no longer present to be beaten, they took their anger and beatings out on Paul instead.

Paul describes being beaten another way in 2 Corinthians 4:9 where he describes himself as *"persecuted, but not forsaken; struck down, but not destroyed."* The phrase *struck down* comes from *kataballó*, which means thrown down. This word literally means cast or thrown to the ground. Thayer has a helpful comment on this where he says the picture of this word "is taken from an athlete or combatant."[36] Therefore, being thrown down could be seen as being body-slammed or punched to the ground. Paul was very familiar with the physical beatings that accompanied being an apostle, teacher, and pastor of Christ, and he endured countless numbers of beatings.

We see that Paul often lived his life and ministry near death because of the sufferings and persecution he endured. If we were to give an outline of 2 Corinthians 11:23–29, verse 23 would be Paul's thesis statement of what he suffered as a steward of Christ and verses 24–29 capture how he suffered. The picture he draws is one of toiling to the point of exhaustion, being imprisoned, being beaten, and often near death.

> **2 Corinthians 11:24** – *"Five times I received at the hands of the Jews the forty lashes less one."*

Paul received the "forty minus one" five times, which refers to the penalty a man was to be given if a judge decided that a man stood guilty. The man was to lie down and be beaten in public with as many as forty stripes but no more (Deuteronomy 23:1–3). The "minus one" was a practice of giving thirty-nine stripes so, they didn't miscount and break this law. There are different accounts of what such beatings looked like. Some accounts detail this as a lashing with cowhide that had three six-inch strands that were used for whipping; some accounts say that the whip had metal attached to the ends; other accounts detail that the victim's arms were spread so the skin was exposed and able to be easily whipped. Regardless of the specific details, the pain inflicted by this punishment was immense. In what is likely a description of the lashes he received which scarred his body, Paul says, *"From now on let no one cause me trouble, for I bear on my body the marks of Jesus"* (Galatians 6:17). How many lashes did Paul receive by the time he wrote 2 Corinthians? This would be a total of 195 lashes to his body. Most likely, the Jews had Paul lashed for preaching the gospel. Thus, we see that Paul suffered religious persecution by the Jews, his own kinsmen, for the sake of Christ and the gospel.

2 Corinthians 11:25 – *"Three times I was beaten with rods. Once I was stoned. Three times I was shipwrecked; a night and a day I was adrift at sea."*

We see that Paul was beaten with rods three times, and he was stoned. As mentioned earlier, there was an account of Paul being beaten with rods in Acts 16, but there were two other accounts that were not recorded. Additionally, we see that Paul was stoned. This account is detailed in Acts 14 where the Jews persuaded those in Lystra to stone him after he had exhorted them to turn from vain things to the Living God. After they dragged him out of the city and stoned him, they left supposing he was dead. Stoning was a horrendous way to die. A group of people would stone the victim by throwing rocks and boulders at the person (Deuteronomy 17:6–7), or they might throw the victim down a precipice and then roll a large stone on their body. Paul was treated as an infidel, a Sabbath lawbreaker—someone who turned people away from the Living God—even though he was proclaiming the gospel as the only way to be saved. For his faithful duty, he was stoned and beaten with rods.

Paul was shipwrecked three times during his missionary journeys. Not only was there hardship and persecution in his ministry from opposition, but there was also difficulty as he traveled. In fact, we read that he was shipwrecked three times and that he was in the deep sea for a full day. This speaks of Paul's perseverance. Regardless of the elemental forces he faced, he continued in ministry. Yet these hardships did not deter him from fulfilling his mission to proclaim the gospel.

> **2 Corinthians 11:26** – "*On frequent journeys, in danger from rivers, danger from robbers, danger from my own people, danger from Gentiles, danger in the city, danger in the wilderness, danger at sea, danger from false brothers.*"

Notice that Paul was in constant danger. In this verse alone, Paul emphasizes the peril he endured when he uses the word *danger* eight times. The word *danger* comes from *kindunos*, which means "peril" or "risk." This word can refer to spiritual or physical danger, but in this context, it refers to physical danger. It's a way for Paul to say that his whole life was one of being in danger. He was in danger because of the natural elements of rivers and flooding when he traveled. He was in danger from robbers who would look to rob him and leave him for dead when he traveled. He was in danger from the Jews who sought to slander him, lash him, and stone him. He was in danger when he went to different Gentile cities where riots were started (Acts 17:1–10). He was in danger when he went to Jerusalem (Acts 21:10–13). He was in danger of shipwreck when he traveled at sea. False brethren constantly sought to undermine his message and the gospel (Galatians 2:4). No matter where Paul went, he faced danger.

Not only was Paul in danger from false brothers, but he was even deserted by true brothers in 2 Timothy 4:16 where he says, *"At my first defense no one came to stand by me, but all deserted me. May it not be charged against them!"* When Paul was standing trial at his first defense, he was abandoned by everyone. The word *deserted* comes from *egkataleipó*, which conveys the action of leaving someone behind and even implies a sense of forsaking or neglecting. Paul is indicating that it wasn't that people were unable to make it to his first defense, but rather, they forsook him, abandoned him, and deserted him on purpose. Perhaps they didn't want the persecution, or perhaps they didn't want the association. Regardless, we see Paul dealing with abandonment from true brothers with amazing graciousness and asking the Lord not to charge it against them.

2 Corinthians 11:27 – *"In toil and hardship, through many a sleepless night, in hunger and thirst, often without food, in cold and exposure."*

We see that Paul endured all of this in wearisome labor. The word *toil* comes from *kopos,* which means "laborious toil to the point of weariness and fatigue." This word conveys the idea of laboring while being fatigued and facing hardship. Additionally, Paul says he toiled. This word for "toil" comes from *mochthos,* which means "hardship" or "trouble." This speaks of strenuous effort accompanied by suffering and difficulty. Paul's ministry was one of suffering, hardship, toil, and difficulty. In 1 Thessalonians 2:9, Paul uses these same two words when describing how he worked where he says, *"For you remember, brothers, our labor and toil: we worked night and day, that we might not be a burden to any of you, while we proclaimed to you the gospel of God."* Paul wasn't just a proclaimer of the gospel, he was also a tentmaker (Acts 18:3). Therefore, we can see that he not only traveled, proclaimed the gospel, and was in danger, but he did all of this while he supported himself through his trade, and he worked to the point of continually being exhausted by his labor.

Paul mentions that he had many sleepless nights. The phrase *sleepless nights* comes from the original word *agrupnia*. Luke records a picture of this when Paul gave a speech until midnight and then conversed with Christians at Troas until daybreak (Acts 20:7–11). So we see that it may have been Paul's way of life where he worked by day and preached by night, or he preached by day and worked by night. In either case, Paul went through sleepless nights as he both worked, taught, and preached.

We see that Paul struggled just to maintain the essentials to live. He notes that he was constantly hungry. The word *hunger* comes from *limos*, which can also mean "famine." In this context it is used to denote a scarcity of food, which leads to hunger. We also see that he was constantly thirsty. The word *thirsty* comes from *dipsos*, and in this context, it speaks of the longing desire for water. From other Scripture passages, we know that Paul was often cold. For example, when Paul was being held in prison, he asked Timothy to bring his cloak, which would be for warmth (2 Timothy 4:13). We also see that Paul was without clothes. The phrasing suggests the kind of exposure that comes from *gumnotés* and speaks of a state of vulnerability or exposure but also suggests physical nakedness. Thus, we can see that Paul's struggles included lacking basic elements needed to live such as food, water, and clothing.

Paul details his persecution in 2 Corinthians 6:8–10 where he says:

> *Through honor and dishonor, through slander and praise. We are treated as impostors, and yet are true; as unknown, and yet well known; as dying, and behold, we live; as punished, and yet not killed; as sorrowful, yet always rejoicing; as poor, yet making many rich; as having nothing, yet possessing everything.*

We can restate this another way to shed light on what Paul is describing. Paul was honored to be a minister of Christ, yet he was dishonored by false teachers, false brothers, apostates, and sometimes even true Christians who deserted him. Paul was slandered by false teachers and yet praised by true believers. Paul was accused of being an impostor by the false apostles, yet he was a true apostle. Though Paul was a former Pharisee, he was treated as one who is unknown by unconverted Jews, yet he was known by the churches and apostles. He was physically dying yet he was alive and being transformed into the image of Christ. He was being punished as Christ was punished, yet he had not been killed. He was sorrowful over his sin and the body of death, the concern over the churches and yet he was joyful in Christ. He was poor in wealth, yet he was making others rich in Christ. Though he had very little in this world, he possessed Christ which is everything. This was Paul's paradox of suffering. Though he suffered tremendously and was sorrowful, he was joyful in Christ.

2 Corinthians 11:28 – *"And, apart from other things, there is the daily pressure on me of my anxiety for all the churches."*

We see that although Paul suffered much persecution and hardship, he was deeply concerned for the churches. Here, we see an incredible picture of Paul's love, concern, and sympathy for the churches. Though Paul was being slandered, reviled, stoned, lashed, beaten with rods, imprisoned, going without food, going without water, being shipwrecked, lacking sleep, in danger from false brothers, in danger from Gentiles, struck down, and much more, he was deeply concerned with the well-being of the churches. Paul had a constant pressure and concern for the purity of the church. He was concerned when the Galatians were attacked by the Judaizers who gave a false gospel. He was concerned when the Colossians were attacked by false teachers who taught asceticism, visions, and legalism; and attacked the deity of Christ. He was concerned when the Corinthians were creating sects, becoming proud, allowing ongoing sexual sin into the church, abusing the Lord's supper, abusing worship, and lacking love for the brothers and sisters in Christ. Paul loved Christ, and he loved Christ's church. He desired to win others to Christ, see the churches grow into maturity and Christlikeness, and remain firm in Christ. He knew the churches were constantly under attack, and he had unending concern for their spiritual well-being.

2 Corinthians 11:29 – *"Who is weak, and I am not weak? Who is made to fall, and I am not indignant?"*

We see that Paul demonstrates great care and empathy for the churches. When the churches were either physically or spiritually weak, he felt their pain. When they suffered, he suffered. Additionally, when the churches were led into sin, he burned with righteous indignation. When the churches were taught false doctrine, he burned with a holy anger. Paul's love for Christ's church, despite his hardships, was astounding. He loved the churches and cared for them as a nursing mother tenderly cares for her children (1 Thessalonians 2:7–8). Paul taught the churches, prayed for the churches, preached to the churches, cared for the churches, confronted the churches, led the churches, and didn't want to burden the churches. Though Paul suffered tremendously, he loved Christ's bride, the church.

As we close this chapter, let's reflect not just on the persecution, suffering, and hardships that Paul endured, but let's look at his hopeful outlook in Christ. In Romans 8:35, Paul asks whether these hardships will affect his salvation: *"Who shall separate us from the love of Christ? Shall tribulation, or distress, or persecution, or famine, or nakedness, or danger, or sword?"* What is the answer to Paul's question? He suffered tribulation, distress, famine, nakedness, danger, and the threat of death. Can such persecution and hardship affect his salvation? Paul gave us this magnificent answer in Romans 8:37–39:

> *No, in all these things we are more than conquerors through him who loved us. For I am sure that neither death nor life, nor angels nor rulers, nor things present nor things to come, nor powers, nor height nor depth, nor anything else in all creation, will be able to separate us from the love of God in Christ Jesus our Lord.*

So how should one respond to persecution, slander, reviling, beatings, stoning, suffering, hardship, and danger? Remember what Jesus said in Matthew 5:11–12; the true pastor can respond in joy and gladness for great is his reward in heaven. And Paul's ringing proclamation reminds the Christian that neither life nor death, nor angels nor demons, nor things present or yet to come, nor height nor depth, nor anything in all creation can separate him from the love of God in Christ Jesus (Romans 8:37–39). This is how the true pastor is graced to suffer persecution. Paul commanded Timothy to join him in such persecution: "*Therefore do not be ashamed of the testimony about our Lord, nor of me his prisoner, but share in suffering for the gospel by the power of God*" (2 Timothy 1:8). Paul commands all true pastors to suffer as he did for the sake of the gospel.

Chapter 7

A Man Who Has the Grace of God Poured Out on His Life to Address Sin in the Church

As for those who persist in sin, rebuke them in the presence of all, so that the rest may stand in fear.

—1 Timothy 5:20

In this chapter, we will see how the grace of God is poured out on the true pastor to address sin in the church. Church discipline and church membership are not highly valued in the church today. Church membership for the purposes of having individuals committed to the rest of the body of believers has been replaced with casual attendance and feigned commitment. The notion of disciplining the sinner for the purposes of restoring the sinner and maintaining the purity of the church seems to be a thing of the past. Biblical church discipline has been replaced by simply removing the troublesome members, cleaning up the membership list, and taking inactive members who are no longer attending off the list, and avoiding the topic of sin altogether for the sake of false unity.

However, the true pastor does not take any of these views. The true pastor sees church discipline as necessary for maintaining the unity of the church, maintaining the purity of the church, winning and restoring brothers and sisters back to fellowship, and presenting Christ's bride as spotless and blameless to Him. The true pastor is not concerned with superficial church growth because it is Christ who builds the church. Therefore, the true pastor seeks to deal with sin in the church according to the Master's instructions. Additionally, the true pastor is not seeking to address every single sin of every single person on a personal one-on-one basis. Not at all. The pastor seeks to instruct the church on how it should deal with sin, and he seeks to lead the church to obey the Lord in His instructions. He is not seeking to instruct just the elders, the deacons, or a small group of men in leadership. No, the true pastor is seeking to teach the entire church how the Lord instructs that sin be dealt with in the church. Thus, we see that the grace of God has been poured out on the true pastor to lead and instruct the church on how to deal with sin in the church.

To get a better understanding of what this looks like, we will perform a brief exposition of Matthew 18:15–20, which speaks of church discipline, and 1 Timothy 5:19–22, which speaks of disciplining sinning pastors or elders. Before we get started, consider John MacArthur's helpful insight on church discipline: "Somewhere along the line we have to decide whether we're going to protect the man or protect the God the man says he serves. For if we have a God who tolerates sin, then we have defamed the name of God."[37]

Addressing Sin in the Church

Matthew 18:15 – *"If your brother sins against you, go and tell him his fault, between you and him alone. If he listens to you, you have gained your brother."*

We see that sin in the church is to be dealt with. Discipline in the church is not to be done out of retaliation or self-interest or personal vengeance or any of the like. Church discipline has many purposes which include:

- Admonishing lovingly as the Lord admonishes His children whom He loves for their own good (Hebrews 12:4–13).

- Keeping the purity of the church (Ephesians 5:27).

- Keeping the unity of the church by removing sinful living and errant doctrine (1 Corinthians 5:11–13, Galatians 5:9–10).

- Restoring brothers and sisters back to useful service (Matthew 18:15), so that we may fulfill the law of Christ and build one another up through love and service (Galatians 6:2) and so that the Lord's

name is not blasphemed and dishonored (Romans
2:23–24).

Therefore, we should see that although confronting sin in
the church often has a negative connotation, the purposes for
church discipline are never to be for retaliation or self-interest,
but for the purposes mentioned above. Likewise, because the
Lord owns the church, builds the church, and has set forth
instructions on how He wants sin dealt with in the church,
the true pastor is one who seeks to deal biblically with sin and
teach the church the biblical instructions for how to deal with
sin in the church.

We need to understand what kind of sin should be
addressed. As discussed earlier, God abhors sin; it is rebellion against Him, and He cannot look upon it with favor.
Therefore, when Jesus is speaking about sins being committed
against someone, we should understand that this could be any
sin as Jesus uses the word *hamartanó*, which can refer to any
sin. The Lord does not specify sins that are excluded. Additionally, addressing sin in the church must be distinct from
legalism and man-made rules (Colossians 2:20–21). There is
a difference between someone who is slandering and someone
mowing their lawn on Sunday. There is a difference between
someone committing adultery and someone choosing to send
their child to a public school. There is a difference between a
man teaching a false gospel and a pastor who has chosen to
change the worship service time by thirty minutes. There is a
difference between someone who is buying and using drugs

illegally and someone who smokes a cigarette legally. We must distinguish between outright sin and trespassing man-made rules when addressing sin in the church.

We should seek to understand what it means when "someone sins against you." John MacArthur has a helpful word on this where he distinguishes between directly and indirectly "sinning against you."[38] Directly sinning against you could include someone who comes to you and hits you, steals from you, abuses you, or attacks you. Indirectly sinning against you would include a sin that defames and stains the church and God's people. For example, if a man has a crass and crude mouth, which is known by his neighbors; if his neighbors learn where the man goes to church and vow never to go to that church because of the man's sin and crudeness, this would be indirectly "sinning against you" because he is staining the name of the church and the rest of the church assembly. Therefore, when Jesus says, *"if your brother sins against you"* (Matthew 18:15), we understand how this could apply both directly and indirectly.

We should see that discipline is in the context of the church because Jesus uses the word *brother*, which comes from the word *adelphos*, which is a designation for fellow believers. Paul had this to say about judging those inside the church versus those who are outside the church when he was addressing the discipline of a brother in the Corinthian church who was committing incest: *"For what have I to do with judging outsiders? Is it not those inside the church whom you are to judge? God judges those outside. Purge the evil person from among you*" (1 Corinthians 5:12–13). Here, we see that Paul made a distinction between those inside the church and those outside the church. We know that those outside the church will not have regard for God and obeying and trusting Him. However, those who claim to be Christians and know God are the ones that the church is to discipline. In a similar statement regarding discipline and judgment, Peter says this in 1 Peter 4:17: "*For it is time for judgment to begin at the household of God; and if it begins with us, what will be the outcome for those who do not obey the gospel of God?*" Therefore, we should understand that Jesus seeks for this discipline to take place in the church.

We should also see that it is the believer's responsibility to address the one sinning. It's important to note that addressing sin is not just the responsibility of the pastor, the elder, the deacon, or the church leadership. This is the responsibility of every believer. We see this when Jesus says, "*go and tell him his fault*" (Matthew 18:15). The word *go* is written in the present tense and imperative mood, which means that this is a command that is to be continually carried out until the sinning brother is rebuked. It does not say to go and run to the pastor and set up a meeting. No, it commands that the believer go tell the sinning brother his fault.

Next, we see the phrase "*tell him his fault*" comes from the word *elegchó*, which means "to rebuke." We discussed the meaning of *elegchó* earlier; it means to show someone is wrong using biblical evidence. It's also important to know that the word *reprove* is written in the aorist tense and imperative mood, which is a command that calls for immediate obedience. It gives the sense that when the rebuking believer goes to the sinning believer, the rebuking believer is to be thorough, forthright, and clear as to how the sinning believer has sinned.

This rebuke is to happen between just the rebuking believer and the sinning believer. Let's remember that the point of discipline is not retaliation, retribution, self-righteousness, or any self-seeking purpose. This discipline is to be done out of gentleness, kindness, and love for the purposes that we mentioned earlier of maintaining purity, unity, restoration, and honoring the Lord. In fact, Galatians 6:1 gives us a picture of how the rebuking believer is to address the sinning believer where it says, "*Brothers, if anyone is caught in any transgression, you who are spiritual should restore him in a spirit of gentleness. Keep watch on yourself, lest you too be tempted.*" Here, we see that the rebuking believer must be gentle and meek. This word *meek* does not mean weak. Rather, it implies strength under control. This is not a meekness that is void of conviction. Rather, it is a gentleness that is under God's control. Additionally, we see that in Galatians 6:1, Paul reminds us that we should keep watch on ourselves so that we're not tempted. This means the rebuking believer goes to the sinning believer in humility and gentleness knowing their weakness and vulnerability to fall into the same temptation and into sin.

One of the purposes for rebuking the sinning believer is to gain him. This word *gain* comes from *kerdainó*, which means "to win" or "to profit." In a metaphorical sense, this is talking about winning the brother over for gaining spiritual benefits. When a believer is living in ongoing sin, the Lord has prescribed that the church is to seek to restore the sinning believer. As it says in Galatians 6:1, it is the goal to restore the sinning believer. The word *restore* comes from *katartizó*, and it speaks of restoring something to its intended state or equipping someone for a task. The purpose of this rebuke is not only for the purity of the church, but also to restore the sinning believer to usefulness and good works (Titus 2:14). The rebuking believer is to have the same mindset and intention of the Lord in Matthew 18:10–14 who goes out and finds the sheep who has gone astray, restores the sheep, and rejoices over the restoration of the lost sheep.

Matthew 18:16 – *"But if he does not listen, take one or two others along with you, that every charge may be established by the evidence of two or three witnesses."*

If the sinning believer does not listen to the rebuking believer and remains unrepentant, the rebuking believer is to take one or two fellow believers to address the sinning believer. If a sinning believer will not listen to the biblical rebuke and remains recalcitrant and unrepentant, it is then the obligation of the rebuking believer to bring one or two other believers. Let's note that the word *take* is written in the aorist tense and imperative mood, which means that this is a command that is to be fully completed with urgency. Sin does not get better with time. Sin does not age well. No, sin permeates and has a negative influence. When sin is left to linger and remains unaddressed, this downplays the seriousness of sin. When sin is left to permeate the church, this shows a lack of understanding of what the Triune God thinks of sin. Therefore, this is a task that is to be done both prayerfully and with discernment but not allowing the sin to linger. Additionally, Jesus commands that there be two or three witnesses present. This is a command from Deuteronomy 19:15, which reads:

> *A single witness shall not suffice against a person for any crime or for any wrong in connection with any offense that he has committed. Only on the evidence of two witnesses or of three witnesses shall a charge be established.*

The purpose of bringing the witnesses is to protect against false accusations and to strengthen and confirm what is said between the rebuking believer and sinning believer. This is not about having strength in numbers or using intimidation, but rather, for the confirmation and the discernment of other brothers. The other brothers can affirm the attitudes of both the sinning believer and rebuking believer, affirm that the rebuking believer is rebuking in gentleness and love, affirm the rebuking believer is using Scripture and not appealing to man-made rules, and affirm whether the sinning believer is demonstrating repentance and understanding. This is to be the purpose of having two or three witnesses.

Matthew 18:17 – *"If he refuses to listen to them, tell it to the church. And if he refuses to listen even to the church, let him be to you as a Gentile and a tax collector."*

Jesus commands that if the person remains unrepentant after bringing two or three witnesses, the rebuking believer is responsible to tell this to the church. At this point, we see that the sinning believer remains unrepentant, and so Jesus now commands that this is told to the church. One may ask the question, "Who should be informed of this?" In a sound church, it would be a good practice to notify the elders because they are the ones who are keeping watch over the souls of the congregation who will have to give an account to the Lord and who can best discern how to let the entire congregation know of the sinning brother (Hebrews 13:17). However, in this verse, the Lord commands that the sin be told to the church. In fact, He uses the word *ekklésia*, which refers to the whole assembly and not simply the elders. Therefore, discernment must be exercised to know how to inform the elders and the congregation.

Next, the whole assembly is to reach out to the sinning believer. Let's note the Lord's love for the sinning believer. The Lord doesn't want just one or two people reaching out to restore the sinning believer, He wants the whole assembly to reach out to restore the sinning believer. This is a stunning act of mercy and graciousness by the Lord. The Lord is a forgiving God, and He wants His people to be Christlike and demonstrate His character when they love, forgive, and restore as He does. These are the tens or hundreds or perhaps thousands of people who plead with the sinning believer to repent and be restored out of love. This is the magnificent picture of hands and hearts reaching out for the sake of one sinning believer and earnestly hoping, praying, and pleading with the person to repent. D. L. Moody said this regarding forgiveness, "The voice of sin is loud, but the voice of forgiveness is louder."[39] This is to be the picture of how the church is to respond and call the sinner to repentance and restored fellowship. Paul gives us this picture of the sinning believer who was restored to repentance where he counsels how the repentant believer should be treated in 2 Corinthians 2:7, "*So you should rather turn to forgive and comfort him, or he may be overwhelmed by excessive sorrow.*" We see how far the modern church has fallen when they simply remove inactive members from the church membership roll or simply take a sinning church member off the membership list without earnestly pursuing them. This is not the Christlike attitude of the Savior who pursues His lost sheep (Matthew 18:10–14).

We should see that if a sinning believer remains unrepentant, they are to be treated as a Gentile or tax collector. When Jesus says they are to be treated as a Gentile or tax collector, He does not mean that they should be stoned, persecuted, or any of the like. Rather, He is simply saying that they must be treated as an unbeliever. It's also important to note that when the Lord says that they be treated as unbelievers, this is written in the present tense and imperative mood, which means that this is a command to be continually obeyed. Paul gave this command regarding how to associate with unrepentant and ungodly people who call themselves a brother or Christian:

> *But now I am writing to you not to associate with anyone who bears the name of brother if he is guilty of sexual immorality or greed, or is an idolater, reviler, drunkard, or swindler—not even to eat with such a one.*
>
> —1 Corinthians 5:11

When Paul says they are "*not to associate*" with those who bear the name "brother" but are ungodly, he uses the word *sunanamignumi*, which means "to associate with," "to mix with," or "mingle with." This word conveys the idea of mingling or associating within an intimate interaction. Paul did not want the Corinthian church to be associated with those who called themselves Christians but were ungodly in their lifestyle. He did not want them even to eat with them because eating and dining with people in Paul's day showed association and affection, and one could even be influenced by the ungodly. Therefore, Christ commands that the sinning believer who is unrepentant, must be treated as unbelievers, and they must not be associated with as true believers.

Once a person has been put out of the church, the church must not treat them as an enemy, but admonish them and call them back. In 2 Thessalonians 3:14–15, Paul gives further instructions on dealing with a sinning brother where he says, "*If anyone does not obey what we say in this letter, take note of that person, and have nothing to do with him, that he may be ashamed. Do not regard him as an enemy, but warn him as a brother.*" Though believers are not to associate with the person, they are not to treat them as an enemy either, and they are to warn them. The word *warn* comes from *noutheteó* and conveys the idea of warning someone with the intent of correcting the behavior with gentle but firm guidance. Though the person has been put out of the church, the church is still to warn and call the person back to fellowship in repentance.

Matthew 18:18 – "*Truly, I say to you, whatever you bind on earth shall be bound in heaven, and whatever you loose on earth shall be loosed in heaven.*"

When church discipline is administered according to Christ, we can know that heaven agrees. The word *bind* comes from *deó*, and it means "to tie," "to bind" and can also mean "to declare to be prohibited and unlawful." The word *loose* comes from *luó*, and it means "to loose," "to release," "to dissolve." This word could also mean "to declare lawful." When something is "bound," it is the same as saying that someone is not forgiven or bound in their sins, and they are unrepentant. When something is "loosed," it is the same as saying someone has been loosed from their sins or forgiven, which would mean they are repentant. Therefore, when the church carries out discipline according to the Lord's instructions as described above, the Lord declares that heaven agrees because the Lord is the one who gave the instruction. When discipline is followed according to the Lord's instruction, heaven agrees that someone is bound in their sin and not forgiven or loosed of their sin and forgiven.

Addressing Sinning Pastors

1 Timothy 5:19 – "*Do not admit a charge against an elder except on the evidence of two or three witnesses.*"

The pastor is not only responsible for teaching the church how to address sinning believers in the church, but he is also responsible for teaching the church how to address elders who are in sin. If any pastor is caught in sin, the true pastor should give the church instructions on how they are to discipline and deal with him. Therefore, the true pastor is one who fully acknowledges this task and instructs his congregation how to deal with a sinning pastor.

We see that the pastor is not to receive an accusation against another pastor or elder unless there are two or three witnesses. As we mentioned above, having two or three witnesses is important. The purpose of bringing two or three witnesses in this case is to protect against false accusations and to confirm the charge against a sinning pastor. This is not for having strength in numbers or using intimidation, but rather, having two or three witnesses is for the confirmation of the truth. The other brothers or sisters are to affirm the sin they have witnessed the pastor engaged in to avoid speculation, hearsay, and false testimony. This is the purpose of bringing two or three witnesses.

1 Timothy 5:20 – "*As for those who persist in sin, rebuke them in the presence of all, so that the rest may stand in fear.*"

We see that those pastors who persist in sin are to be rebuked. The word *persist* is not in the original language. Rather, Paul puts the word *sinning* in the present tense and participle mood, which speaks of sin that is an ongoing and continual pattern of life. Pastors who have been caught in an unbroken pattern of sin in their life are to be rebuked. Once again, the word *rebuked* comes from *elegchó*, and it means to show someone is wrong using biblical evidence. The pastor's sin is to be exposed using Scripture. Additionally, the word *rebuke* is in the imperative mood, which means this is a command. To not rebuke a pastor is to sin. To hide the pastor's sin is wicked. To overlook and ignore the pastor's transgression is perverse. The Lord Jesus Christ commands that the pastor's sin be rebuked. Note that there is no instruction about putting the man back in ministry. This is not to say that the pastor cannot be restored to fellowship in the church. However, it is to say that he may be temporarily or permanently disqualified as a pastor. We'll see this when we get to 1 Timothy 5:22.

Note that the unqualified pastor is to be rebuked before the whole congregation. The phrase "*in the presence of all*" comes from the original word *enópios*, which means "before the face of" or "in the eyes of" and *panton* means "all." This is not to be a secret rebuke where only a few members of the leadership know of the pastor's sin. This is not to be a select group that is made aware of the pastor's sin. No! The pastor who has been caught in sin is to be rebuked in the presence of the entire congregation. The whole congregation is to be made aware and knowledgeable of the pastor's unrepentant sin. When it has been established that the pastor has been caught in sin and is no longer above reproach, he must be exposed and removed. Why should there be such drastic consequences? Paul exhorted the Corinthians to imitate him as he imitated Christ (1 Corinthians 11:1). Paul told the Corinthians that he was sending them Timothy who was his son in the faith and would remind them of his ways in Christ (1 Corinthians 4:17). It is a high calling to be a pastor. Teachers will be judged with a stricter judgment (James 3:1). Pastors are called to preach, teach, and walk before the face of God. God is jealous for His church and for the godliness of the man who leads His church. The pastor is to be an example of Christ in speech, conduct, love, faith, and purity (1 Timothy 4:12).

The pastor is to rebuke a sinning elder in front of everyone so everyone may stand in fear. One may ask, "Is this the fear of sinning against God or the fear of the Lord?" The answer would be yes. Proverbs 8:13 says this regarding the fear of sin and the fear of the Lord: "*The fear of the Lord is hatred of evil. Pride and arrogance and the way of evil and perverted speech I hate.*" The rebuke of a sinning elder should cause the congregation to fear the Lord and fear committing the sins the Lord hates. This public rebuke is to have a purifying effect on the church. It is to show the holiness of God and His disdain for sin. It is to have the congregation stand in fear of committing the same sin the pastor or elder is guilty of committing.

1 Timothy 5:21 – "*In the presence of God and of Christ Jesus and of the elect angels I charge you to keep these rules without prejudging, doing nothing from partiality.*"

Timothy is solemnly charged to obey this command. The word *charge* comes from *diamarturomai*, and is used to convey the act of solemnly testifying or earnestly charging someone with a truth or command. It often implies serious or emphatic full and clear testimony. Not only is this charge serious, but we also find that it's a continuous charge as it is written in the present tense and indicative mood.

Moreover, this solemn charge to keep these rules is to be carried out in the presence of God, Christ Jesus, and the elect angels without partiality. It's as if Paul is telling Timothy and every pastor, "Timothy, I charge you to keep these commands before all of heaven. Timothy, I charge you in the watchful eyes of God and Christ Jesus and His elect angels that you are to keep these rules without partiality, without bias, without favoritism, and without prejudice." This is a serious charge. It is disobedience to not discipline sinning elders. It's a serious trespass to not discipline a pastor who gives a false gospel. It's a serious sin to not bring a pastor into discipline because of partiality. The word *partiality* comes from *prosklisis*, which means "an inclination" and conveys a sense of devotion or attachment. Timothy and the true pastor are to discipline sinning pastors even if the sinning pastor is a friend or family. There is to be no bias or partiality. Timothy and the true pastor have been given this charge to obey this command before the face of God the Father, Christ Jesus, and the elect angels.

1 Timothy 5:22 – *"Do not be hasty in the laying on of hands, nor take part in the sins of others; keep yourself pure."*

Paul charges Timothy to not be quick to put men into ministry as elders. The laying on of hands was symbolic of commissioning (Deuteronomy 34:9, Numbers 27:18) and identification (Numbers 8:10–11), receiving the power of God (Acts 8:17), and receiving blessing (Matthew 19:15). However, in this context, the laying on of hands would be symbolic of commissioning and identification. The laying on of hands would mean that the elders identified the pastor or elder as one of their own and that the man was suitable, qualified, and approved by the elders to be commissioned as a pastor. Paul is telling Timothy that he should not be quick or hasty in making men pastors.

We've gone through the several reasons why it would be foolish to put a man into the position of a pastor without properly testing and discerning his giftedness and qualifications. The other pastors or elders must understand whether the man is a true convert; they must understand if the man's character fits that of the biblical qualifications; they must understand if the man is proclaiming the true gospel; they must understand if the man is skilled in teaching; they must understand if the man is knowledgeable in Scripture; they must understand if the man is devoted to Scripture; they must understand if the man will stand firm against opposition; they must understand if the man has impure motives; they must understand whether the man can address sin in the church, and more. Men that desire the position of a pastor is a good and noble thing (1 Timothy 3:1). However, as we learned earlier the man's tongue, teaching, and character can have both positive and detrimental effects. Therefore, Timothy is to be slow, discerning, prayerful, and wise when laying his hands on and ordaining men.

Finally, we see that Timothy and the true pastor are culpable and liable if they lay hands on a man who is unqualified. Paul makes this clear when he says, "*nor take part in the sins of others.*" In fact, the phrase *take part* comes from *koinóneó*, meaning to "participate" or "have fellowship." This word conveys the idea of having a common part or fellowship in an activity, experience, or possession. As we discussed earlier, we will be able to identify a true or false teacher by their fruits— the fruit of their life and the fruit of their teaching (Matthew 7:15–20). If Timothy were to put a man into the position of a pastor who had an abhorrent and false doctrine or was sloppy and unskilled in teaching the Word, Timothy would be a partaker and fellowship in the man's sin because he commissioned him and didn't adequately discern that the man was not skilled in teaching and handling God's Word. If Timothy were to put a greedy man into the position of a pastor or allowed women to be pastors, Timothy would share in the man's sin because he was not wise in discerning the man's true intentions. Therefore, Timothy and the true pastor must not hastily and quickly commission a man for ministry because they must realize that they are culpable and do not want to share in the man's sin. If Timothy and the true pastor have thoroughly evaluated a man's life, character, doctrine, and teaching, then they are not culpable. Paul makes this point that there are some whose sins go before them and are obvious, but there are others whose sins appear later (1 Timothy 5:24). Thus, Timothy and the true pastor must not lay hands on men whose sins go before them and who demonstrate a lack of biblical qualifications and God-given giftedness of a pastor.

As we close this chapter, we have examined the purpose of practicing church discipline for pastors as well as the entire congregation. The purpose of such discipline is not retaliation or retribution. The purpose for church discipline is to maintain the unity and purity of the church, and to win and restore brothers and sisters to fellowship, presenting Christ's bride as spotless and blameless to Him, and for the glory of God. The true pastor has a burden for addressing sin in the church as he knows the purpose for the discipline and plan for Christ's church. The true pastor is also slow to put men into the position of a pastor because he knows that he would share in the culpability and sin of an unqualified man if he does not properly vet the man. An unqualified man or even a false teacher will have devastating effects on the church. The true pastor is not seeking to be the sole executor of church discipline, but rather, he teaches the church the Lord's instruction for discipline and seeks to do so faithfully as one who feeds, guides, and guards the flock (Ephesians 4:11–16).

Chapter 8

Unspiritual, Not a Pastor, Not Recognized, and Ignorant - A Man Who Permits Women Pastors

I do not permit a woman to teach or exercise authority over a man; rather, she is to remain quiet.

—1 Timothy 2:12

In this chapter, we will take some time to demonstrate that a woman is not and can never be qualified to be a pastor. There has been a significant increase in the number of women pastors in the contemporary church. Women pastors can be found in such protestant denominations as the Evangelical Lutheran Church of America, Alliance of Reformed Churches, Reformed Church in America, Presbyterian Church USA, Kingdom Network (A Community of Reformed Churches), Christian Reformed Church, American Baptist Churches

USA, The Assemblies of God and Foursquare Church, charismatic churches, and many others. Increasingly, more believe that women can be pastors, elders, or hold offices or roles of authority in the church. Therefore, it is important to understand what the Bible says about women being pastors.

Not only will we address the biblical perspective of women pastors, but we will also address men who are pastors or in positions of church leadership who allow women to be pastors, elders, and take positions of authority and leadership over men. The Bible has stern words of warning for men that allow women to be in the position of pastors, preachers, elders, lay-shepherds, and positions of authority over men. In this chapter, we will perform an exposition of 1 Timothy 2:11–15 and then 1 Corinthians 14:33–38.

This chapter is not written to demean, degrade, or minimize the role of women in the church or even in the family. One of the reasons for including this chapter is because there are men in churches and denominations that were once biblical and scripturally sound who have caved to society and who have abandoned Scripture when it comes to not allowing women to be pastors. It is not a small thing for a man to allow women to be pastors. In fact, Paul has a shocking statement that is backed with the full authority of the Lord Jesus Christ regarding anyone, including men who are called pastors, who allow women to be pastors. Men who allow this to occur must heed what Paul says in 1 Corinthians 14:37–38: "*If anyone thinks that he is a prophet, or spiritual, he should acknowledge that the things I am writing to you are a command of the Lord. If anyone does not recognize this, he is not recognized."*

Women Not Permitted to Teach or Exercise Authority Over a Man

1 Timothy 2:11 – *"Let a woman learn quietly with all submissiveness."*

Today, it is often thought that equality equals fairness and that if there is not equality, then things are not fair. For example, the world says that women must make the same wage as a man for doing the same position; this appears to be a fair concern if the experience and skill are the same. However, the world does not try and push for job equality for women. For example, there is not a push for there to be equal numbers of women to men in jobs such as construction workers, electricians, garbage truck drivers, roofers, demolition laborers, plumbers, oil rig workers, drilling operators, prison guards, welders, maintenance technicians, autobody workers, and other jobs that require hard and demanding physical labor, which can be dangerous.

This is to say that there are differences between men and women, which are God-given distinctions. These God-given differences do not make males or females superior or inferior to one another. Rather, the differences reflect God's plan and order for both male and female. In fact, Paul emphasizes the equality of men and women when he says, *"But I want you to understand that the head of every man is Christ, the head of a wife is her husband, and the head of Christ is God*" (1 Corinthians 11:3). In this short, but powerful statement, we see that woman and man both have equal worth and value. How can we know this? Paul states that "*the head of Christ is God.*" We know that Jesus is coequal with God the Father and God the Holy Spirit. Jesus is not of more value or worth than God the Father and God the Holy Spirit, and He is not of lesser value or worth than God the Father and God the Holy Spirit. The subordination or different roles in the Godhead do not make the Father, Son, or Holy Spirit lesser or greater. When Paul makes this statement that "*the head of Christ is God*" and "*the head of a wife is her husband,*" we should understand this to mean that although both man and woman are of equal worth and value, but they have different roles.

Paul emphasizes this once again in 1 Corinthians 11:11 where he says, "*Nevertheless, in the Lord woman is not independent of man nor man of woman; for as woman was made from man, so man is now born of woman. And all things are from God.*" Paul is essentially saying that the man and woman or co-dependent; unlike God who is self-sufficient in and of Himself. It's true that Eve was made from Adam's rib, but it's also true that man came forth from Eve. Therefore, both are of equal value and worth, but have different roles. This is of most importance as we examine these verses.

First, note that Paul desires women to learn Scripture. The word *learn* comes from *manthanó*, which means to "learn" or "understand." It implies a process of understanding or comprehending something that was previously unknown. In this context, Paul is referring to Scripture. As we learned earlier, Christ gave the church pastors, evangelists, and teachers so that the body of Christ, including women, may grow in knowledge of the Son of God, be equipped for works of service, and become mature and Christlike. Paul is not barring women from learning Scripture. Rather, he is advocating that they be taught Scripture, so they can become mature in the faith and not be deceived by false doctrine and false teachers (Ephesians 4:12–16).

Second, we see that Paul desires women to learn quietly and with all submissiveness. The word *quietness* comes from *hésuchia*, which means "silence" or "tranquility." This word pictures a state of calmness and self-control. Additionally, Paul commands that women learn in all submissiveness. The word *submissive* comes from *hupotagé*, and it means "subjection" or "obedience." This word implies a voluntary yielding or arranging oneself under authority or leadership of another. When Paul says women should learn quietly and in submission, he uses the present tense and imperative mood, which simply means that these are commands that are to be continually obeyed. Not only this, but Paul says that women are to learn in "*all submissiveness.*" This is strong language and shows that there is no area in the church where women are not to be under the submission of men in the church. Women are not to be loud, noisy, or boisterous when they're learning, and they are to be completely submitted to their husbands and the male leadership. They are not to be seeking to overthrow the pastors, elders, their husbands, or other men. Rather, they are to learn Scripture quietly, self-controlled, and in full submission.

> **1 Timothy 2:12** – *"I do not permit a woman to teach or to exercise authority over a man; rather, she is to remain quiet."*

Third, Paul gives instruction that a woman is not permitted to teach over a man. The question we need to answer is what does it mean when a woman is not allowed to teach? We see that in Titus 2:3–4, that women are allowed to teach younger women where it says, *"Older women likewise are to be reverent in behavior, not slanderers or slaves to much wine. They are to teach what is good, and so train the young women to love their husbands and children."* Therefore, we can know that more mature women in the faith can teach younger women or women who are not as mature in the faith. Additionally, we see that in Proverbs 1:8 that women are to teach their children: *"Hear, my son, your father's instruction, and forsake not your mother's teaching."* Therefore, we know that the Bible allows women to teach other women as well as their children.

However, we see that a woman is not permitted to teach a man. The word *permit* comes from *epitrepó*, and it means to "to allow." The original word for "not" is *ouk*. The word *epitrepó* implies a sense of authority or control, where one party grants permission to another. In this verse, *epitrepó* is written in the present tense and indicative mood, which simply means that this is a truth that will continually be true. Additionally, when Paul uses the phrase *to teach*, he uses the present tense. Now that we know some of the verb tenses and word meanings, we could render the verse this way, "I do not allow, and I will never allow a woman to ever teach a man." Paul's clear instruction is that women are never to teach men in the church. There are no exception clauses for this instruction; rather, there is simply a clear statement that women cannot teach men in the church. It does not matter if the woman is gifted to teach other women and is gifted in teaching her children. Even though God has gifted the woman to teach other women in the church, she is not to teach men. Not once. Not ever.

Fourth, not only are women not to teach men in the church, but they are also not to take authority over men. The phrase "take *authority over*" comes from the original word *authenteó*, which means "to have authority over," "to exercise authority over," or "to dominate." This word conveys the act of exercising authority or dominion over someone. There are debates and arguments over this specific word with some scholars arguing that *authenteó* speaks of authority in a negative sense such as bullying. However, in the context of this verse, this would not be the correct interpretation or convey what Paul is stating. In fact, in the subsequent verses, Paul will articulate what he means when he says that women cannot take authority over men in verses 13–14. Paul is saying that women are to take no positions of teaching and no positions of authority over a man, which includes the office of pastor or elder. The verse could also be rendered in this way, "I do not allow, and I will never allow a woman to have authority, exercise authority, usurp authority, hold authority, or have dominion over a man in the church." This is very strong and clear language. No matter how gifted or godly a woman is, she is never, not once, and under any circumstances permitted to teach over a man or take authority over a man.

1 Timothy 2:13–14 – *"For Adam was formed first, then Eve; and Adam was not deceived, but the woman was deceived and became a transgressor."*

Fifth, we see that Paul appeals to creation for why a woman should not teach or take authority over man. When we look at the Creation account and the fall of man, we can see Paul's point. In Genesis 2:15, we see that Adam has been created and put in the Garden of Eden, but Eve has not yet been created. The Lord commands that Adam can eat of every tree in the garden but not from the tree of the knowledge of good and evil because when he does, he will surely die (Genesis 2:17). Then the Lord saw that Adam was alone to work the land, and He saw that it would be good for him to have a helper (Genesis 2:18–20). The Lord caused Adam to fall asleep and formed Eve from one of Adam's ribs, and Adam and Eve were husband and wife (Genesis 2:21–25).

As we turn to Genesis 3, we see that Eve was with Adam when the serpent came to deceive her (Genesis 3:6). The devil then tempted Eve to touch the fruit and eat the fruit all while in the presence of Adam; he deceived her into believing that when she ate the fruit, she would not die but become like God knowing good and evil (Genesis 3:3–5). We also see that Eve was aware that God had commanded them not to eat from the tree of the knowledge of good and evil (Genesis 3:3). But when Eve saw that the tree was good for food, looked delightful to her eyes, and believed it would make her wise, she was deceived, ate of it, and sinned (Genesis 3:6). This all took place while Adam was with her as it says in Genesis 3:6, "*She took of its fruit and ate, and she also gave some to her husband who was with her, and he ate.*" Adam knew the command of God. Adam was supposed to teach Eve not to eat of the tree; he was supposed to guide her, and he was supposed to watch over her. Yet, he failed to protect his wife and obey God. In fact, the word for deceived comes from *exapataó*, which means to be thoroughly deceived and implies that Eve fell into a deep level of deception. Thus, Adam's failure to protect his wife led to Eve's deception and transgression.

In 1 Timothy 2:13–14, Paul makes a distinction in that he says the woman was deceived and became a transgressor. However, in Romans 5:12, Paul makes the argument that sin entered the world through Adam and not Eve where he says, "*Therefore, just as through one man sin entered into the world, and death through sin, and so death spread to all mankind, because all sinned*" (NASB2020). The one man who brought sin into the world was Adam (Romans 5:14). So, although Eve transgressed first, Adam was blamed for the fall of humanity. We even see that God questioned Adam for his sin before He questioned Eve (Genesis 3:9–13). Adam obstinately disobeyed God and knowingly sinned against God's command. Adam was not misinformed or misled; he decided to rebel against God and listen to his wife (Genesis 3:17). Instead of Adam teaching, guiding, and protecting his wife, he listened and followed his wife, which was a reversal of God's ordained roles.

This is Paul's argument. Paul is saying that man is responsible for teaching his wife, leading his wife, and guarding his wife. Adam was responsible for teaching his wife that she must not eat from the tree of the knowledge of good and evil. Adam was responsible for leading his wife away from the Serpent and not allowing her to be deceived. Adam was responsible for guarding his wife so that she would not be deceived and fall into temptation. God's plan was and is for man to teach, lead, and guard his wife. Likewise, God's plan for the church is for men to teach, lead, and guard the church. Just as Christ is the Head of the Church and is the true teacher (Matthew 23:10), true guide (John 14:6), and true protector (John 10:11), so men are to lead the church, and husbands are responsible to lead their wives. When Paul appeals to the Creation account, he wants us to see that man is to be the head of the woman (1 Corinthians 11:3). When we survey 1 Corinthians 11:3, we see Paul lay out this order: God is the head of Christ; Christ is the head of man; and man is the head of woman. Additionally, in Ephesians 5:22–24, Paul gives this instruction on women's submission to their husbands:

Wives, submit to your own husbands, as to the Lord. For the husband is the head of the wife even as Christ is the head of the church, his body, and is himself its Savior. Now as the church submits to Christ, so also wives should submit in everything to their husbands.

God's order is that Christ would be the head of the church, and the church submits to Him; man is the head of woman, and woman submits to him. Therefore, when Paul says that he does not permit a woman to teach or take authority over a man, he means to bring us back to the creation account to recall the God-ordained order that began in Creation. He also wants to remind us of the disastrous result when these roles were not followed. Therefore, Paul is clear that women are not to teach or take authority over men, and he cites the Creation account and fall of man as evidence for this God-ordained order.

1 Timothy 2:15 – "*Yet she will be saved through child-bearing—if they continue in faith and love and holiness, with self-control.*"

Sixth, we see that God has a plan for women in the church and home. Paul makes a statement that women will be saved through childbearing if they continue in faith and love and holiness with self-control. We can know that Paul is not saying that women are saved because they have children because we studied the gospel earlier and understood that the Lord calls for repentance and faith in Him to be saved. Man is justified before God through faith in Christ as we discussed in Chapter 3 when we explored the nature of saving faith in Christ.

Therefore, we must understand that Paul is not speaking of childbearing as another way of salvation.

So far in this section, we have seen that a woman was deceived, stepped out of her God-ordained role, and became a transgressor. Scripture states unequivocally that women are not allowed to teach over men and are not allowed to take authority over men in the church. Some women at this point might ask, "What role do I play in the church?" Paul gives a surprising answer, and John MacArthur says it best when he explains the woman's God-given role:

> They have caused the race to fall by stepping out of their God-intended design, but they also are given the priority responsibility of raising a godly seed . . . women led the race into sin, but bless God; God has given them the privilege of leading the race out of sin to godliness.[40]

Paul gives an excellent example of this with Timothy. In 2 Timothy 1:5 Paul says this regarding the faith of Timothy's grandmother and mother, "*I am reminded of your sincere faith, a faith that dwelt first in your grandmother Lois and your mother Eunice and now, I am sure, dwells in you as well.*" Additionally, in 2 Timothy 3:14–15, he says this about Timothy's upbringing:

> *But as for you, continue in what you have learned and have firmly believed, knowing from whom you learned it*

and how from childhood you have been acquainted with the sacred writings, which are able to make you wise for salvation through faith in Jesus Christ.

So what role did Timothy's grandmother and mother play in his life? From his childhood, his mother taught him the Scriptures. She was an Old Testament believer with sincere faith who impressed upon Timothy the truth of Scriptures, which pointed him to faith in Jesus Christ. Since women can't teach or take authority over a man, what role would God have for them? Though women do not have the role of teaching or authority in the church, women have a unique role to nurture their children, care for them, teach them the Word, show forth the character of a godly woman (Proverbs 31), and teach their children of Christ and lead them to a knowledge of Him. This is what Paul means when he says women will be saved through childbearing. Therefore, let us know, understand, and appreciate the important and vital role that a woman plays in the church for bringing up and teaching her children about the Lord Jesus Christ.

Not a Spokesman for God, Not Spiritual, Ignorant, and Unrecognized – The Man who Permits Women to Teach and Take Authority Over Men

1 Corinthians 14:33 – *"For God is not a God of confusion but of peace. As in all the churches of the saints."*

Earlier in 1 Corinthians 14, Paul gives the Corinthians instruction for conducting orderly worship, including how to handle the use of spiritual gifts such as speaking in tongues for the building up the saints. In verses 33–38, Paul will begin to explain that orderly worship in the assembly of the saints does not permit women to speak in the church and then he ends with a warning to those who allow disorderly worship, which includes women preaching and teaching in the church. We will start our exposition at 1 Corinthians 14:33.

We see that just prior to giving the instruction for not allowing women to speak in the church, Paul notes that this is a universal practice in the church. We can know this because Paul says that this is the practice "*in all the churches of the saints.*" Therefore, this isn't the rule for a minority of churches or even most churches; this is the practice of all the churches of the Living God with no exceptions. None of the churches allowed women to speak in the church without exception; this is a very important point.

1 Corinthians 14:34 – "*For they are not permitted to speak but should be in submission, as the Law also says.*"

We see that Paul gives a command that women must be silent. The word *silent* comes from *sigaó*, which means "to keep silence" or "quiet." This word denotes the act of being silent or refraining from speech, and it implies a deliberate choice to withhold words where speaking might be inappropriate. When Paul says that women are to be silent, we know from our exposition of 1 Timothy 2:11–15 that Paul does not mean that women must never speak in the church because there is a place for women to teach women and children (Titus 2:3–4). Additionally, Paul is not suggesting that they are never allowed to talk or converse among themselves because the saints gather to fellowship amongst one another.

If we look back at 1 Corinthians 14:26–33, we see that Paul is talking about orderly worship in the church and the order that must take place when the whole church assembles. In fact, the concept of speaking orderly when the church assembles is a dominant theme in this chapter. There must be order if someone is speaking in tongues, and there must be an interpreter (1 Corinthians 14:27), there must be order in prophesying where no more than two or three are allowed to speak and each in turn (1 Corinthians 14:28), and the people are to discern what is being spoken (1 Corinthians 14:29). What Paul is saying is that women are not allowed to speak in the church when it comes to prophesying, preaching, or teaching over men. How can we know this? In 1 Timothy 2:11–15, we understood that women are not to teach or take authority over a man. When Paul says that women must be silent, the verb is written in the present tense and imperative mood, which means this is a command that is to continually be obeyed. The verbs "permitted" and "speak" are also written in the present tense, which means that this to be the continual practice of all the churches of God. We could even render the verse this way: "Women are commanded to continually be silent in the churches. For it is not allowed and will never be allowed for them to speak." Women are to continually remain silent and refrain from preaching and teaching over men. This is to be the practice of the churches of God with no exception.

Women are to be in submission. To whom are women to be in submission? We answered this question earlier in the chapter. Women are to be in submission to their husbands as well as the pastors and elders. They are not to seek to take authority over a man, their husband, or a pastor (1 Timothy 2:11–12, 1 Corinthians 11:3, Ephesians 5:22–24). When Paul says that women are to be in submission, he writes this in the present tense and imperative mood, which means this is a command to be continually obeyed. Therefore, we know that women are to be silent and not teach or preach over men, and they are to remain in submission to their husbands as well as the pastors which can only be men.

We see that the law demands that women remain silent. What law is Paul referring to? As we learned earlier from our exposition of 1 Timothy 2:11–15, the law that Paul is referring to is most likely from the Creation account and fall of man. When Paul commands that women are not to teach or take authority over a man, he appeals to the Creation account, Adam's leadership role, Eve's subordinate role, and the disastrous result that occurred when Adam did not lead Eve. Therefore, the law that states that women are not permitted to speak is most likely the account of the Fall. However, it is also likely that Paul has in mind the Old Testament where men were priests and prophets. Likewise, kings were also men. There are rare exceptions where women took roles over men such as Deborah (Judges 4), but the dominant theme is that men held the positions of religious leadership over women.

1 Corinthians 14:35 – *"If there is anything they desire to learn, let them ask their husbands at home. For it is shameful for a woman to speak in church."*

We see that the husband is to be knowledgeable in Scripture and teach his wife. The husband is responsible for teaching his wife Scripture. Let's recall what we learned about Adam and Eve. Adam was responsible for teaching his wife, guiding his wife, and guarding his wife. This was to be the order in marriage. Husbands have this same responsibility, which is to love their wives self-sacrificingly and teach them Scripture in order to protect, guard, and guide their wives. We see this in Ephesians 5:23, 25–26 where it says:

For the husband is the head of the wife even as Christ is the head of the church, his body, and is himself its Savior. . . . Husbands, love your wives, as Christ loved the church and gave himself up for her, that he might sanctify her, having cleansed her by the washing of water with the word.

We see in Ephesians 5:25 that man is to love his wife self-sacrificingly as Christ loved the church and gave Himself up for her. We also see in Ephesians 5:23, that just as Christ is the Savior of the church, so man is responsible for acting as a savior for his wife. One may ask, "How is it possible for a husband to be a savior to his wife when the Lord Jesus Christ is the only Savior of mankind?" It's true that husbands cannot live a perfect and sinless life, die a substitutionary death for sinners, and take the place of Christ. However, it is possible for the husband to act as one who saves and rescues his wife spiritually. Jude 23 says that Christians are to "*save others by snatching them out of the fire.*" Paul speaks of acting to save people where he says this in 1 Corinthians 9:22, "*To the weak I became weak, that I might win the weak. I have become all things to all people, that by all means I might save some.*" James speaks of saving those who wander from the truth when he says, "*My brothers, if anyone among you wanders from the truth and someone brings him back, let him know that whoever brings back a sinner from his wandering will save his soul from death and will cover a multitude of sins*" (James 5:19–20).

Therefore, we can and should know that just as Christ loved the church and gave Himself up for her and is the church's Savior, so the husband is to also mimic Christ and act as a "savior" to his wife by living a life of submission to Christ and conducting his life in such a way that guards, protects, feeds, and saves his wife spiritually. Tim Conway has a helpful word on what it means for men to act as a savior for their wives:

Clearly the concept "Savior" can be applied to husbands

without it meaning that they have to go to the cross and atone for the sins of their wife. Men, I don't think Paul tacked that phrase on the end of verse 23, "and is himself its Savior," in order to confuse us, to get us doubting whether or not a husband can really be a savior or not. I think he put those words there so that you and I would use our brains and our thinking and literally just behold Christ saving and realize in that imagery, I have a responsibility toward my wife that is as that is. As much as it can be as that [as Christ saving His bride]. As much as a Christian can be as his Savior, into whom he is being transformed into that image, but as much as he can resemble Christ in that capacity, I believe that's what Paul wants us to do . . . . Think what the term "Savior" is all about. Savior has the idea of rescuing, protecting, preserving . . . We were in danger brethren, and this is exactly what Paul wants us to see. He wants us to see the glories of Christ who came in. Brethren, God literally came in and kicked open the dungeon that we were chained in! He came in and He tore those shackles off us! He picked us up and He put us on His shoulders, and He rescued us! He rescued us! He rescued us from death! He rescued us from the law! He rescued us from the wrath of God! He rescued us from the devil! Did He not brethren?! From the power of sin! He just ripped them apart! He took us out of that dungeon! He is the Rescuer! Paul wants us to see that and be filled with the glory of that. And men to take that and say, "OK, as much as it lies within my capacity to be a preserver and a protector and a savior and a rescuer of my wife then that I will be." . . . Men, Paul goes through all these dealings here and he goes into the next chapter, and he goes right out into describing the Christian warrior. This is what we need to be! We need this! We need husband warriors! Men. We need men like are described there. Warriors who take up the whole armor of God! Men of faith bearing their shield! Men of confident assurance of their standing with God! Have you read that? You see what's there? Men with their feet gospel shod! Men with belts of truth and breastplates of righteousness! Men with helmets where they have assurance they have a confidence that God is there! They have a shield, brethren, of faith! They look at God's Word, they're men of God's Word, they're men of God's promises, they're men who take these and live on that Word, they believe that Word, they seek to guide their families by that Word. Men of prayer and men who bear this sword, the sword of the Word of God. That's what we need."[41]

When Paul tells the women to ask their husbands at home, this is what he has in mind. The husband is not some lazy man who is ignorant in the Word. Not some apathetic husband who is indifferent to the Word. Not some weak husband who does not have the courage to stand upon and remain firm in the truth of God's Word. Not some husband who only loves theology but does not practically apply it to himself. Not some man-pleasing husband who would rather make friends with the world than be pleasing to God. Not some authoritarian husband who rules with a heavy hand, sharp tongue, and unforgiving demeanor. Not at all! This man is to be strong in the Word, strong in faith, strong in the gospel, strong in conviction, strong in Christ, and submissive to Christ. This is a high calling for men to submit to Christ and love their wives sacrificially as Christ loved the church. This includes teaching, guiding, guarding, feeding, praying for, protecting, and nurturing one's wife. When Paul says that women are to ask their husbands at home, let us not forget the high calling of the man to not only know Scripture, but to act as a savior to his wife and be responsible for "*cleansing her by the washing of water with the word*" (Ephesians 5:26) or rather, self-sacrificingly loving his wife and teaching her Scripture. For a man to be unknowledgeable in Scripture and not teach his wife is a neglect his duty as a husband. Such a man who will not protect, nurture, guide, and guard his wife will be required to give an account of his duties of a husband to the Lord on that final day of judgment. If you're a husband, take heed of this command!

We see that it is shameful for a woman to speak in church. The word *shameful* comes from *aischros*, and it means "base" or "dishonorable." This word conveys a sense of moral or ethical repugnance and highlights actions that are dishonorable and indecent. For a woman to speak, teach, or preach over a man in church is shameful. It is shameful for the woman who is disobedient to God. It is shameful for the man who allows his wife to be unsubmissive. It brings shame on the Lord's name because it is His church, and His instructions for worship are to be obeyed. There is nothing but shame and dishonor when a woman speaks, teaches, or preaches in the church over men.

1 Corinthians 14:36 – "*Or was it from you that the word of God came? Or are you the only ones it has reached?*"

In this verse Paul is using sarcasm to show the Corinthian church that they are acting in ignorance of God's Word. Paul has just shown that the universal practice of the church is not to allow women to speak; he has commanded that women are not to speak, and he has shown that Scripture does not allow women to speak; that is to teach or preach over a man. To paraphrase what Paul is saying, we could render his sarcasm this way, "Did the Word of God originate from you or from God? Hasn't the Word of God and His law been spoken long before you?" Essentially, Paul is saying that this is not something new. These laws and principles have been in place long before the Corinthians came into existence. God's Word has not changed on this matter. The churches of God do not practice what the Corinthians are practicing. Therefore, Paul uses sarcasm to show the Corinthians that they are out of line with the Word of God and the other churches of God.

1 Corinthians 14:37 – "*If anyone thinks that he is a prophet, or spiritual, he should acknowledge that the things I am writing to you are a command of the Lord.*"

We see that anyone who considers himself a prophet, a preacher, a spiritual or spiritually gifted person will acknowledge that these are the Lord's commands. The true pastor, the true teacher, and the true preacher will acknowledge that this is the command of the Lord. This word *acknowledge* comes from *epiginóskó*, which conveys a deep, thorough, experiential, and intimate knowledge of God's truth. This is not just intellectual knowledge, but relational and experiential knowledge. All true pastors, teachers, and preachers who know God will know that this command for women to remain silent in the churches and not to teach or preach over a man is a command from the Lord. The true pastor, teacher, or preacher will not try to water down the command, make exceptions for the command, or choose to disobey the command. No, the true pastor will fully acknowledge and seek to obey this command from the Lord. Remember, that women remaining silent in the church is the practice of all the churches of God; no church of God is to allow women to teach, preach, or take authority over a man. Every church of God is to follow this command and recognize that this is God's instruction and plan for the church. To disobey this command is to bring disgrace upon oneself, rebel against God's command, and fight against God's plan for the church.

1 Corinthians 14:38 – *"If anyone does not recognize this, he is not recognized."*

Those who do not recognize this as a command from the Lord are not to be recognized. This is incredibly strong language from Paul. The word *recognize* comes from *agnoeó*, and it means "to be ignorant" or "to not know." This means that if someone considers themselves a pastor, a preacher, or a teacher and does not recognize this, he is not recognized as a pastor, preacher, teacher, or a spiritual or a spiritually gifted person. If someone does not recognize that women are not to be pastors, preachers, teachers over men, then they are ignorant and they must be ignored and not recognized as a pastor, preacher, teacher, or a spiritual person. This is strong, strong, strong language. For a man, a denomination, a synod, or any of the like to advocate for women to be pastors, preachers, and teachers over a man is to say that these men, synods, and denominations are ignorant and not recognized by the Lord. John MacArthur has some helpful and strong comments for those who allow women to be pastors and teachers over men:

> If you don't recognize the command of God, we don't recognize you as a preacher or a spiritual person. What Paul wrote is the Lord's command. Violate that command and you're not a preacher and you're not spiritual; you're a fraud. The Word of God is clear.[42]

Not only does John MacArthur comment strongly on this point, but other commentators give similar statements about the so-called pastor who does not recognize God's command in their exposition of relevant Scripture passages.[43]

- *Ellicott's Commentary for English Readers*: "This would signify that any man who knows not this truth is not known of God."

- *Barnes' Notes on the Bible*: "At his own peril, let him remain so, and abide the consequences. I shall not take any further trouble to debate with him. I have stated my authority. I have delivered the commands of God. And now, if he disregards them, and still doubts whether all this is said by divine authority, let him abide the consequences of rejecting the law of God. I have given full proof of my divine commission. I have nothing more to say on that head. And now, if he chooses to remain in ignorance or incredulity, the fault is his own, and he must answer for it to God."

- *Matthew Poole's Commentary*: "In some copies it is, he shall not be known: in the day of judgment Christ shalt say unto him: Depart from me, I know you not."

- *Gill's Exposition of the Entire Bible*: "Let him be ignorant: let him be treated and despised as an ignorant man; and let his ignorance be no hinderance to any in receiving these rules and directions as the commandments of Christ; for no regard is to be had, or pity shown, to a man of affected ignorance, and willful obstinance; such a man is not to be known and owned, but shunned and rejected"

As we close this chapter, let's remember that God is the one who gifts, equips, and commissions men to be pastors to serve

His church (Ephesians 4:11–16). The purpose of this chapter is not solely to show that women are not to be pastors, but to also demonstrate that there are many frauds and phonies who call themselves pastors and who allow and endorse women to be pastors in churches, denominations, and synods. Though these men call themselves pastors, Paul and the Lord Jesus Christ would call these men ignorant and unrecognized and proclaim that they're not pastors, preachers, spiritual or spiritually gifted. Men who do not recognize this command from the Lord are not to be recognized.

Chapter 9

A Man Who Has the Grace of God Poured Out on Him to be Devoted to Prayer and Blessed by His Sheep

Let the elders who rule well be considered worthy of double honor, especially those who labor in preaching and teaching.

—1 Timothy 5:17

In this final chapter, we will see that the true pastor is a man who depends on the Lord for all he has been commissioned to do, and he is to be honored by the sheep he oversees. As we've learned throughout this book, the true pastor has been tasked with many things. The true pastor is to watch over his life and doctrine carefully. He is to devote himself to Scripture. He is to teach with skill and handle the Word of God carefully. He is to proclaim the gospel. He is to stand and oppose false teachers. He will be persecuted by those outside the church and those inside the church. He is to watch over, feed, guard, and guide the sheep. Therefore, he is a man who is dependent on the Lord.

The true pastor is dependent on the Lord for everything he does in ministry. He is to be a man who can relate to the apostles who said this regarding the primary importance of their ministry: *"But we will devote ourselves to prayer and to the ministry of the word"* (Acts 6:4).

The true pastor is to be one who is devoted to the ministry of the Word and to prayer. The Lord Jesus Christ had this same practice of devotion to prayer as Scripture says, *"But he would withdraw to desolate places and pray"* (Luke 5:16). It was the common practice of Jesus to go alone to pray to His Father. Paul said that we should pray about everything: *"Do not be anxious about anything, but in everything by prayer and supplication with thanksgiving let your requests be made known to God"* (Philippians 4:6). There is nothing that the true believer and true pastor should not be prayerful over. In 1 Thessalonians 5:17, Paul says, *"Pray without ceasing."*

The true pastor is a needy man:

- He prays for grace to preach the gospel with clarity (Colossians 4:3).

- He prays for kings and those in public positions (1 Timothy 2:2).

- He prays for other believers (1 Timothy 1:3).

- He gives thanks when he prays (Ephesians 1:16).

- He prays for a greater knowledge of God for the sheep under his care (Ephesians 3:17–19).

- He prays for spiritual wisdom and understanding for his sheep (Colossians 1:9).

- He prays that his sheep walk in a manner worthy of the Lord (Colossians 1:10).

- He prays to be delivered from hardship (2 Corinthians 12:8–10).

- He prays for those who persecute him (Matthew 5:44).

- He prays that believers have peace and be sanctified in their whole spirit, soul, and body and to be kept blameless (1 Thessalonians 5:23).

The true pastor is a man who prays to God for help in all he does, for the souls of his people, for the souls of the lost, and for the glory of God. This is to be the posture of the true pastor who loves his Master and the Bride for whom the Master laid down His life.

Worthy of Double Honor

> **1 Timothy 5:17** – "*Let the elders who rule well be considered worthy of double honor, especially those who labor in preaching and teaching.*"

The true pastor who rules well and who labors in preaching and teaching is worthy of double honor. Earlier, in this book, we described what it means to preach the Word and teach the Word with skill, accuracy, and clarity. Those who work tirelessly to rule, oversee, guide, and lead the church in preaching and teaching are worthy of double honor. In this context, "honor" would be referring to wages or compensation; this is made clear in 1 Timothy 5:18: "*For the Scripture says, 'You shall not muzzle an ox when it treads out the grain' and 'The laborer deserves his wages.'*" Those men who are faithful, lead well, and labor in preaching and teaching are to be honored and compensated. I will not go into more detail regarding what their compensation looks like. Those church members who understand the precious gift that God has given them will take this verse to heart to discern the best way to honor their faithful pastor.

Discern and Pay Attention to What the Pastor Teaches

> **Acts 17:11** – "*Now these Jews were more noble than those in Thessalonica; they received the word with all eagerness, examining the Scriptures daily to see if these things were so.*"

One of the things the flock can do to honor the pastor is to eagerly examine the true pastor's teaching. Just because a man holds the office of a pastor does not mean the sheep are not to examine and judge what the pastor is teaching is correct. Therefore, one way of honoring the pastor is to eagerly and diligently search to see what the pastor is teaching is the truth. Such diligence is noble and keeps the true pastor accountable and the sheep attentive.

Share All Good Things

Galatians 6:6 – "*Let the one who is taught the word share all good things with the one who teaches.*"

The true pastor is also to be blessed by his congregation in seeing the progress of the sheep he shepherds. For those that are under the pastor's teaching, preaching, guidance, and guardianship, it is a good and wonderful thing when the pastor sees the sheep growing and maturing. John speaks of this in his letter to the lady in 2 John 4 where he says this regarding the joy of a pastor: "*I rejoiced greatly to find some of your children walking in the truth, just as we were commanded by the Father.*" Seeing the sheep growing in maturity and walking in obedience is a great joy to the pastor. One of the ways the sheep can bless the pastor is by sharing these good things with their pastor as this is a source of his joy.

Obey Your Leaders

Hebrews 13:17 – "*Obey your leaders and submit to them, for they are keeping watch over your souls, as those who will have to give an account. Let them do this with joy and not with groaning, for that would be of no advantage to you.*"

The true pastor also finds joy when the sheep obey the leaders of the church. As mentioned earlier, the true pastor is not seeking to use authoritarian control, manipulative schemes, or deceitful practices. Rather, the true pastor watches over the sheep as one who must give an account to the Lord, and he watches over them willingly, eagerly, and not under compulsion. As the pastor submits to God, so the sheep submit to and obey the pastor and the leaders. Thus, the response of the sheep is to submit to the leaders in the church, so that it may be a joy and not anger or grief for the pastor because this would not be profitable for the sheep. Peter teaches the same thing in 1 Peter 5:5 where he says, "*Likewise, you who are younger, be subject to the elders. Clothe yourselves, all of you, with humility toward one another, for 'God opposes the proud but gives grace to the humble.'*" Therefore, the sheep can honor and bless the pastor by obeying and submitting to him and the other pastors or elders.

As we close this chapter, we see the high calling the pastor has been entrusted with, and we see how God calls the sheep to honor and bless the pastor. From the brief exposition in this chapter, I trust that true believers see how great is the love of God to give His church such gifted men and that, in turn, they respond to God in thankfulness and love and honor their pastor.

> *Now to Him who is able to do far more abundantly than all that we ask or think, according to the power at work within us, to Him be glory in the church and in Christ Jesus throughout all generations, forever and ever. Amen.*
>
> —Ephesians 3:20–21

Notes

_____

_____

_____

_____

_____

_____

_____

_____

_____

_____

_____

_____

_____

_____

Notes

Notes

Endnotes

1. John MacArthur, "Building the Body of Christ, Part 1," Sermon, August 27, 1978, Grace Community Church, Sun Valley, California.

2. Adrian Rogers, *The Berean Call*, December 1996, p. 3

3. MacArthur, "Looking at the Face of Jesus, Part 1," Sermon, August 28, 1994, Grace Community Church, Sun Valley, California.

4. Charles Spurgeon, "Greek Word Studies: Trickery (2940) *kubeia*, SermonIndex.net, accessed May 2025, https://www.sermonindex.net/modules/articles/index.php?view=article&aid=35982.

5. Charles Spurgeon, "Greek Word Studies: Methods (3180) *methodeia*, SermonIndex.net, accessed May 2025, https://www.sermonindex.net/modules/articles/index.php?view=article&aid=34452.

6. Tim Conway, "Listen to Jesus, But Not Paul?" Sermon, May 1, 2016, Grace Community Church, San Antonio, Texas.

7. Lasciviousness (766) Aselgeia, *SermonIndex*, accessed June 2, 2025, https://www.sermonindex.net/modules/articles/index.php?view=article&aid=34347

8. Steven Cole, "Greek Word Studies: Devout (3741) *hósios*, SermonIndex.net, accessed May 2025, https://www.sermonindex.net/modules/articles/index.php?view=article&aid=33867.

9. William Barclay, *The Letters of James and Peter*, rev. ed., The Daily Study Bible Series (Philadelphia: Westminster Press, 1976), 312.

10. John MacArthur, *Titus*, The MacArthur New Testament Commentary (Chicago: Moody Publishers, 1996), 23.

11. William Barclay, *The Letters to Timothy, Titus, and Philemon*, rev. ed., The Daily Study Bible Series (Philadelphia: Westminster Press, 1975), 222.

12. Richard Owen Roberts, "The Use of the Words of God in Preaching," Sermon, January 4, 2015, G3 Conference.

13. Roberts, "The Use of the Words of God in Preaching."

14. Vance Havner, "Greek Word Studies: Preach (proclaim) (2784) *kerusso*, SermonIndex.net, accessed May 2025, https://www.sermonindex.net/modules/articles/index.php?view=article&aid=34638.

15. Dwight L. Moody, "Greek Word Studies: Preach (proclaim) (2784) kerusso, SermonIndex.net, accessed May 2025, https://www.sermonindex.net/modules/articles/index.php?view=article&aid=34638.

16. Jonathan Edwards, *Works of Jonathan Edwards, Volume One*, accessed May 2025, https://ccel.org/ccel/edwards/works1.ix.iv.html#:~:text=I%20should%20think%20myself%20in,the%20nature%20of%20the%20subject.

17. Kenneth S. Wuest, "Greek Word Studies: Confidence (boldness) (3954) *parrhesia*, SermonIndex,net, accessed May 2025, https://www.sermonindex.net/modules/articles/index.php?view=article&aid=33717.

18. Charles Spurgeon, "Tetelestai–Paid in Full, "Precept Austin, November 7, 2022, https://www.preceptaustin.org/tetelestai-paid_in_full.

19. A. W. Pink, "Tetelestai–Paid in Full, "Precept Austin, November 7, 2022, https://www.preceptaustin.org/tetelestai-paid_in_full.

20. A C. Gaebelein, "Tetelestai–Paid in Full, "Precept Austin, November 7, 2022, https://www.preceptaustin.org/tetelestai-paid_in_full.

21. Warren W. Wiersbe, *The Bible Exposition Commentary*, vol. 2 (Wheaton, IL: Victor Books, 1996), 220.

22. Ian Murray, *The Life of Arthur W. Pink* (Banner of Truth, 1981), 107.

23. Wuest, *Word Studies from the Greek New Testament* (Eerdmans Publishing Company, 1980), 25.

24. *2 Timothy 2:15-19 Commentary," Precept Austin, accessed June 2, 2025, https://www.preceptaustin.org/2_timothy_215-19*

25. Richard Baxter, *The Poetical Fragments of Richard Baxter*, 4th ed. (London: Pickering, 1821), 35.

26. Steven Cole, "Preaching and Hearing God's Word (2 Timothy 4:1–5)," *Sermon Index*, accessed June 2, 2025, https://www.sermonindex.net/modules/articles/index.php?aid=34730.

27. Barclay, *The Daily Study Bible*, 207.

28. Barclay, *The Daily Study Bible Series*, Rev. ed. (Philadelphia: The Westminster Press), 35.

29. Spurgeon, "Christ's Indwelling Word," Sermon #2679, *Spurgeon's Sermons*, https://www.spurgeongems.org/sermon/chs2679.pdf.

30. Lewis Guest IV, "This Day and That Day: The Pressures of Today and the Returning King," *Desiring God*, September 25, 2020,

31. MacArthur, "Survival Strategy of Apostate Times, Part 3," Sermon, August 8, 2004, Grace Community Church, Sun Valley, California.

32. Paul Dowling, "Disgraceful Pastors and the Coming Doom" Sermon, September 2, 2007, https://www.sermonaudio.com/sermons/920717235510.

33. William Penn, *No Cross, No Crown: A Discourse Showing the Nature and Discipline of the Holy Cross of Christ* (London: Andrew Sowle, 1669).

34. "1 Peter 1:6 Commentary," *Precept Austin*, accessed June 2, 2025, https://www.preceptaustin.org/1_peter_16-12.

35. Mike Riccardi, "The Surpassing Value of Knowing Christ, Part 1," *The GraceLife Pulpit*, June 28, 2015, https://www.thegracelifepulpit.com/sermons.aspx?code=2015-06-28am-MR.

36. Joseph Henry Thayer, *Thayer's Greek-English Lexicon of the New Testament*, s.v. "καταβάλλω."

37. MacArthur, "Restoring Biblical Eldership, Part 2," Sermon, January 18, 1987, Grace Community Church, Sun Valley, California.

38. MacArthur, "The Discipline of God's Children, Part 2," Sermon, January 23, 1983, Grace Community Church, Sun Valley California.

39. Emma Moody Fitt, *Day by Day with D. L. Moody* (Moody Publishers, 1977), 316.

40. MacArthur, "God's High Calling for Women, Part 4," Sermon, March 2, 1986, Grace Community Church, Sun Valley, California.

41. Conway, "Husbands Save your Wives," Sermon, February 27, 2011, Grace Community Church, San Antonio, Texas.

42. MacArthur, "Does the Bible Permit a Woman to Preach?" Sermon, November 3, 2019, Grace Community Church, Sun Valley, California.

43. "Commentaries, 1 Corinthians 14:38," Bible Hub, accessed May 2025, https://biblehub.com/commentaries/1_corinthians/14-38.htm.

www.ingramcontent.com/pod-product-compliance
Lightning Source LLC
Chambersburg PA
CBHW062041080426
42734CB00012B/2523